ZOOLOGIES

Also by Alison Hawthorne Deming

POETRY
Rope
Genius Loci
The Monarchs: A Poem Sequence
Science and Other Poems
Poetry of the American West: A Columbia Anthology (Editor)

NONFICTION
Writing the Sacred Into the Real
The Edges of the Civilized World: A Journey in Nature and Culture
Temporary Homelands
Anatomy of Desire: The Daughter/Mother Sessions (Coauthor)
Girls in the Jungle
The Colors of Nature: Culture, Identity and the Natural World (Coeditor)

ZOOLOGIES

On ANIMALS

and the HUMAN

SPIRIT

Alison Hawthorne Deming

MILKWEED EDITIONS

Published 2014 by Milkweed Editions
Printed in the United States of America
Cover design & illustration by Mary Austin Speaker
Author photo by Cybele Knowles
The text of this book is set in ITC New Baskerville.

19 20 21 22 23   5 4 3 2
First Edition

Milkweed Editions, an independent nonprofit publisher, gratefully acknowledges sustaining support from the Bush Foundation; the Jerome Foundation; the Lindquist & Vennum Foundation; the McKnight Foundation; the voters of Minnesota through a Minnesota State Arts Board Operating Support grant, thanks to a legislative appropriation from the arts and cultural heritage fund, and a grant from the Wells Fargo Foundation Minnesota; the National Endowment for the Arts; the Target Foundation; and other generous contributions from foundations, corporations, and individuals. For a full listing of Milkweed Editions supporters, please visit milkweed.org.

Library of Congress Cataloging-in-Publication Data

Deming, Alison Hawthorne, 1946-
  Zoologies : on animals and the human spirit / Alison Hawthorne
Deming. -- First edition.
      pages cm
  Includes bibliographical references.
  ISBN 978-1-57131-348-5 (paperback) -- ISBN 978-1-57131-899-2
(ebook)
  1. Animals. 2. Human-animal relationships. 3. Nature. I. Title.
  PS3554.E474Z36 2014
  814'.54--dc23
                          2014004104

Milkweed Editions is committed to ecological stewardship. We strive to align our book production practices with this principle, and to reduce the impact of our operations in the environment. We are a member of the Green Press Initiative, a nonprofit coalition of publishers, manufacturers, and authors working to protect the world's endangered forests and conserve natural resources. *Zoologies* was printed on acid-free 30% postconsumer-waste paper by Thomson-Shore.

For Lincoln and Raymond

Contents

The dragon tipped up his great tusked head, stretched his neck, sighed fire. "Ah, Grendel!" he said. He seemed that instant almost to rise to pity. "You improve them, my boy! Can't you see that yourself? You stimulate them! You make them think and scheme. You drive them to poetry, science, religion, all that makes them what they are for as long as they last. You are, so to speak, the brute existent by which they learn to define themselves. The exile, captivity, death they shrink from—the blunt facts of their mortality, their abandonment—that's what you make them recognize, embrace!"

JOHN GARDNER
Grendel

The human species emerged enacting, dreaming, and thinking animals and cannot be fully itself without them.

PAUL SHEPARD
Coming Home to the Pleistocene

Though human beings have created much of the beauty of the world, they are only collaborators in a much vaster project. . . . Beauty is a call.

ELAINE SCARRY
On Beauty and Being Just

ZOOLOGIES

Introduction

The Aberdeen Bestiary, written and illuminated in England around the twelfth century, is a luxury book intended "to improve the minds of ordinary people, in such a way that the soul will at least perceive physically things it has difficulty grasping mentally." Its pages are rich with burnished gold, plush reds and blues. It is a work of theology, not natural history, glorifying the Christian wisdom tradition, an instruction manual in the art of the sermon and moral education used to train monks in medieval monasteries. The position of thumbprints at the center top page, notes the University of Aberdeen's historical collections site, indicates that the book was held open and shown to others, probably in the teaching of unlettered lay brothers. The animal images are exquisitely rendered, the lessons varying from parable to metaphor to oblique celebration of art as a way of knowing.

One page shows a ram, "a virile beast," bounding gracefully, its muscles contoured in elegance that predicts the sharp lines of art deco, its wool as articulated as chain mail, its eye Egyptian in black-rimmed intensity. Propelled by the pleasure of its strength, the ram's head breaks through the ornate frame of its rectangle. Beneath this image is a smaller illustration of a lamb, "a pious creature," a two-dimensional cotton puff that skips happily within the confines of its golden roundel. Piety, it would seem, asks a sacrifice of certain pleasurable capabilities the body offers. I imagine the artist's hand and mind, the hours spent in contemplation

while he worked, the hand speaking a truth more complicated than that of the mind and will.

The hyena was considered unclean. It was thought to
change its sex, one year being male and the next year being
female. It inhabited tombs of the dead and fed on their bodies. Thus it is depicted in the bestiary boasting a pronounced
double set of gender gear—full, open labia and the holy
male trinity of testicles and penis suspended just below the
opening. The hyena is scavenging a man's limp body that lies
on a tomb. The beast seizes a mouthful of the man's naked
shoulder, using feet more like dragon claws than dog paws
to pin down the corpse, the animal's ears exaggerated into
devilish horns, its spine—thought to be rigid—depicted as a
chain of metallic barbs lying on the outside of the creature's
back and extending to the tip of its tail. It is a viciously cautionary tale against the unresurrected body.

Some entries come closer to natural history observation
than moral teaching. Of deer, the bestiary writes:

> Stags, when it is time to rut, rage with the madness of
> lust. Does, although they may be inseminated earlier, do
> not conceive before the star of Arcturus appears. They
> do not rear their young just anywhere but hide them
> with tender care, concealed deep in bushes and grass,
> and they make them stay out of sight with a tap of the
> hoof. . . . The offspring of the deer are called *hinnuli*,
> fawns, from *innuere*, 'to nod,' because at a nod from their
> mother, they vanish from sight.

And some entries conflate the two realities—what is and
what one imagines—into devotional poetry:

> The dove, with its silver-colored feathers, signifies every
> faithful and pure soul, renowned for the high esteem
> accorded to its virtues. The dove gathers as many grains

of seed for food as the soul does examples of righteous men as models of virtuous conduct. The dove has two eyes, right and left, signifying, that is, memory and intelligence. With one it foresees things to come; with the other it weeps over what has been.

The book's sources lie in Indian, Jewish, and Egyptian legend, filtered through the classical texts on natural history of Aristotle and Pliny, alloyed with the early Christian philosophy of Origen, who was also responsible for coalescing texts that became the New Testament. The Aberdeen Bestiary is descended from the *Physiologus*, a work of animal allegories, author unknown, that had varied iterations in the ancient world. It may have originated in Alexandria in the third or fourth century. No copy of that Greek text has survived, only later Latin versions in both prose and verse, which were among the most popular books in the Middle Ages. "Physiologus" is often translated as "the naturalist," but the works were not intended to be natural history books. Rather, the *Physiologus* was, as Michael J. Curley writes, the voice of "one who interpreted metaphysically, morally, and finally mystically the transcendent significance of the natural world." The Aberdeen Bestiary is a catch basin for works of wisdom and imagination inspired by animals from antiquity into the medieval era.

An earlier work drawing on traditional lore is Aesop's *Fables*, the compendium of animal stories said to be authored by a sixth-century BCE Greek slave and storyteller. Either Aesop existed or did not, was a slave by capture or by birth, was a black African or a white Thracian, gathered fables from India or Libya or Egypt or Sumer or Sudan or Ethiopia or all of these places. The history clearly is muddled. The stories embody human traits in animals. In antiquity they were something of a toastmaster's jokebook used to poke fun at dynamics of human power and weakness, wisdom and folly.

The fables are cited by Aristophanes and Socrates, and their influence extends into contemporary children's stories and our colloquial lexicon: "The Fox and the Grapes," inspiring our expression "sour grapes"; "The Ant and the Grasshopper," an advisory on planning for future need; "The Ass and the Wolf," teaching that "those who seem to legislate according to justice cannot even abide by the rules which they themselves have established and decreed"; and "The Tortoise and the Hare," lauding discipline over natural talent.

◆

As a child growing up in the deciduous woods of the Northeast, I was enthralled by animals. The agility of gray squirrels leaping tree to tree, their furry tails bigger than their lithe bodies. The gentleness of circus elephants that came to our town by train and paraded in a ring, lifting front legs to the backside of the beast in front, until they had made a daisy chain of clumsy grace and turned their gargantuan cement-colored bodies into animated sculpture. The threat of the copperheads that inhabited our woods, the diamond-shaped pattern of their skins perfectly camouflaged in the rust and brown of fallen oak and maple leaves. The beauty of a deer, so perfectly at home in the leafy dapple of forest that when one would venture near our lawn it seemed stunned at a reality it could not comprehend. The insomniac night song of the whip-poor-will on hot summer nights when I tossed in my bedroom tucked under the eaves, the sound so irritating and the bird's name so menacing that I imagined the bird to be the size at least of a vulture. I am surprised to this day when I see a photograph of this harmless little woods dweller smaller than a white-winged dove.

At age three, I was brutally initiated into the animal kingdom. Two dogs, kennel boxers escaping their chain-link pen, bolted down a forest path in wild enthusiasm to be free. I was in their way. They tore me, thrashed me, clawed me. My face was stitched back together. I remember running my fingers over the scabs on my scalp that their claws had left and tracing each scar on my face as a token of mystery. I had no memory of the event as a child nor do I now, but I saved a newspaper article that reported the attack. I hid it in my closet and took it out in secret to read it again and again throughout my childhood. It seemed important to know that this had happened. A dog attack is news.

What effect this experience had on my psyche remains a mystery—perhaps a code—deeply woven into the skeins of neurons that make me who I am. I have a strong startle reflex at the sound of a barking or growling dog. But that outcome one could predict. More uncannily, I have a strong attraction to animals, and I sometimes think that my animal self knows that I am of their world, that they have claimed me, humbled me, and left their mark on my body and spirit. I feel I owe them my attention.

◆

A cormorant the size of a human thumb has been found in the Hohle Fels cave in Germany's Swabian Alps. One of three figurines carved from mammoth ivory, the find provides the earliest evidence that our human ancestors made figurative art more than thirty thousand years ago, the period during which bison, mammoth, and lion images began to transform European caves into shrines. All three carvings in the recently discovered cache depict animals: one horse's head, one half-lion/half-human creature, and one bird with body and neck extended into the graceful tension of a cormorant rising toward water's surface after a feasting dive, rising from the invisible underwater world into the air. The beauty of animals called these ancestors to acts of creation.

The figures, which do not appear to be the work of amateurs though they may be among the earliest artworks made by human beings, are polished from constant handling, as one might rub a beach stone or hardwood burl, letting the oil of one's fingers raise the object's sheen while the thumb's repetitive motion against that smoothness leads the mind to that clean place one comes to when staring into space and thinking. Rather than being savages, our forebears were sculptors, painters, and contemplators, their minds like ours in a daydream. As long as we've been human, we've been making art. Or perhaps it is more accurate to place this eagerness to participate in creation at the center of what it is to be the animal we are: as long we've been making art, we've been human.

Art from the primal world draws the imagination back into the unthinkably deep well of time it took for the human mind as we know it to evolve. "We" may have been around as toolmakers, language users, dietary omnivores, cosmological celebrants, nomadic socializers, and combatants for five hundred thousand to two million years, depending what markers you use to start measuring protohumanity. But it is not until forty thousand to one hundred thousand years ago that fossil forms look indistinguishable from those of modern human beings. And as we dig up more and more of the last remote places on Earth looking for the bones that will teach us the nature of what we are, we keep turning up art and asking, What does it mean?

It means what it is. Mammoth tusk transformed to waterbird by a creature who, seeing the beauty and mystery of the bird, was moved to hold it in mind and hand, to become intimate with the bird, and so carved a likeness that would preserve and keep it close. And so begins the long human braiding of art, nature, and the idea of the transcendent: the bird transcends the limits of its birdness by flying through water, and the carving transcends the circumstance of the human encounter with the waterbird, prolonging the interaction for as long as the hand and mind desire and providing the opportunity to share it with others. Our deepest human memory, one so deep we cannot see the shape of it on the surface of our thinking, may be our capacity to read and preserve and share our encounters with animals. Early humans may have learned this capacity in surviving the threat of predators, but we get to carry it forward as an acuity to animal beauty that gives meaning to our lives.

✦

Animals surrounded our ancestors. Animals were their food, clothes, adversaries, companions, jokes, and their gods. In the Paleolithic period of the Great Hunt, Joseph Campbell writes, "man's ubiquitous nearest neighbors were the beasts in their various species; it was those animals who were his teachers, illustrating in their manners of life the powers and patternings of nature." In this age of mass extinction and the industrialization of life, it is hard to touch the skin of this long and deep companionship. Now we surround the animals and crowd them from their homes. They are the core of what we are as creatures, sharing a biological world and inhabiting our inner lives, though most days they feel peripheral—a wag from the dog, an ankle embrace from the cat, the pleasure of sighting a house finch feeding outside the window, the thrill of spotting a hedgehog waddling along a park path in Prague or a fox trotting across the urban campus in Denver. Animality and humanity are one, expressions of the planet's brilliant inventiveness, and yet the animals are leaving the world and not returning.

What do animals mean to the contemporary imagination? We do not know. Or we have forgotten. Or we are too busy to notice. Or we experience psychic numbing to cope with the scale of extinctions and we feel nothing. Or we begin through our grief to realize how much we love our fellow creatures and we tend to them. Or we write about them, trying to figure what the experience of animals is and how they came to be so ingrained in human mind and emotion, to remember what it feels like to be embedded in the family of animals, to see the ways animals inhabit and limn our lives, entering our days and nights, unannounced and essential.

I am tired of the conventional palette with which the lives of animals are painted. Most renderings feel too saturated with gratuitous piety, weighed down by ceaseless elegy, or boastful about heroic encounters on the last islands of wildness. I want something closer to the marrow of our lived days, as in childhood, when an animal story or encounter could make me wonderstruck. In that mind I could feel my responses to animals inviting me into continuity and connection with forces larger than myself, a feeling for which I hunger today.

This is a spiritual hunger—an attraction to the energy present in all living things that cannot be explained by their material qualities. This energy is mothered by matter. *Mater.* Living creatures apprehend it in each other. *Anima,* the ancients said, meaning breath, life, soul. Perhaps it is an energy that pervades the universe and becomes concentrated in creatures, so that we feel kinship and intensity in their presence. Magnetism. I want to test this sense of presence as we live it during this time of diminishment of Earth's biodiversity. I do not want to write an elegy for the lost and dying animals. Who wants to hear again the sad summary of loss? I want to write of presence, not absence, to feel the spiritual force of animals as one might encounter or contemplate them on any day and in any place—not only on a hike, safari, expedition. All of the world still teems and steams with the shared breath of creatures.

But how can I be honest with myself or anyone else if I do not speak of diminishment, the grief and panic attendant to the loss of so many compatriots? What's the future for life on Earth? For lions, tigers, and polar bears—no future at all. Except in captivity. Or experimental breeding. "Why should I read this?" complained a woman in the audience, when she heard my story of feasting bluefish terrifying thousands of tiny alewives to leap to their deaths on a Cape Cod beach. She didn't want to hear another depressing word of what I had to say. She wanted to find hope for team optimism. I wanted it too. But I knew the only way I could arrive at hope was to travel through grief. What would Anne Frank's faith in humanity add up to, if she hadn't arrived at it during the worst of times? People have rituals for dealing with grief. When a loved one dies, they overcome their loss by talking it out, keening their way into spiritual reflection, gathering together to mourn and help one another to move on. "An hour or two sacred to sorrow," wrote Sir Richard Steele, "revived the spirits without firing the blood."

I want to count the costs to the human spirit of our losses, to attend to the wild and the not so wild, to write about animals and about myself as animal. I want to evoke the range of feeling that animals have inspired in me—terror, anger, happiness, sadness, disgust, surprise, love. There is desire behind every work of art—desire as a religious and erotic and aesthetic force—that drives a person beyond reason into an intuitive sense of what one must do. This bestiary for the twenty-first century is my gratitude, my reverence, my penance, my secular prayer for the beauties and beasts of Earth.

Murray Springs Mammoth

On an autumn day, the yellow-leaved cottonwoods light the passage where the San Pedro flows. This is the last undammed desert river in the American Southwest, a migratory refuge for millions of songbirds. For hundreds of years, cottonwoods have torched the way for people crossing arid land in the American West. Even when no water flows, the thirsty giants mark the place where digging might lead to water. Now in the Late Oil Age the trees converse not with pioneers but with commuters heading west for Tucson and tourists heading east for the faux Old West of Tombstone. These travelers too feel relief to see the grand old cottonwoods, if only for the visual surprise they offer after miles of lowly scrub and sprawl.

I'm cruising east from Sierra Vista, the pop-up city inspired by Fort Huachuca, where intelligence officers learn the language of war and techniques for interrogation, our regional training site for service in hell. The city has been scrawled out in haste as the business of war burgeons. I always wilt driving through this place, nodding to the latest Target, Safeway, Ace, and Subway, knowing that the world has lost another precious quantum of openness. It doesn't help to know that war makes this city thrive or that its growth will mean the end of the San Pedro River as the city's needs lower the aquifer and the river sinks into that absence. Where will the migratory birds go when there is no water left to harbor them as they pass through the desert? At least the Huachuca Mountains hold their ground outside the city limits, though velocity roars at their feet.

I drive out of town, heading for the dip in the road that announces a narrow wash. The brown U.S. Forest Service sign is smaller than a rural mailbox. I could easily breeze on by, but I've come for just this destination to quarry out some firsthand sense of the Murray Springs mammoth site. I turn in to the gravel road, jounce to its end, and hike the black brush scrub to the place where water has gouged out a streambed lined with cut banks taller than a Winnebago. Nothing is flowing in the wash at this time of year. Late autumn, the watercourse has grown thick with shoulder-high rabbitbrush tasseled into full golden plume. The fluff drifts and spins in the air like cirrus clouds of tiny moths. This is a land of ghosts, their history traced in layered soil exposed by erosion. I walk the sand, a sere and hostile place: little shade, little shelter, little vegetation free of thorns. No refuge in sight across the flat, scorched desert, where coyotes and javelinas scratch out a life on rodents and roots. The Dragoon Mountains rise in the distance, stark and raw.

✦

"We have something to match the pyramids of Egypt," Paul Martin boasts when I visit him at the Desert Laboratory on Tumamoc Hill, mischief flickering across his face like campfire light. "We have giant ground sloth shit." He sits behind his desk at the research site established in Tucson by the Carnegie Institution in 1903, the acropolis of arid land studies. He shows off the prizes in his glass-covered display case: a healthy fistful of fossilized sloth dung from Rampart Cave in the Grand Canyon and the incisor of a woolly mammoth. He recites the names of megafauna that once roamed the Americas.

Preptoceras (shrub oxen). *Symbos* and *Bootherium* (woodland musk oxen). *Stockoceros* (four-horned pronghorns). *Libytherium* (dwarf pronghorns). *Tanupoloma* and *Titanotylopus* (llama-like camels). Woolly rhinos. *Gomphotheres* (one of three families of elephants). Glyptodons (armadillos the size of a car). American cheetahs. Short-faced bears. Dire wolves. Dozens more.

During a long and heckled career, Martin has gathered evidence from ancient packrat middens where fossil pollen shows what plants lived in a place and what animals ate them as far back as ten thousand years ago. Globe mallow, Mormon tea, and saltbush were the main forage for extinct giants. Grass kept the eight-ton woolly mammoths alive. Lots of grass. A time traveler visiting this landscape fourteen thousand years ago, before humans had appeared in the American landscape, would witness mammoths, camels, horses, and sloths grazing along the shores of the San Pedro, an American lion dozing in the shade.

"We've been selling out our past," Martin continues, warmth softening a face that might otherwise appear weary with years. "There are whole orders extinct from this continent as important as the elephants in Africa. We don't even know what was here. We haven't gone back far enough."

Martin has worked at the Desert Lab since the 1960s and has seen his ideas dismissed, debated, and, as recently as 2007, celebrated in *Scientific American.* He has hypothesized that the great mammals of the Americas became extinct because early human hunters slaughtered them. The hypothesis has been dubbed the "Pleistocene overkill" theory. On our continent 75 percent of the large mammals that became extinct disappeared shortly after the hunters arrived, following prey across the Bering land bridge. The pattern of extinction has moved with "deadly syncopation" around the globe for at least fifty thousand years. Martin turns to a strangely poetic music of invented words to dramatize his theory, a single percussive syllable for human arrival, and another for their outsized animal assault.

In an *American Scientist* interview he sums it up:

As humans first arrive ("ka!"), they rapidly increase in numbers and trigger megafaunal extinction ("tunk!") in a few thousand years at most: 50,000 years ago in Australia ("ka-tunk!"), 11,000 years ago in America ("ka-tunk!"), 5,000 years ago in Cuba and Haiti ("ka-tunk!"), and less than 1,000 years ago in New Zealand ("ka-tunk!").

Mind-boggling as it is to imagine a small group of hunters armed with stone-tipped spears standing up to a ten-ton Columbia mammoth that looms thirteen feet at the shoulder and swings tusks the length of a Buick, such was the scene again and again and again, the little bipeds outcompeting their bestial rivals.

"How was it possible?" I ask Martin.

"I haven't wanted to use the word. But I have to say . . . genocide. They enjoyed killing. You see it all over the world today. Look at Rwanda. The death camps of Darfur. We haven't found a way to stop it. They did it for no reason other than . . . it could be done."

Martin's manner is gentle and friendly, despite the deadening weight of his claim. He doesn't want to cause a ruckus with his ideas. They are just what he has come to after a lifetime of scientific research and contemplation. I suspect his good humor has helped him to weather forty years of being treated like either a crackpot or a genius. He speaks of hunters today who pay anything to bag a certain species in Africa, accomplishing their full complement of trophy kills. I roll my eyes in disgust.

"It's in the genes, Alison," he soothes, his voice surprisingly empathic. Material explanation is not absolution, but it makes forgiveness come easier. He recalls his childhood. He and other boys tortured pigs with sticks for the fun of it. For a high school graduation present, he got to take his father's car to Florida on a bird-watching trip. He started running down cats in the road. He made an ethical argument for himself to support his actions. The cats are not on our side, since they are killing birds. Later, when he was a student at the University of Michigan, he shot and tagged birds for a natural history collection.

"There was more to it than science," he confides. "There was the pleasure human beings take in killing. With hyenas and other animals, it's been called 'surplus killing.' Look it up."

The Pleistocene killings occurred, in Martin's view, because the hunters were skilled and took pleasure in their skill. The animals, innocent of human beings for millions of years, did not recognize the bipeds as predators. They were probably weakened by the Ice Age, drought, and habitat changes that came in synchronicity with the hunters. What if they burned off the grasses to have a clear view of the land and flush out game? The American megafauna were easy marks. In Africa the animals had coevolved with hominids and understood them to be dangerous. There, both human hunters and animal prey had grown strong, fierce, and wily under the pressures they exerted on each other. In places where the fauna had no selection pressure from hominids, they were likely to have behaved as did the Galapagos birds and beasts when Darwin arrived. Oblivious. Unconcealed. Vulnerable.

Martin would like schoolchildren to know that horses and camels originated in the Americas. He'd like them to know that, for millions of years, American cheetahs hunted pronghorn antelope on American grasslands. He'd like to see elephants and lions return to the San Pedro and other regions of the West set aside for reinhabitation of the great mammals. He'd like to study fruit dispersal and forest tree ecology under conditions similar to what prevailed before the extinctions.

"That," he asserts with good and wistful will, "was a great time for Earth."

✦

I pick my way through the dry scrub at the Murray Springs washout. In 1966, researchers found here sixteen Clovis spear points, a wrench carved from a mammoth bone, fossil remains of a young female mammoth, eleven bison, camels, horses, wolves, and a hunting camp stocked with flensing stones and cutters. Pine needles were found in the middens, remnants of the piñon and juniper that grew where now blackthorn and rabbitbrush gain ground. I came here to wrap my senses around the place, not that the terrain looks much like it would have when those hunters tracked the mammoth and her young into a swampy thicket, circling them when the beasts came to drink at a water hole dug with their tusks. The hunters must have divided the labor, separating the calf from the mother, circling it, shouting courage and caution to each other, until they were close enough to land spear blows. The agate points, none much larger than a human palm, broke into the calf's flesh—one near the base of the skull, one near the scapula, two lodged between ribs, and then the killing blade slipped between two vertebrae, severing the spinal column and knocking the calf off its feet. The din of animal screams and human shouts quieted as the young mammoth fell. The mother withdrew, a spearhead lodged in her gut that would bleed her dry, so that the calcified remains of her would surface ten miles downstream in another arroyo. The bladed stone rested in its nest of bones as the body fell. It was silted over until it became hidden and remained so for ten thousand years.

I run my finger along the Clanton clay, the black strip of sediment that marks the cut bank about three meters below ground level, algal deposits laid down in the days when mammoths tusked into the mud to dig their wallow. Arid sandy soil lies over the black mat, a measure in dirt, silt, and dross of the long interval between the mammoth's life and my own. The streambed is as dry as ash. The air, dry and hot as an oven. Inching my finger gently at the sand and clay, I'm startled to touch one tiny calciferous dwelling after another packed into the marly bank. A spiral tube, a horn shape, a clamshell, a miniature conch. Mussels and snails. Then pointing out from the black stratum, a knuckled bone like the thigh joint on a chicken leg grabs my eye. I pick the bone loose. It is frailer than an eggshell and as hollow.

What bird sang on this stream bank at dawn and dusk in those years when hunters flensed meat from gigantic bones and hung it over pine rails to dry? What mind listened to the song and, exhausted from the day's labor, felt joy settling into evening? What body slept inside the long ache of good work, riding dreams into the underworld, and then startled awake at dawn to an exaltation of birdsong?

The white bone crumbles at my touch.

Spotted Hyena

On a dark and moonless night of storms, Hans Kruuk observed a pack of spotted hyenas engaging in a predatory orgy of killing. The Dutch biologist had spent three and a half years living with Serengeti hyenas, documenting their complex matriarchal clan structure and cooperative hunting strategies, and keeping a full-grown hyena named Solomon as house pet. Hyenas make a living by scavenging and hunting. Their large jaw muscles and bone-crushing premolars give them chewing ability stronger than a brown bear's. They eat and digest parts of dead animals other predators leave for waste, including bones. Their gut is so efficient that their feces are white and powdery. Hyenas rival primates in intelligence and skill at cooperative hunting. In captivity, pairs of hyenas, given the challenge to pull two ropes in unison to get a food reward, learned the skill quicker than chimps given the same task. They rivaled the chimps too in passing on the skill to inexperienced clan mates.

Spotted hyenas are weird looking. Cute teddy bear ears. Fluffy, mottled coat. The cantilevered stance, hind legs much shorter than forelegs, makes the animal look somehow taller than itself and always ready to lunge. There is menace in the darting eyes. Their whooping cry has earned them the nickname "laughing hyena," though it sounds nothing like laughter except in bedlam. They live in clans of five to ninety members, led by an alpha female whose offspring will inherit her role. Aristotle thought hyenas resembled hermaphrodites. There is little sexual dimorphism in their genitalia. The female hyena has a six-inch clitoris that can become erect. The labia are fused in a sac resembling a scrotum. This confusing equipment entered oral tradition as protoscience: in medieval bestiaries, the hyena was said to change its gender at will or with the season. For the female hyena, this gear means difficult childbirth, as the young emerge through the clitoris.

Kruuk observed that during a violent storm in the Ngorongoro Crater, a herd of Thompson gazelles became frenzied and disoriented. The hyenas became excited and gave chase, pursuing the gazelles with a zeal matching the storm's intensity. They slaughtered eighty in a night—far more than the pack could possibly eat. He named the behavior "surplus killing," and it is now known that many carnivores do this. It may be more likely to occur when predators are overstimulated and prey weakened by ill health or weather. Kruuk reported that three crows went on a binge, caching seventy-nine mice in slightly over two hours. Other reports of surplus killing tally red foxes in north Scotland killing two hundred black-headed gulls in a night, and similar binges by minks feeding on terns, killer whales on seal pups, and even among spiders hunting flies. Surplus killing is not the norm, but it is common enough in the carnivorous world to say that the capacity for this behavior is a component of the animal spirit.

Surplus killing looks brutal and gratuitously violent to the human eye, though our species too is quite accomplished in acts that have earned those descriptors. But for an animal that must kill to live, it makes sense for the hunt and the kill to be pleasurable. If you don't kill, you don't eat, and if you don't eat, you die. Nature's clever trick is to make behaviors that enhance survival among a creature's keenest pleasures: eating, having sex, maternal bonding, social cohesion. Animals engaged in surplus killing may simply be thrilling in their physical being—their skill and strength and muscular joy. Human beings add a new element to the repertoire of the animal spirit. In finding the behavior excessive, vicious, causing unnecessary suffering and death, humanity identifies itself as a creature holding values and making ethical judgments. Just because it feels good doesn't mean you should do it.

I visited the Ngorongoro Crater in the company of two Peace Corps volunteers, a traveling companion, and a Chaga guide. My safari offered no opportunity for the sustained observation I so admire in a researcher of Kruuk's dedication. What conclusions could I draw from a week of casual observation made through the roof of a Land Rover?

Surely not science. A casual observer can testify only to the moment. And what one sees will always be colored by what one longs to see. The unsettling truth is that most safari visitors coming to the last great animal spectacles on Earth long to see the kill. It thrills and arouses the imagination. It stimulates an atavistic hunger to live in a body so perfectly suited to meeting its needs. I saw no kill and counseled myself that I should not be disappointed.

Yes, I saw the dried pelt of a gazelle hanging from a baobab tree where a leopard had left it after supper. Yes, I saw the dismembered head of a zebra lying in scrub, the red gash where it had been severed as loud in mind today as when I saw it through the window of our racing microbus. But what struck me most keenly was the peace of the animals. Cloudlike herds of zebra, impala, and wildebeest drifted across Ngorongoro's great grassy mind, shape-shifting throughout the afternoon. Two cheetahs trotted in purposeful single file toward the opening in the crater that leads to the Serengeti. The pride of lionesses lay on their backs in the high heat of the day, forelegs dawdling up into the air. The black rhino slept, imitating a boulder in tall grass. The Egyptian goose and crown-crested cranes, Fischer's lovebirds and superb starlings, hammerkops and saddle-billed storks dabbled in the shallows of wetlands or clawed up playful clouds of dust. The troupe of baboons sat quietly under a sprawling tree, waiting out a rain squall. The peace of the land, the last islands of this peace, made me feel small. I welcomed the feeling. It was a pleasure to feel insignificant, to let my desires quiet, and feel, in the moment, the human body as an instrument attuned to peace.

The Sacred Pig

Imagine a tired sow with ten impish piglets of varied color—coppertop, red spot, leopard skin, ivory—nuzzling in a slop of straw and spilled water. Their ears and snouts are pink and hairless. Coarse silky bristle thinly covers their bodies. They are nothing like pink cartoon pigs. The piglets nibble on fresh-cut spring grass spread in the trough. They sleep in an intimate mindless pile. When they wake, the noise begins. They poke at the sow. She brushes them aside with her snout. They persist. She goes down heavily onto her chest, then turns to open her teats to them. They squeak and race. She grunts. Together they make a chant. Oh, sweet pig. They all settle into the rhythm. Sucking sounds, squabbles for position, the sow's grunts of peaceful acceptance and pleasure. After they are all calm and satisfied, she gets up and the piglets fall into napping, lined up like a package of hot dogs.

Mitch, who takes care of this small farm, sits in a folding chair in the hog pen to watch the piglets and get to know them. He picks Red Dot to be the next brood sow. She's friendly and easygoing. The others will be raised for meat. When the time comes for weaning, he separates the piglets from the sow in adjacent pens. The piglets cannot see their mother, but the chorus continues. The sleeping sow makes soft contented grunts, and the piglets reply in kind to her reassurance. Mitch was eight years old the first time he shot a cow. His father handed him the rifle: "You might as well do it this time." Now he's the farm manager at Sterling College in Craftsbury

Common, Vermont, the smallest college in the nation where a student can study draft horses, goat farming, or wood living and dead. Before he took this position, Mitch worked for the Quaker Farm and Wilderness camps. He comes from a family of farmers and is mindful in continuing the work.

About the killing, he says that some people read a poem before they do it. Some say a prayer of gratitude. Kids, he says, get into it. On the morning they learn to butcher hens, no one wants to make the first cut. By afternoon, they're having fun and don't want to stop. Mitch says he's silent for a few minutes before he does it. Later one of the students asks me, "Why are the Native American stories better than ours? Do you believe it, for example, when they say the animal gave itself to the hunter?" No. I don't believe the animal gave itself. But I believe that to see it that way helps people to accept the sadness of taking another life. It gives the act a spiritual aspect. Meaning comes into the act when it is seen through the lens of a belief in reciprocity between human and animal, a spiritual presence grounded in the things of the world.

But what am I missing of the metaphysical world? The *meta* that hovers everywhere, of which Paul writes in Romans: "For we know that the whole creation groaneth and travaileth in pain together until now." That "until now" jolts with its confidence that "the earnest expectation of creatures," "the hope for deliverance," is at hand in the word of God, will be manifest to the sons of God. I have no such confidence. For one thing, I am daughter not son. For another, I find continuities not in the desire for them but in their manifestation as cycles of growth and decay, arrival and departure, emergence and disappearance. I am hopelessly materialistic in my spirituality. Is that possible? The lessons will come.

On the day the piglets are castrated, I visit the barn to watch. No one likes the job, but Mitch knows how to do it and the razor is swift. He says his father used to keep a jar of cob-

webs in the barn for clotting blood in the wound. This time
he uses salt. He picks up the piglets in his beefy hands and
steadies them for the cutman who slits the sack and pulls out
the testes in a fast grab. There's a scream from each piglet
and then the job is finished. The little ones curl up to sleep
in clean straw.

✦

In the ancient world, the pig was sacred. The process of pig
domestication began in the Tigris Basin thirteen thousand
years ago; in Cyprus and China, eleven thousand years ago.
Sculptures of pigs have been unearthed in Greece, Russia,
Yugoslavia, and Macedonia. Marija Gimbutas, in her keystone
work *The Goddesses and Gods of Old Europe,* writes that "the fast-
growing body of the pig will have been compared to corn
growing and ripening, so that its soft fats apparently came to
symbolize the earth itself, causing the pig to become a sacred
animal probably no later than 6000 BC." The goddess of vegetation sometimes wears a pig mask. Sometimes the pig figu-
rine, fleshy and round, is scored with traces of grain pressed
into the clay or is graced with earrings. The prehistoric goddess of vegetation dates back to Neolithic times and is predecessor to Demeter, the Greek goddess of fertility and harvest,
whose temple at Eleusis was built in the second century BCE.

The Eleusinian Mysteries became the principal religious
ritual of ancient Greece, begun circa 1600 BCE. Originally a
secret cult devoted to Demeter, the rites honored the annual
cycle of death and rebirth of grain in the fields. The resurrection of seeds buried in the ground inspired the faith
that a similar resurrection might await the human body laid
to rest in the earth. The religious rituals of the Eleusinian
Mysteries lasted two thousand years, became the official state
religion, and spread to Rome. They laid the groundwork for
Christianity's belief in resurrection and were ultimately over-
thrown by the Roman emperor in the fourth century CE.

The canonical source of Demeter's story, the "Homeric Hymn to Demeter," dates from about a thousand years into the practice of these rituals. It is called Homeric because it employs the same meter as *The Iliad* and *The Odyssey*—dactylic hexameter, the rhythm of "Picture yourself in a boat on a river / With tangerine trees and marmalade skies." The foundation of the Mysteries is Demeter's power over the fertility of the land. When her daughter Persephone is stolen by Hades to be his lover in the underworld, the mother's grief is so acute that she refuses to let the fields produce grain. People are in danger of starving, but Demeter resists, saying there will be no crops until she sees her daughter return. When Persephone does come back, after many trials among mortals and much deal making among the gods, Demeter's sudden transformation of bare ground into a "vast sheet of ruddy grain" marks the miracle of fruition returning after the fallow time and sparks the fertility cult of the mysteries. This metamorphosis occurs in mythic time, so it is safe to say that it continues in the present moment for the mind embracing its truth.

Suckling pigs played a key role in the festival of Thesmophoria, a three-day rite that took place in October, the time for autumn sowing of barley and winter wheat. As I write this, the word *sow* catches my eye, as both noun for the female pig and verb for planting seeds. The *Oxford English Dictionary* tells me that the two words come from different Old English roots, but nonetheless history delivers the homograph to modernity still carrying freight from the ancients. Pig = grain. And the corollary, embedded in prehistoric art: pig = Earth = survival.

Persephone was sometimes known as "that sweet young seedling" or "killer of suckling pigs." Some say that when the earth opened to swallow her, a herd of pigs rooting nearby was also swallowed into the underworld. Demeter, when she was wandering in search of Persephone, found her daughter's footprints obliterated by pigs' hooves.

The Thesmophoria was performed exclusively by women, who prepared with sexual abstinence, fasting, and ribald exchanges of insults (a relic of the dirty jokes that had helped Demeter revive from her depression). Piglets, thrown into a pit to decay, were retrieved, placed on altars, mixed with seeds, and returned to the fields to guarantee fertility. Cicero wrote, in praise of the Eleusinian Mysteries, that "we have learned from them the first principles of life and have gained the understanding, not only to live happily, but also to die with better hope."

Oh, sweet pig.

✦

1957. Nevada Test Site.

Operation Plumbbob.

Twenty-nine explosions over five months, May to October. Tower shots. Balloon shots. Tunnel shots.

"It was the world's finest Roman candle, because at night it was all visible. Blue fire shot hundreds of feet in the air. Everyone was down in the area, and they all jumped in their cars and drove like crazy, not even counting who was there and who came out of the area."

Sixteen thousand military personnel from the Army, Navy, Air Force, and Marines. The Department of Defense wanted to learn how foot soldiers would stand up physically and psychologically to the tactical nuclear battlefield.

More than two times as much radioiodine as in any other continental test series—58,300 kilocuries—released into the atmosphere.

Total civilian exposures from Plumbbob explosions: 120 million person-rads of thyroid tissue exposure expected to cause some 38,000 cases of thyroid cancer leading to some 1,900 deaths. Or 11,000–212,000 excess cases of thyroid cancer leading to 1,000–20,000 deaths.

Total nonhuman research subjects (not counting collateral

damage in the desert, which was not part of the protocol): 1,200 pigs that were subjected to blast-effect studies. In the Priscilla shot (thirty-seven kilotons), 719 pigs, about one-third of a mile of piglets lined up snout to tail. They were not, however, lined up in that manner. They were tethered in containers that look like rural mailboxes. Each pig wore a different kind of protective jacket. The researchers wanted to know which jacket would provide the best protection against the nuclear bomb's thermal pulse. In other tests, pigs were placed in pens behind large sheets of glass to test the effect of flying debris on living targets.

Why should I read this?

A poster from the era: Lassie dog posed happily beneath a desertscape upon which a nuclear explosion has blossomed. Caption: "We must thank ANIMALS if good comes from the atomic bomb."

Look it up.

The pigs have been archived on film, their screams and panic preserved in bytes and bits, with ones and zeroes, on celluloid and silicon. Many of the pigs survived, horribly burned and traumatized. One might say they were sacrificed and yet the word weakens at the knees in this context. "Making sacred" is not what has happened, though "giving up" something has. Giving up the notion of living happily, giving up the hope of better dying.

Oh, sweet pig.

rows are ubiquitous in the Connecticut hills and fields, the landscape of my childhood. In sunlight, their feathers shine like obsidian. Over a cornfield, a flock of crows is an elegance. Gleaning grubs from a fallow field, it is a society of peasants. Crows fly with patience, their flapping never belabored. Sometimes they glide. They make their own clothing, feathers grown from their skin, every keratinous cell of the calamus, every black silk fiber of the vane, made by the crow, made thoughtlessly and without effort. There is a hollow place in the quill, a space used by veins to supply nutrients while the feather is alive and growing. But the feathers are dead when the crow wears them, a headdress, wing dress, body dress, basic black, and bearing the lovely sheen of life. For forty million years the iridescence of bird feathers has graced the earth.

But it was the sound of crows that I loved as a child. Ca-aw. Ca-aw. The throaty, emphatic call announced their presence. It rose from cedar trees on the edge of the yard, from that place in the sky just out of sight above the hickory tree or behind the house; it entered the open window of the school bus or the chaotic playground during recess at school. The caws announced some work to be done, some passage to be flown, some sight to be seen, some news to be shared. What was it that made them call like that from the air as they passed on their way? Ca-aw. The syllable bends slightly downward at the end, almost like the Doppler effect of a passing train. It was a sound I knew well and a voice that made me

feel the world was right, that some lives beyond my life were
going about their business, being with their being, and I felt
suddenly larger than my small self. Even now, remembering
it, I feel as if I am opening the door and stepping outside into
the wonder of things. Crows were always a surprise and never
a menace to me.

My father did not like crows. He spent many hours working in his vegetable garden. It was his solace. He started corn
from seed, germinating Golden Bantam stock in Dixie cups,
then transplanting it into hills he had hoed up in the rocky
soil. No sooner had he tamped the seedlings into the ground
than the crows would fly in to pluck up the tender greens. I
saw him storm out of the house with his shotgun many times
to teach them a lesson. I'm sure he failed. I was never shocked
to see his rage. I empathized with that feeling of helplessness
that riled him, though I did not share his hatred of crows.

A group of crows is called a "murder." It lines up in a fes-
tive parade of animal names: flock of sheep, herd of horses,
pack of wolves, parliament of owls, cauldron of hawks, bouquet of pheasants, whiteness of swans, murmuration of starlings, gaggle of geese, improbability of shearwaters, newspaper syndicate of gannets, charm of finches, raft of ducks,
exaltation of larks, unkindness of ravens. The poor corvids
scored low in the judging.

Murder as a group name for crows goes back at least to
the 1400s in England. The American Society of Crows and
Ravens suggests the origin of the name might be in the
folk legend that crows, in their black robes, hold tribunals
to judge and punish members of their flock exercising bad
behavior. A crow that is found guilty would be killed by the
flock. This notion, the society claims, may be based on obser-
vations that a crow will occasionally kill a dying crow that
doesn't belong in its territory or will feed on a dead crow. In
medieval times, crows scavenged human remains at grave-
sides, battlefields, and execution sites.

Crows are smart. Crows use tools. They adapt to city life. They rival primates in cognitive ability. In the wild, New Caledonia crows will use a twig to probe in a tree trunk for grubs. In captivity, two crows sharing an enclosure learned to retrieve bits of pig heart, their favorite food, from a bucket. The male chose the hooked wire, which did the job well, so the female took the straight wire and bent it into a hook, using it to lift the small bucket of food from a vertical pipe. She had no other crows to model the behavior, little training with pliable objects, and very limited experience with wire. Such skill at turning a found object into a tool is rare among animals. Chimpanzees presented with a similar task—using a length of pipe to pass through a hole to retrieve an apple— failed until they were coached.

Since 1990, Japanese crows have been observed using cars to crack walnuts. The trees grow beside a street on a university campus. The birds drop a nut into traffic and when it's cracked, fly down to retrieve the meat. Because traffic can be heavy on campus, the retrieval can be challenging. So the crows have learned to drop the nuts onto crosswalks. Crows and humans line up and wait on the sidewalk. When the cars stop, the bird hops into the street and safely retrieves the snack. Crows in California have been seen using the cross- walk technique. The birds have long known how to drop clams onto rocks to break their shells. But this behavior requires inferential thinking: if I drop this nut here, it will be cracked open by the passing cars.

Crows also demonstrate compassion and companion- ship. Kevin McGowan, working with the Cornell Lab of Ornithology, has studied crows for over twenty years. The group he has tagged and studied suffered an epidemic of West Nile virus that killed one-third of the population in 2002; the following year, another third were lost to the virus. Crows are very social. They roost in murders that can range from one hundred individuals to millions. Crows have

twenty or more calls including alarm calls, hunting calls, and
assembly calls. The call for distress brings other crows. Crows
develop a complex system of helpers. They will defend unre-
lated crows. One crow will wait in a tree watching out for
predators while others forage, making a small personal sacrifice for the good of the flock. Crows in the wild can live fifteen to twenty years. The oldest known wild crow lived nearly
thirty years. They mate for life.

During the West Nile epidemic, when one crow lost a
partner it stayed with the larger family of eight or so birds.
Widowed adults moved in with their parents. Even with
plenty of open territory in which to go off and mate anew,
they chose to stay and care for siblings. When only two sisters
were left, they joined neighbors and helped raise their young.
Researcher Anne Clark reported that the crows that had suffered big losses to their community did not move right away
into the opened territory. It was as if they didn't know who
owned it anymore or they simply didn't want to go back to
the place of so much dying. She called it the "haunted house
effect."

During the epidemic, when a crow was sick and dying
its mate would sit beside it until the end. If the dying bird
had no mate, another member of its blended family would
perch by its side. The researchers concluded that no crow
dies alone. Far from being murderers, a flock of crows might
more aptly be called a caretaking of crows.

Dog Tags

Clamp the S-hook to the collar and the dog has permission to live. If he gets lost, the person who finds him can get your address and bring him home to you. If he gets hit by a car, someone will deliver a definition for the grief you feel at the loss of his company. Every year or two you will renew his license, using pliers or a Vise-Grip to detach the old tag and attach the new one. Then the dog will prance around the living room shaking his head, for a few moments feeling the collar that he had forgotten he wears. You will hear him jingle in the house at night as he scratches his fleas—his fleas, like he is your dog, though unlike this in that he takes no pleasure in their companionship. Because of the metallic jingle, you will hear him stir, turn, and resettle in the night. A stranger who once has been attacked (such a sweet dog, he would never . . .) will be grateful for the music of dog tags that gives warning before the bark or growl or baring of teeth that will trigger the startle reflex, the body's memory of a trauma the mind has suppressed. Once a person has known teeth in her flesh, the dog tags will no longer convince her that anyone owns the dog's wildness except the dog. *Domestic* only means he has agreed to live in the house and we have agreed to welcome him there.

Men and women wear dog tags too, to identify their bodies. In 2001, a twenty-seven-year-old man traveling in Ho Chi Minh City to scout for business opportunities found the dog tags of American soldiers hanging on a string in a back-alley market not frequented by tourists. They were for sale—six or seven for one dollar. He was disgusted. He could not stop thinking about them. Were they real or fake? He returned to buy 620 of them and brought them home. Some of the dog tags belonged to men who are still living. Thirty years after leaving Vietnam, where every one of them must have left a piece of his soul, the soldiers got back their IDs. For them too the dog tags meant, in retrospect, permission to live. Thirty years after their sons died in Vietnam, some parents got back their dog tags. One mother said she felt joy to hold them. For her they meant identifying with her son's body, and he was real and tangible, at least in her mind, as had been the child whose back she had stroked as he fell into sleep on troubled nights.

One morning in Vermont when I lived simple and remote, visitors rare and reminding me that the world extended beyond my house and barn and neighborhood, I picked up a hitchhiker. This was near the Canadian border, so near I had gone several times to a club the size of my living room in the eastern townships of Quebec to hear Jesse Winchester perform. The Memphis-raised folksinger and draft resister had become famous for his love song "Yankee Lady," but he could not perform in the United States without being arrested for evading his 1967 draft notice. That war was everywhere in American society, and it showed up quietly on my dirt road that morning. The hitchhiker looked about the age I then was—twenty-four or twenty-five. He was bearded, scruffy, and carried a dirty backpack, the sartorial style signifying, it seemed to me then, his solidarity with resisting the trim exterior that belied America's vicious heart. To be messy and grow wild was to be truthful about the reality that our nation was a mess and the war had gone wild—a ferocity no one's tidy rhetoric could control. But appearances rarely are what they seem, and I realized soon that I had projected my own ideology on the stranger, instead of learning the story that had brought him to this spot on his tattered map. I know this is beginning to sound like one of the tales we call a shaggy dog story—so much digression you can't see where you're going.

I brought the man to my house for lunch, gave him home-made soup and bread. He wanted a lift a few miles down the road, and I agreed to take him. He pointed to the green area on his map, saying it looked like the biggest stretch of unin-habited forest in the vicinity and asking me if that were true. I said yes and pointed out the window to the Cold Hollow Mountains, which had been my comfort in the landscape that taught me I belonged to something larger and older and wiser than human life. He told me he wanted to see if he could survive in the wild with nothing but his pocketknife and sleeping bag. Did he even have a sleeping bag? I remem-ber so little of this—only that I thought he was crazy or sui-cidal or running from something that must have seemed to him worse than death. It was late autumn and in that region winter brought killing cold, weeks when the morning tem-perature would register at forty below. Why didn't I ask the stranger where he had come from and why? Why didn't I offer him something other than soup and a ride? What would it have been? I was afraid of him and I wanted to protect him, and the contradiction immobilized my good intentions.

After lunch I drove him as far as a car could go on the dirt road that dead-ends on a saddle of those forested moun-tains. This looks good, he said. The maple trees had already lost their leaves and lay crisp with frost on the hard-packed ground. I stopped the car. Are you sure? I began to see that I might be helping a man to kill himself. Yes, he said. And his eyes were sure. What was unsaid hung around us like acrid smoke. Will you do me a favor? he asked. What? He reached in his pocket and took out a set of dog tags hanging on their chain. Put these in the nearest U.S. mailbox. I stared at him. It's okay, he said. I took the tags. I let him out. He walked upslope into the woods. I wanted to call out to him, but what could I have said? I drove to town and put the dog tags in a mail drop at the post office. I felt as if I were committing a crime. I cannot say what his intentions were. Perhaps he'd gone AWOL and would hike north to the border for amnesty. Perhaps he died in the cold woods with not one thing on his body to identify him, wanting to be reduced to the animal, because he felt himself no longer to be human. There were so many men—mostly men in those years—who were lost or could not find a way out of the arguments in their heads over what they had done or not done in the war. I felt ugly to myself, as if by handing in his tags, I was treating a man as if he meant less to me than a dog. I regret still that I did nothing more to help him. What would that have been? Send a letter to his family explaining his confident resolve? Perhaps this account is that letter. Perhaps we, every one of us who has no faith in war, are his family.

Patativa (Sporophila leucoptera)

The passerines make up the largest order of birds on the planet, about half of ten thousand or so bird species. Many passerines are songbirds. The house sparrow (*Passer domesticus*) and tree sparrow (*Passer montanus*). Wood thrush. Veery. Vireo. Hermit thrush. Cedar waxwing. White-throated sparrow. Olive-sided flycatcher. Warbler. Gnatcatcher. Flowerpecker. Mockingbird. Oxpecker. Bulbul. Bird of paradise. Wagtail. Pipit. Weaver. Indigo bird. Grackle. Cardinal. Bunting. Titmouse. Bluejay. Peewee. Lark. Raven. Mockingbird. Honeyeater. Shrike. The extinct passenger pigeon and dusky seaside sparrow were passerines.

All passerines are perching birds, having a special adaptation that allows their feet and talons to tighten and clench when they relax. Their feet are anisodactyl, one of numerous arrangements for bird digits, with the first toe facing backward and the other three facing forward. When passerines start to fall asleep, their feet clench automatically onto their perch, the body acting without consciousness, as in the human startle reflex, to secure their position. Passerines can cling to horizontal or vertical perches, and their legs are super strong, so that they can seem to ascend a tree by bounding hops, branch to branch to branch, as I recently saw a boastfully athletic bluejay do on a tall black spruce. The bird seemed to pop from one branch up to the next and next, never opening wings, a gymnast of branchlets.

Aniso means dissimilar. *Dactyl* means finger. The pterodactyl was a prehistoric, dinosauric bird with "wing-fingers." Other arrangements of bird toes include the zygodactyls such as woodpeckers, with two digits facing forward and two backward facilitating vertical walking up a tree trunk; the raptorial hawks and owls, with four sharp curved nails for grabbing while in flight; and the syndactyls such as the semipalmated plover with its half-webbed toes, and the palmated ducks and gulls with fully webbed toes for wading and swimming in water. All this variety and more is a way of saying birds are very successful players in the evolutionary game, having adapted to every environment on the planet and hung in there for millions of years, despite the steep learning curve that human culture has brought to the world.

Probably 13 percent of bird species are threatened with extinction, with another 12 percent occupying small ranges in danger of habitat destruction. When I mention such statistics to my undergraduate students, some are crestfallen, heartbroken, downed by grief and guilt to be part of the sad human story that has brought the animal planet to its knees. But there are always a few students in the classroom—and sometimes more than a few—who glaze over in boredom. One says, "So what? What does that have to do with me?"

I say, "All art is empathy." I say, "Neruda tells us that artists must always be on the side of the oppressed." I say, "Nature isn't a bank account we can withdraw from until it's empty. Nature is the money and when it's gone, we're gone." I say, "We, the species, not 'we, the people of these United States.'" I say, "Ecosystem science says we're part of a whole and all the other creatures want their lives as much as we want ours. That desire is the planet's gift to all of us, a gift that's perilous to refuse."

I exhort until I have made myself a fool for life.

I say, "Do you remember a time when you saw an animal and it made you startle into wonder? That moment of consciousness is where art and science and religion were born, that moment of snapping awake." I say, "The well-being of life is everyone's business now."

My students are worried about money and jobs and what music to download to their amazing external brains. They are addicts and anorexics and survivors of gangbanging and cancer and of mothers who have hanged themselves. They are part of a wounded whole. They want to become writers because they feel invisible. No matter what they buy and wear and play, they still feel invisible. They think language might help to make them visible, will help to make visible something ineffably seductive about their amazing internal brains that are crackling and flashing at the rhythm of one thousand trillion neural connections in constant electrical flow.

Motto for planet, world, and brain: connectedness is all.

Would it help if I talked about dactyls?

Dactyl means finger. *Dactyl* means a unit of measure in a line of poetry. Dactyl is music. Dactyl is a bird claw. Dactyl is a group of ten small phallic males associated with the Great Mother in ancient myth. Smiths and healers in Hephaestus's employ. The ancients say that the dactyls taught humans mathematics and the alphabet. They say that when the Mother of the Gods gave birth, she went to a sacred cave on Mount Ida. She squatted down in labor and dug her ten fingers into the earth. The dactyl is the Earth Mother's grip on life. A finger has three segments, the first segment being the longest. The dactyl in poetry has three syllables, the first one being the strongest. The dactyl is the basic foot in Greek and Latin epic poetry, usually composed in lines of six feet. Would it help if I asked which came first, the finger or the foot, the bird or the poem?

Yes, all of this would help.

✦

The man called Patativa came out of the backcountry, the dry *sertão*, of northeastern Brazil with hundreds of poems on his lips. He was a peasant, blind in one eye since age four, blind in both eyes since age forty-five. His father died when he was eight and he began working as a plowman, growing cotton and beans. This is the land of the landless where drought and flood and famine rule. The land where coffins are sold in the store next to fruits and vegetables, because death is a daily way of life. It is the land of itinerant singers at the outdoor markets. Before Patativa knew the alphabet, the man was making up poems. And though he became a virtuoso improviser, much of his work was composed in European literary forms, worked out and structured in memory.

"He did not speak in prose, but almost always in rhyme," writes Nicholas Gabriel Arons in "Homer of the Sertão," an account of his visit with Patativa in 2000 when the poet was ninety-one years old. Arons found him "standing at his door, wearing a cowboy hat, a pink button-down shirt that looked as if it had not been changed in two months, and huge black sunglasses. He was a short man, no taller than five feet, and had a full head of gray hair and a round, jolly face weathered from years in the fields, on stages, and in dust storms."

In the poor villages of the state of Ceará, it has long been the custom for people to sit outside sharing folk songs and *cordel* poems. This was how people got the news before the cell phone and the satellites brought everybody's news everywhere. The songs were vessels for praise, lament, and protest. They were a record of lives. Thousands of popular poets and singers from this land of the forgotten have carried forward poetic traditions for at least two hundred years. *Cordelistas, repentistas, poesia da bancada, poesia cabolca*, sonnets in metrics after the sixteenth-century Portuguese poet Luís de Camões. Northeast ancestry—like the language of Brazilian Portuguese—is a mix of indigenous, African, and Portuguese lineage. Songs and poems have been passed generation to generation through oral tradition. Oral poets held sway in rural communities. One might hear the news on the radio, but one believed the news that was sung by an oral poet.

✦

On my 2012 visit to Fortaleza's Centro Cultural dos Cordelistas do Nordeste, a man nicknamed "Sparrow" hosted a program of *cordel* literature. This region of the northeast has the greatest economic disparity in Brazil and the richest tradition of oral and traditional poetry and song. The *cordelistas*, working in a tradition coming from the Iberian Peninsula and taking root here in the 1830s—"cord" poets, because the poems were printed into small chapbooks, often with woodcut illustrations, and hung on a string in the street markets and fairs for sale. This poetry comes out of the arid backcountry, the *sertão*, where life is tough, poverty common. Some poets are vaqueros among whom, the sparrow told us, their cows and bulls listen to the sounds produced by the poet and they understand.

We heard an hour or so of performances and toured a gallery of historic and contemporary *cordel* literature, a dozen men lined up at tables selling handmade, stapled brochures—poems about an encounter between a cricket and a butterfly (both depicted with human heads), about a man who took a shit in church, about a wildcat (*gato-do-mato* or "cat of the bush") who "quenched his hunger" by procuring a guinea pig, about a cat who escaped a lion, leaving it in tears. One man sang that he had never worn shoes, until he went to town to find a wife. The women laughed and rolled their eyes. One man said that when he told his mother he would become a poet, she beat him. He sang that the *cordel* reports on "the travels we go through" (so said our simultaneous translator, though I wondered if the poet meant "travails"). "Many things are reported about the drylands," he sang. "Our culture has been forgotten in other regions. The land is talking to man. The earth says it is not happy."

The poems sounded syllabic, end-rhymed, and rhythmic as a troubling memory. The poets were loud. Very, very loud.

As if decibels alone could invoke feeling. We saw a film clip of two *repentistas*, rough-hewn men in work clothes, banging guitars and competing in a verse challenge. They can go on for fifteen minutes or an hour. There is a tray where people can give money. Whoever has the most money at the end wins. Back and forth they went in fierce passion.

"No one can beat me. My verse is very tough."

"The police, when they hear him sing, want to take him to jail."

"My voice is very tough and I will be the winner."

"Whoever sings without feeling carries his own cross."

✦

Patativa was born Antônio Gonçalves da Silva in 1909 in the town of Assaré, which means, in the language of a local indigenous group, "battered earth." The region has a climate plagued by alternating droughts and floods. Patativa started out playing guitar and reciting poems at local parties in his town. A journalist heard him, published his poems in the newspaper, and gave him the nickname Patativa do Assaré when he was nineteen. He never learned to read. He composed poems in his head, memorizing them as he plowed and hoed and harvested. While he was known as a "popular" poet—a kind of second-class citizen in the hierarchy of cultural esteem—he could hear a complex literary form and master it. He worked as he made the turns of the furrow and row. Verses, we say, meaning in Latin a row or line. He worked and reworked the poem to the rhythm of his passage on the land. When he had a final version, he fixed the poem in memory and remained faithful to it when he recited or sang it. At age sixteen he convinced his mother to sell a goat so he could buy a guitar. He had only four months of schooling. *Literatura pobre,* some critics called it, meaning both literature of the poor and poor literature. He called his poetry "raw" and said it "grew out of the earth."

Patativa composed poems in many forms—the sonnet, the *sextilha nordestina* (six lines, seven syllables, rhyme scheme ABCBDB), the *décimal* (four-line intro followed by four ten-line stanzas)—and improvised forms like those made up in the moment by *repentistas* in response to a challenge. Many of these formal traditions came to Brazil from the Iberian Peninsula with the early Portuguese settlers. Farmers and cowboys have kept the forms alive for centuries. At age ninety-three, Patativa could recite hundreds of poems he'd composed in the fields. Many were reports of the hardships and injustices suffered by rural workers.

"The Sad Farewell," made up while he was planting beans, traces the drought cycle through a year and the farmers' struggle: "terrible drought / devouring everything / throwing them out / of the native grounds." The poor farmers head south hoping for a better life and end up living "like slaves" in São Paulo. He fought for amnesty for imprisoned and exiled political leaders. He was a spokesman on stages and in stadiums for human rights and dignity. He gave hope to the oppressed in "Lesson of the Chick," which became an anthem for the powerless. A frail little bird is trying to break out of its shell: "Work is needed. / Prick with the beak. / Prick with the beak, / little bird, to get free."

Patativa's first book, *Northeastern Inspiration*, was transcribed by a friend and published in 1956. His first vinyl record came out in 1979. Pop singers took up his songs and made them hits, national anthems for the dispossessed and displaced. Any money he made, he turned back to the town for irrigation and to help the poor. His daughter told Arons that Patativa was "the poorest person in this town." Once when the governor asked whether he wanted a new car or a new home, Patativa asked for a new cowboy hat. He died in 2002.

Now in the eternal present of electronic time, I can see the old man walking to the fields with a handmade hoe slung over his shoulder, the rough handle fashioned from a sapling stripped of bark. A gourd of water hangs from the shaft, swaying as the man limps along heading for work. I can see that his face is square at the forehead, narrow at the chin. He wears aviator shades. He wears beat-up chinos, a plaid button-down shirt, and a floppy straw hat. His skin is the terracotta color of the desolate soil he has spent a life working, a land riven by the ghosts of conquest.

And now after his death it is virtually impossible to walk in any city of Brazil's northeast and not see Patativa's face graffitied on a wall or mounted in a public square or postered in a tourism office. He has become the brand for local pride and empathy for the poor, while the poor continue to starve, pine coffins for sale hanging on the wall of the corner store. Patativa is a statue, library, motorway, museum, cartoon, multiple honorary degrees, national theater, cultural center, pop song, course of study at the Sorbonne, and the voice of resistance spurring the Movimento dos Trabalhadores Rurais Sem Terra (the Landless Workers' Movement) with over 1.5 million members—the largest and most influential social movement in Brazil, working for agrarian reform and land distribution and against the control of seed production by transnational corporations.

✦

Fifty years ago, 80 percent of Brazil's population lived in rural areas. By the 1990s, 76 percent had become urban, many living in desolate shantytowns built of scrap material. Prior waves of migrants had washed into the cities ever since colonial times. In the eighteenth century former slaves having no land and no work came and settled into makeshift quarters. In the nineteenth and twentieth centuries industrialization brought further waves, hundreds of thousands of rural migrants abandoning their homelands in search of work or displaced by development or taking on temporary jobs that left them homeless and broke. By 2011, 11.4 million people, 6 percent of Brazil's population, lived in slums. In 1969, there were three hundred "subnormal agglomerates" in Rio. Now there are twice that number. The poor live in *favelas* (named after a skin-irritating tree that soldiers had encountered while at war), *invasões* (invaded properties), *grotas* (slums in deep valleys), *baixages* (southern lowlands), *comunidades* (communities), *vilas* (villages), *ressacas* (backwaters), *mocambos* (shacks), *palafitas* (stilt houses in water).

✦

The *patativa-chorona* (*Sporophila leucoptera*) is a small, gray, white-bellied passerine, a seed eater equipped with a stout, strong beak suited for the job of opening seeds. It has a wide range in South America, though it is not that common. A solitary bird that doesn't socialize very much, it can live well in disturbed habitat and deforested land. It is in the conservation category of least concern among bird species because its population is stable even in the drylands, the region described by novelist João Guimarães Rosa as a "harsh, wavy and tragic landscape which spreads to the infinite." Poor land, poor people, bird adapted to poor circumstances.

It's impossible to parse the syllables of the *patativa's* singing, though I have been studying recordings made both in nature and in cages. Chirps, twits, trills, runs, and cascades. Some elements repeat. Some are melancholy. Some frenzied. Some melodious. Some sharp. What birds are singing in this scrub? There must be numerous species. But here is one *patativa* in a cage, its throat pumping with muscular effort, its head cocked in intensity, its songs filling up space, the score veering into something new, second by second. It can barely stop to take a sip of water from its dispenser. I'd like to see a musician's transcription of the *patativa's* singing. I'd like to be able to discern and better describe syllable, pattern, and melody.

I've never been very good at parsing bird song. When the

bird book says the white-throated sparrow sings "Old Sam Peabody, Peabody, Peabody," I scratch my head because what I hear of this bird in the dawn chorus is three notes, one low, two high at an interval that sounds like a perfect fifth. I'm like a student who cannot hear the difference between a dactyl and an anapest, an iamb and a trochee. I still can love the song, but my ear lacks discipline. I suffer from a lack of ornithological literacy. For now, my task is to praise the literacy that comes from aesthetic experience. This lightness of bird being and of human singing. This insistence that the voice move as a measuring device to keep track of all the territorial unrest of the world. This new attempt to gather listeners within a net of song. This old practice that the passerines have carried generation to generation for sixty million years like a bowl of embers kept alive since before the great rending that sent the continents adrift.

Ant Art

At the end of World War II, Jean Dubuffet began searching for spontaneous and anonymous types of art, works produced without regard for rules or conventions of the day. He called what he was looking for *art brut*. He wanted work that owed nothing to works on display in museums and galleries, but instead would "appeal to humanity's first origins." He gathered art made by self-trained, marginal artists—psychiatric patients, prisoners, recluses, peasants, and nomads. He believed true art can be found where you least expect it, that it requires secrecy and silence. "Art detests being recognized and greeted by its own name," he wrote. "It immediately flees."

Dubuffet's collection of works made by individuals disconnected socially and psychologically from their society includes statuettes made from chewed bread; drawings dictated by the dead; the fifteen-thousand-page saga made by a hospital janitor titled "In the Realms of the Unreal" featuring the seven "Vivian Girls" (all male); huge machines made of branches, rags, and wire lubricated with human excrement; pictures drawn in tincture of iodine with brushes made from locks of human hair; ballpoint drawings touched up with coffee grounds, tobacco juice, and wine, then browned over with a cigarette lighter; five hundred tiny drawings each containing thousands of minuscule faces made by the Polish shopkeeper who, after the Germans occupied his town, took refuge in his brother's attic, refusing entry to anyone, and never left his confinement until his death twenty years later.

I have found works made by untrained artists in the back lot behind my desert house—dozens of cones randomly arrayed in an area twenty feet square shaded by a large mesquite tree. The cones all have a collapsed center like a volcano and range in diameter from sixteen to nine inches across. The tallest are six inches high. The widest crater is nine inches across, measuring from one crisp lip to the other, sides falling outward like a skirt. The cones are constructed of coarse brown sand and fine gravel, the particles no larger than peppercorns, as smooth and regular as if they had passed though a flour sifter. The sifter in this case is the body of an ant. The anthills lie in various phases of construction and destruction: some, long neglected, have lost their shape, melted by rain into messy heaps; some have been dug at by coyotes, claw tracks gouged into the dirt scattering their symmetry into chaos. In the desert's flowering seasons the anthills may be skirted with yellow petals from paloverde trees or purple petals from Texas Rangers (*Leucophyllum frutescens*), diaphanous tissue cut into shreds like confetti. In winter the site is still and lifeless. One day I found the anthills had become a working construction site, with a ten-foot line of ants flowing into the colony and another line flowing out, as workers delivered mesquite leaves to the farmers below. The ants flowed like water over a bumpy streambed, each bearer carrying a needle-like leaf over its head, so that it looked like a parade marshal. The ants staggered as they made their way along the dirt. I left them, then returned hours later to find them still at work. I tore a leafy twig off the mesquite tree and tossed it on the ground a foot away from their parade line. Within seconds a handful of scouts had branched off and begun severing the green from the wood, then flowing from their tributary back into the ant river.

Ants are little chemistry kits sensitized for making and detecting scent. They get around by following the chemical trail left by ants that have gone before them, and they do so with minimal help from vision, hearing, and feeling. They learn by imitation, not teaching. Researchers following the scent trail of the *Atta texana*, as ant aficionado E. O. Wilson reports, calculate that one milligram of trail pheromone would lead a column of ants three times around the earth. Ant scent is laid down by a gland and evaporates to create a scent trail that hovers over the ground. Ants use their antennae to follow this trail, appearing to stagger as they bring first the right antenna over the vapor space, proceeding in that direction until losing the scent, then turning until the left antenna crosses the trail and heading in that direction until they again lose the trail, and so forth, so that following a straight line for an ant requires zigzagging left and right.

The most elementary ant pheromone is carbon dioxide, which fire ants use to hunt subterranean prey. Ants can also produce alarm pheromones and attractant pheromones. A death pheromone signals the need to dispose of a corpse; they will remove anything placed in their nest if it is marked with this chemical. Some ants make slaves, raiding nearby colonies and carrying prisoners back home to labor for the colony. They do this by spraying an alarm pheromone on the enemies, which frightens and disperses them, making them easy captives. Wilson calls these "propaganda substances," one of which can provoke the victims to fight among themselves.

Most people's response to insects is not to build a professional career out of a relationship with them. Most people are creeped out by bugs. They arouse fears of infestation, toxicity, destruction, contamination, pestilence, and ultimately the occupation of the corpse by the devouring swarm. People slap them, sweep them, spray them, burn them, poison them, turn them one against another to exterminate them, these tiny agents of transformation that have lived for fifty million years on Earth. Their familiars will have their day with our meat and bones, cleaning us up for the final judgment that

I suspect will be made by no authority greater or lesser than
Earth, which can only welcome us back as fresh material.

I value the scientist's eye for particulars and the patience
that researchers exhibit in exercising that eye to understand
the peculiarities of each creature's existence. When I asked
my friend Elizabeth Bernays, who has made a distinguished
career of her relationships with insects, about my flower-
cone builders, she smiled as if she were boasting about some
accomplished members of her own family. She told me they
were leaf-cutter ants and that their colonies go three feet
under the ground. They spread the flowers out to dry, then
when the petals have lost enough moisture, the ants carry
them down into the nest, a structure that is one of the largest and most complex made by any animal, where the ants
use the flowers to farm gardens of fungus, and the fungus
produces enzymes that break down the plant material into a
form the ants can use. The queen ant, who may live for ten
or twenty years, spends her entire life in the fungus garden.

I know it is wrong to call the flower cones art, a word that
implies intentionality and an inner life rich enough to produce the contradictions that make art necessary. What I had
seen as an aesthetic construction was an artifact of utilitarian enterprise, only a phase in the ants' menu planning. But
why is it that the arrangement of the petals is so symmetrical,
the sculptural appeal so tactile, the pattern of cone building
repeated with such precise craft? How do chemicals tell the
mindless ant to create form, symmetry, pattern, beauty? Do
human beings misapprehend art as a goal or product, when
it too is an artifact of a process that meets a biological need?

Field Notes on Hands

The granite of Deer Isle, Maine, goes five miles deep. On the surface the stone looks pink, crystalline, and sparkles with quartz. The slosh and seethe of Atlantic tides wear the outcrops into sloping mounds. There's a quarry in Stonington, but for the most part the massive granite keeps its five-hundred-million-year-old memories to itself. Small coves dent the shoreline, pocket beaches covered with sand made of broken clam and barnacle shells so white that when the tide flows in the water glows as if lit from below. Henry David Thoreau, walking one cold morning in Massachusetts, saw ice crystals lying on top of granite rock and called the quartz crystals "frostwork of a longer night." I have always loved that phrase. It helps me to wrap my mind around the enormity of geologic time. It helps me to remember that what's observed on a small scale is a message about the nature of the universe as telling as the gorgeous images flying back to Earth from the Hubble Space Telescope.

The soil is very thin on Deer Isle, a veneer over which moss and lichen spread. Spruce and hemlock trees tower up in the woods. Dove, osprey, thrush, warbler, and raven make a big fuss about the details of the day. Dusk gives them something substantial to talk about. On my first evening at Haystack Mountain School of Crafts, I walked through their loud exhortations, heading through the woods to see where the root-laced trail would lead. Walking is a good strategy for gathering ideas, and in this case it proved better than I could have imagined. I had come to write an essay about the pleasure of making things with one's hands—a grand theme of human history—to watch people experience that pleasure while working on ceramics, blacksmithing, drawing, making glass beads, assembling mixed media and fiber projects. What questions had I brought with me? None. I wanted to walk, look, write, and see what the experience would deliver.

I came to a low promontory, the woods thinning out to a water view. It was as calm as shellac out there. A few small islands packed with spruce trees appeared to float on rafts of granite. Pebbles on shore clicked and clacked in the wobbling disturbance of waves—all just what a pastoral daydreamer might expect on the Maine coast, until something odd came into view. A pair of yellow hands rose up from the water, reaching on spindly arms for the sky. I clambered through the scrub to find a tree limb, pale and ghostly, bobbing in the shallows. Two branches veered up like a cheerleader's arms. Two yellow work gloves gave the branches their hands. Aha, I thought, synchronicity is at work, and I'd best follow its lead: your focus, says the universe, will be hands.

Where the hands had come from was a question I didn't really want to answer. Perhaps a lobsterman casually slipped them on the branches while baiting his traps on shore, then forgot them when he went home for lunch and returned to find his gloves carried off by the tide. Unlikely. Fishermen are pragmatic and observant, especially when it comes to tides. More likely, I had stumbled upon an art joke, a visual quip made by one of Haystack's artists, who saw in the driftwood branch a gesture so human it demanded acknowledgment. The brand-new pair of chamois work gloves were small sacrifice to clinch the deal. But when synchronicity strikes, asking cause-and-effect questions is beside the point. Such an image makes the brain buzz because it says nothing about cause and effect, but something about how significance can pop up anywhere like a weed.

I am not a craftsperson, though I play one in my university writing seminars, where I teach the craft of writing. In creative writing classes, *craft* refers not to the medium but to the method. A craft class in poetry might explore metaphor, music, line endings, and word choice; in nonfiction, narrative voice, scene, summary, and reflection. Such classes try to take apart works of literature to see how they are made, with an eye to culling devices to clarify, enhance, or complicate one's own creative process. To make it more interesting. Writing takes place in the head and on the page, so it is difficult to see the raw materials that go into the making of a poem or story. Words, sure, but where do they come from? They arrive at the tail end of a long daisy chain that goes all the way back to the hominid past. It's difficult to articulate how head and page connect—though hands are generally required.

At Haystack, *craft* refers to the medium, the material used in the making, each discipline developing a language specialized for its practice. The glassmakers "gather" glass to shape it. They engage in "feathering," "festooning," and "furrowing," finally "annealing" the beads against breakage. Metalworkers "shoulder" a steel rod to move metal into a mass that becomes a spoon. They find "the sparking place" where fire pulls oxygen out of the metal and speeds up the molecules. In the ceramic studio, the potter "slaps" the clay to compress it, tightening the molecules. She "pulls the lug" to shape a handle on a mug. She describes how a "reduction firing" deprives the kiln of oxygen so that the fire must suck the element out of the glazing chemicals, thus transforming their colors. In mixed media, anything goes—deer bones, laminated wire, sepia postcards, and bait boxes are elements in a Joseph Cornell world where detritus becomes luminous, where the messy falls into pleasing order. The fiber workshop, dubbed "the rhizome lab" by its exuberant collaborators, defined its terms by refusing to define them. The rhizome is, they wrote in the course catalog, "fungus, the internet, suburban sprawl, brain mapping, oceanic pollutants." They drew on the work of philosophers Gilles Deleuze and Félix Guattari, who brought philosophical resonance to a botanical term. *Rhizome* means an image of thought that allows multiplicity. On the workshop wall, a definition in progress grew. "Rhizome is what is not: symmetrical, hierarchical, inwardly seeking, knowable."

✦

When I try to remember making things with my hands as a child, I come up with a paltry list. Rolling out piecrust and shaping it to fit the plate. Cutting out biscuits or cookie dough. Playing pick-up sticks with its acquired vocabulary of maneuvers (slide, tunnel, flip, pivot) for retrieving single sticks from a heap without disturbing the pile. Ironing shirts after dampening them with water from a spray bottle and rolling them into tubes, so that the moisture would disperse throughout the cloth. (This was before the invention of the steam iron, though at least the thing, unlike the old cast iron ones, plugged into a power outlet.) Sewing on a button using the exact steps my grandmother taught me—wrapping thread, circle after circle, around the connecting stitches to strengthen the bond.

My grandmother was a French dress designer in New York City during the first three decades of the twentieth century. She got the season's fashion books from Paris, and her customers arrived by limousine to look over the pages, pick the designs and fabrics. Then she and her seamstresses, beaders, and *corsetière* set to work. By the time I was born, such home-based artisanship had long been replaced by the sweatshop. Being taught to sew on a button by such a woman was like being taught to play "Chopsticks" by Stravinsky. There was no questioning such knowledge, and though the task seemed trivial, the skill did not. I was learning a manual heritage.

One of my grandmother's creations has survived both the decline of elegance and the digestion of moths. She made a black velvet opera coat for my mother. On the collar, rivulets of gold lamé run through mounds of black velvet. Pink moiré silk lines the entire garment, and along the bottom foot of the lining a row of crescents has been cut and appliquéd; they look like a whole baker's window of puffy soufflés. It takes a few French words even to describe the cape's beauty. My grandmother's hands were knobby, spotted, clawed, and old in the years she lived with us. She always wore a few diamond rings—her "solitaire," she called one of these. She was hardly a woman who stared idly into a pack of playing cards looking for the jack of hearts. Marie Bregny Macnab made a living and put her daughter through private school with the work of her hands and a highly refined sense of aesthetic judgment. Her special gift was designing gowns for women with unusual flaws—a humped back or a sunken shoulder. She could cut the fabric to measure by eye and hand, never using a pattern.

✦

"Pleasure in handling is 'hard-wired' into human nature," writes Ellen Dissanayake in *Art and Intimacy*, because "it predisposes us to be tool users and makers." Another of nature's little tricks, making life-enhancing behaviors give pleasure: eating, sex, talking, and friendship help to keep life going. Imagine little *Homo habilis* flaking a flint two million years ago (which takes us roughly halfway back in the four-million-year hominid line), delicious fantasy of a fresh grilled steak drifting through his mind. Imagine her weaving a basket from fragrant grass, placing with her fingers one sweet morsel of wild fruit into the mouth of her child. Think of the child's hands reaching out in eager delight for the mother, the grasping fingers a language without words expressing need and delight.

Hands-free bipedalism has been good for the human brain. Evolutionary biologist Francisco Ayala has said that bipedalism made it possible for early hominids to develop "a runaway brain." Bipedalism freed the hands to make tools. You make a tool for a purpose, and anticipating its use means you must have an image of it in mind. Tool making enlarges the brain. A larger brain means more capacity to learn how to make more tools and solve more problems and enjoy the pleasure of making things with your hands and the daydream your mind falls into during the making. Suddenly consciousness begins to get more interesting. And cultural evolution begins to kick in alongside genetic evolution as an agent of change on the planet. Rather than waiting for the genes to adapt to environmental conditions, you make the environment change to meet your genes.

Cultural heredity is transmitted by teaching and imitation. Hands carry, gather, shape, chip, peel, tie, splice, lash together, braid, throw, pull, stroke, rub, arouse, comfort, greet, beg, shrug, exclaim, and warn. Neurologist Frank R. Wilson writes in *The Hand*, "Any theory of human intelligence which ignores the interdependence of hand and brain function, the historic origin of that relationship, or the impact of that history on developmental dynamics in modern humans, is grossly misleading and sterile." The genes dispose. The hands compose.

This means, of course, that hands, bare hands, can slap, punch, wring, bruise, gouge, shun, insult, threaten, knock out, torture, mutilate, and kill. I'd like to think these acts are a perversion of human handiness, but the record of history and prehistory suggests that cruelty and violence are difficult if not impossible to subdue. They too are part of the human heritage. All the more reason to hold up like a festival banner those experiences of dexterity, competence, pleasure, and joyfully benign folly discovered with one's hands.

✦

On day one of the workshops, I visited the rhizome lab. Instructors Susie Brandt and Kristine Woods, colleagues at

the Maryland Institute College of Art, had invited participants to bring objects from home as an index for who they
are. Each had a rich and curious vocabulary. One offered
a knee-high heap of glasses, sunglasses, glasses frames—
enough to fill a pillowcase. A woman from New York City
brought a shiny Ziploc Mylar bag she had found on the street,
a cheery "Hello" printed on the outside, and inside a poem
and phone number. She thought about calling but did not.
"It's perfect just the way it is," she said. "I walked past it three
times. I did that stalking thing. I thought it was meant for
someone else." Another participant presented paper plates,
each piled with a totemic heap—gel caps, white plastic x's
used as spacers for laying tile, steel wool pads, balls of white
cotton twine. They looked clean, stark, elegant, these objects
that are made for utility and had been removed from that
context to become simply forms and repetitions of form that
make a pattern. The guy with the paper plates placed a whole
wheat cracker on a blank white paper. "It's not a blank page,"
he said, "it's a negation of stuff."

A woman who had moved seventeen times in the first
twenty-four years of her life presented a brick that had fallen
off her 120-year-old house. She had raised five kids in the
house. She also brought dirt and her grandmother's handker-
chiefs. "My nana was the foundation of my life," she said. "She
was older than dirt." A gray-haired Michigander, interested
in excess and waste, demonstrated how she irons blue plastic
bags (in which her *New York Times* comes to her house) and
netted vegetable bags (her daughter is a raw foodist), pressing them between sheets of baker's parchment. The bags melt,
distort, and fuse into glistening pastiched "fabrics." "This one
looks like the tank suits I used to wear." She held it up against
her body, gave a coy smile, and told about the hip replacement
she recently underwent. She makes plastic rust. "It's not easy."

I was struck with the joy they all displayed handling
their objects, telling their stories, feeling the eyes of others

attentively focused on them, everyone sensing that ordinary objects can lift into the extraordinary at the drop of . . . The shrill cry of an osprey interrupted the class. "Clew! Clew!" The group rushed out onto the deck to watch it soar.

✦

In the blacksmith shop, sculptor Hoss Haley demonstrated how to make a cone, heating a steel plate in the coal-fired forge, pounding it on the anvil until the metal moved. Then he demonstrated how to hammer out a bowl and a leaf. "Who cares about a metal leaf?" one bone-weary, ear-weary student scoffed after pounding steel for a day and half. Days later, the cone, bowl, and leaf had been welded together to become a giant bosc pear, the inanimate transformed into an icon of delicious life. Hoss asked students to choose an object, then change its scale. They had begun to look sooty and worn, a few bandaged from their persistent engagement with metal and fire. Days later, a spoon the size of a mailbox, a kayak the size of a purse, and a goat the size of a miniature poodle had somehow been fashioned from steel—sheet, cone, leaf, bowl—simple elements combined and transformed by heat, pressure, grinding, pounding, and glistening welds.

Yoko Sekino-Bove, teaching assistant in the clay studio, lured me from my gawking. "Do you want to make a plate?" Her enthusiasm made it hard for me to resist, though my ceramic skills had been dormant since elementary school. We slapped the clay to compress it, rolled it out like piecrust, turned up the edges to shape the plate, after which I could not resist fluting the edge like pie dough. I pressed my turquoise beaded bracelet into the plate's smooth surface to add texture and interest to that empty field. The studio hummed with the labors of two dozen makers of pots, plates, mugs, and bowls whose skills went far beyond my grade school level of dough rolling. But I felt welcomed as a dabbler and knew childish pride in my accomplishment.

Yoko explained the chemistry of glazes and of firing—and how some of the words to describe firing come from pastoral England. "Bisque" firing from "biscuit." "Cheese hard" from cheddar cheese, which originated in the village of Cheddar in Somerset, England. Language, like craft and art making, is a work in progress. "Ceramics is the only craft," she told me, "that requires a chemistry class to get a degree." Think of glaze calculations, their astronomical and engineering uses, ceramic tiles on the Space Shuttle.

When I visited the drawing studio, David Dodge Lewis was talking to his students about the golden section. They'd been drawing plumb bobs, and they stopped to ask why certain shapes, certain patterns are so pleasing to us. He drew a rectangle, then made a square inside it using three of the rectangle's sides, leaving a smaller rectangle of the same proportions as the first, and so on until the series spiraled down to the tiniest rectangle possible to draw. The ratio expressed in these shapes is the same ratio expressed in the spiral of a sunflower's head, in the branching of sneezewort and other plants, and even in the human body, in which the length from the top of the head to the navel and the length from the navel to the toes hold the same ratio. It was known by the ancient Greeks as the golden section or divine proportion. Pythagoras said that all things are numbers. The ratio informs many works of art and architecture. One of its recent popularizations is the poetic form the Fib, based upon the series of "golden numbers" called the Fibonacci sequence (1, 1, 2, 3, 5, 8, 13, 21 . . .) that follow the same ratio. (Each number in the sequence tells you how many syllables to use for each line of the poem.) Nature does its work with numbers in mind, though the mind of nature is unconscious. Artists often do the same, though when they make conscious the numerical underpinnings of form, this only adds to the pleasure of making. As Stravinsky said, "If you give me form, you give me freedom."

✦

My only craft-making credentials come from a summer in my twenties when I ran the broom shop at Shaker Village Work Group in New Lebanon, New York. This summer program was held on the grounds and in the gracefully grand buildings of the former historic Shaker community, and while its purpose was to give teenagers an experience of democratic self-governance (which included marvelously contentious "town meetings" during which teens struggled to find a collective voice), the substance of our days was spent making reproductions of Shaker crafts, giving tours of the historical site to visitors, and performing Shaker song and dance. It was one of the oddest and most satisfying convergences of structure and freedom that I've ever experienced.

I ran the broom shop, not because I knew anything about making brooms, but because the sexier crafts (making oval wooden boxes, molding candles, weaving, photography, folk dance) were spoken for. I came to love many elements of the enterprise: the fragrance of broom corn soaking in a bucket of water to make it pliable; the way the thick stalks could be bent to form the hips of the broom; the treadled clamp that held the stick taut while wire wound round its neck; the wooden vise that held the broom at eye level for stitching; and the little agrarian guillotine where the broom was placed and trimmed to have a flat bottom for sweeping.

The Shakers, a Protestant religious group founded in England by Mother Ann Lee in 1772, became the most successful American experiment in communal living. In the mid-1800s, they had eighteen major communities in eight states and smaller communities in others. Their fate, however, was set with their vow of celibacy. Though they made converts and adopted Civil War orphans, this was not sufficient to make their communities sustainable. They lived an austere, agrarian life and made furniture of simple but beautifully proportioned design. They were so tidy that when they left a room, they hung their ladder-back chairs on the wall.

The Shakers had a saying, "Hands to work, hearts to God," a perfect expression of the balanced life they sought and for some time found. There's truth in this slogan that bears cherishing, even if both ideas have become remote in our twenty-first-century, first-world minds. We seem to be working harder and harder in order to do less and less with our hands, while the idea of God, for many of us living in secular society, produces more anxiety than comfort as it is passionately invoked to wage war. And yet the truth remains: working with one's hands can lead one to an experience of transcendence and transformation.

✦

My favorite Haystack outing was the trip to the Deer Isle transfer station with Graceann Warn and the participants in her mixed-media workshop. It's the most organized dump I have ever seen. Mounds of refuse are piled up like the Presidential Range in New Hampshire: Mount Mattress, Mount Refrigerator, Mount Tire, Mount Toilet, and Mount Ash. The workshop participants scattered and gathered as if this junk were their subsistence food. There was a mixed-media heap containing smashed Sheetrock, insulating foam, roofing shingles, boats, bikes, buckets, and some little grids of plastic-coated wire that had been snipped out of lobster traps. There was a mess of ceramic waste—cracked pots, broken coils of clay, little curlicues like macaroni, and a ghostly clay human head that looked like a death mask. There was a neighborhood for circuit boards, computer towers, gauges, and controlling devices. There was a valley for dead deer, skin and bones and rotting heads, left by hunters for scavengers to finish off.

"You can tell a whole social reality from a dump," Graceann said. And so it was. Raven feathers had floated down here and there. The song of northeastern peewees and yellowthroats wafted over the wasteland like a cooling breeze.

My best find was the control panel from some long gone machine—a boat or tractor or backhoe. The brand was Stewart-Warner. The functionless gauges announced their interest in amps, oil, fuel, and water temp. They were nested into a metal dashboard that was dented, rusted, and oily to the touch. I took it, along with a handful of raven feathers and a homemade bucket made from plastic-coated wire, back to the studio.

Why did it interest me, this relic of somebody's work, some small act of industry that mattered in the progress of the town? It was powerless in my hands, but it smelled of the power to shape things to human desires—a power at once thrilling and terrifying. It was a perfect statement of contradiction. I went to the tool shop and asked the crew for help disengaging the gauges. I worked with needle-nose Vise-Grips and wrenches and penetrating oil to loosen the locknuts. A young guy in the shop helped me find the tools and looked lustfully over my shoulder at my instrument panel. When I got them free, I lined up the gauges on the deck outside my studio door. That's all I really wanted to do with them, make them objects of contemplation. When I left Haystack, I turned the disempowered gauges over to the shop guy. I hope he still has them pedestaled on his workbench.

The workshop participants were way more industrious—more aesthetically industrious—with their junk. One day later I toured their workbenches to find objects selected, cut, buffed, rounded, polished, and dipped into beeswax. They'd made assemblages that nested in boxes and wax bowls and on stretched canvases. Some works had swinging doors to protect their secrets. A bait bag had become a yarmulke. A weathered wooden box had been laminated with purple wrapping paper, the lowly risen to the status of regalia. A sheet of onionskin paper (a relic itself!) had been graced with a few typewritten words, then painted with beeswax. It hung, a golden trophy, tanned and tallowy as an animal hide.

"There is no source that is not sacred," Seneca wrote, and thus is spirit made manifest in matter.

✦

As a writer I take pleasure in words—their meaning, music, and sources. I love the way words become vessels for time travel, carrying one back through the history of their use, often all the way to a primal connection with Earth. When my companion and I were driving to Haystack, we crossed the causeway that joins Greenlaw Neck to Stinson Neck.

"How come it's a causeway and not a bridge?" asked my Oklahoma-born friend. Coming from arid terrain where everything lies exposed, he's new to the varieties of watercourses, soggy bogs, and woodsy obscurity that we New Englanders call home.

"What's the difference between a bog and a marsh?" he asked. "How can there be so much shoreline?" he protested, as we meandered our way down and around yet another amoeboid peninsula. He kept me on my bioregional toes.

"I think it's a causeway because it's built right in the water and not in the air."

We looked it up. "Causeway: a raised path or road over water." It derives from "causey: a mound or embankment to retain water." This usage for the word goes back to the Middle English spoken in the fifteenth century. A "causey way" then might have referred to the old Roman roads built in the British Isles. Earlier yet, the word may derive from the Latin word for heel, *calx*, suggesting the method used for trampling earthen roads one layer at a time, most likely by employing the heels of slaves. One word used to describe a landscape feature of coastal New England carried us all the way back to the bloody heels of Roman slaves. *Handmade* perhaps tells only half the story of human history.

Such an excursion opens a dimension of time in the words that fall into our brains, a feeling for deep time, to which we are all connected through our understanding of Earth's story, our own handiness, our reflective consciousness, and the tools, including language, that we use to bind ourselves together in common purpose. Vladimir Nabokov writes in his luminous memoir *Speak, Memory* that "the beginning of reflexive consciousness in the brain of our remotest ancestor must surely have coincided with the dawning of the sense of time." The sense of time that dogs most of us these days is "I don't have enough of it." Such is the velocity that robs us of depth.

Jung wrote that making things, transforming matter with hands, gets to that place in the human psyche that lies "beneath the personal psyche" into "the world of primitive man within myself." This is the place in consciousness where "the primitive psyche of man borders on the life of the animal soul, just as the caves of prehistoric times were usually inhabited by animals before men laid claim to them." Jung spoke of "the transcendent function," and I believe he meant not that people transcended nature, but that in certain experiences conscious and unconscious aspects of the mind work together to transcend the feeling that we are not part of nature. We are back home in the old web of connections from which we have sprung and feel once again that we belong.

The kick of transforming a material from one state to another, from one use to another—or to none—is alchemy in any language. It's a ticket into the marvelous, which is where we live every day but forget to notice, because otherwise we'd never get the errands done. Imagine the exhausting euphoria if our minds registered astonishment every time we saw water turned to steam or to ice.

✦

I continued taking walks in the woods at Haystack, and found other art jokes: tiny porcelain eggs scattered on a granite ledge, a bouquet of rockweed tied with green thread to a rootlet crossing the trail, a blue blaze replaced by mussel shell for a trail marker. I left a few of my own—crab shells arrayed in a paddock of birch branches laid out on the forest floor. Valueless, quite possibly noticed by no person, giving me a few minutes of unaccountable joy, my construction disappeared the day after I made it. Ravens perhaps or a raccoon had carried the crab shells away in hope of a morsel—or simply in the ritualistic behavior of picking up shells that is characteristic of their kind. The yellow hands drifted south down the coast and lodged ashore in a narrow cove. I missed the animated motion of their rocking in the water. It was like seeing the trailer of a film after you've already watched the whole show.

✦

How old is our human pleasure in making? How early did our manual skills become refined? Tool making is only a part of the story. In 1965, a farmer digging in his cellar near Kiev, near the juncture of the Ros and Rosava Rivers, felt his spade click on something hard. It turned out to be the lower jaw of a mammoth. He had stumbled upon remnants of the oldest human city, a cluster of huts built fifteen thousand years ago entirely of mammoth bones, one jawbone inserted into the bottom of another like a child's building blocks. The roof supports were mammoth tusks. There was also a drum made from a skull, a xylophone made from a femur. Another thirty bone huts turned up in the Czech Republic—the oldest dated to be twenty-seven thousand years old. It took one hundred animals to make one hut, the bones of which weighed twenty tons. Competence and pleasure in making things with human hands is not only utilitarian, not only aesthetic. It's where and how we have lived.

Elephant Watching

"**O**h, we are stuck. We are really stuck," lamented John Mtalo, our safari driver, slapping his hands against the sides of his head. He was disgusted with himself and with the mud that had mired us in the rain-flooded savanna. Surely it is very bad form to strand tourists in the African bush at sunset as the lions, leopards, and hyenas are waking from their afternoon naps. It was a moment that might have turned perilous but did not. He rocked the vehicle ferociously back and forth, gaining a few inches with each pull of the diesel engine. Then we were free and rolling toward the comforts of roast lamb and rhubarb pie at the park's lodge.

Being stuck is how any Earth celebrant might feel these days, confronted by the habitat-hogging reign of human culture over the planet. But one of nature's contributions to human character is that our better intentions can be fueled by the simple contemplation of natural beauty. Whether our empathy for other species is sufficient to motivate the level of care that the damaged world requires remains an open question. But to feed one's wonder and love for the varieties of Earth's self-expression is one of our better desires.

I visited Tanzania's Lake Manyara National Park, not a celebrity location on the safari circuit but a site nonetheless bountiful with savanna elephants, baboons, hippos, lions, zebras, and those varieties of antelope whose names alone can make a poet's heart soar: dik-dik, klipspringer, bushbuck, waterbuck, impala, and gazelle.

I watched a solitary bull elephant, a huge old veteran, amble across the grassy plain. Behind him lay the soda lake, its flamingos dissolving in the hazy equatorial heat. And beyond them rose the escarpment of the Great Rift Valley, that long gouge running from Syria to Mozambique that has opened secrets of the deeply layered evolutionary past as it has rent the land. The old bull at first strode slowly, head bent low, lumbering along so slowly he looked like a billboard. Then his interest picked up, the head rose, ears flapped back as if opening to hear, knees bent high with the purposeful gait. Some appetite had called him forward. Can an elephant trot? Perhaps not. But he did speed-walk across the low weeds and barren dirt, land grazed to the nub and beginning to flourish anew from recent rains.

When the bull arrived at the wallow, he dug tusks down into the mud, bent onto one knee, until lower and lower the great head fell into the sloppy wallow then rose, spraying, slathering, and washing. He sat in the mud, he reared like a horse in the mud. He shot water droplets in glorious arcs over his shoulder. It was impossible not to see the joy in his movements.

By this time another bull had appeared, wandering out from behind the scrub near where we were parked, at the head of a small bachelor herd—maybe six or eight elephants in all—that had trailed the great bull. This one looked younger, perhaps an adolescent still learning the ropes of male society, having recently left the refuge of the matriarchal herd. If this was the case, he might have been twelve years old. He might have spent the first eight years of his life never more than fifteen feet from his mother. He might have followed the rumbling calls of the great bull, kept his distance in deference to his elder.

But now he was distracted by the white Range Rover with four human heads sticking out through its roof. He stared. He stepped closer. He looked away, the trunk lazily plucking yellow flowers out of the grass. He looked again at us, stepped closer, focused a dead-straight gaze into our eyes. His head was high, ears wide, an alert stance. Did he mean to challenge or only to match our desire for encounter? He stared. He stepped closer. He looked away, the two-fingered trunk plucking again at tiny weeds, such delicate motion a surprise in an organ that can rip down a tree or dig a wallow out of dry dirt. After this dance of approach and avoidance continued for long enough that John had started the car's engine and turned it off two or three times—should we flee or stay calm?—the young bull lost interest in us and walked off to join his comrades.

Several of the beasts met with trunk caresses, others with tusk locking. It did not look hostile, but it was clear to me that my ability to read elephant behavior was very limited. One of the young bulls carried his own trunk draped in one of his tusks, as if the weight of the appendage was just plain tiring.

✦

I've read about Kenya's Mount Elgon elephants. For hundreds of generations the herd has followed caves tunneling hundreds of meters into the mountain. Decade by decade the elephants have walked further and further into the dark, following their salt hunger along the path worn into rock by their ancestors. They feel their way in the dark by smell and the sensitivity of their table-like feet. Each generation must go deeper into the mountain to find the friable cave walls, where they gouge out chunks of salt, milling the mineral between their gigantic molars. The walls are scored with tusk furrows that look like the marks of a miner's pick. Calves make the journey at their mother's side, learning this skill, as they do so many others, under maternal tutelage.

I've read how the matriarchal herds collectively raise their young. Mothers must teach calves to use their trunks. Without instruction, the calves trip over the bulky nuisance hanging from their upper lip. Elephants share the mothering and nursing of the young. They grieve their dead, standing vigil beside a body for hours, even days, and covering the dead with twigs and leaves. They will attempt to raise an elephant that has fallen, weeping and despairing at their loss, stroking the teeth and bones of the dead one with their trunks, as they do in greeting a living member of the herd. Elephants communicate when they are miles apart through rumbles deeper than the human ear can hear, though a person standing close enough can see their foreheads vibrating. In a crisis the herd will follow the matriarch's lead, waiting to see what they should do by observing her actions. Hunters know this and shoot the matriarch first, causing the herd to mill in confusion and become easy marks.

During the 1970s and 1980s African elephants declined due to ivory hunting and loss of habitat. Poaching became as profitable as drug dealing, and the elephant population fell from 1.3 million in 1981 to 750,000 in 1986. There were losses of up to 80 percent in eastern and central Africa. A 1989 moratorium on ivory trade shared by most of the major importing countries (Japan, India, Hong Kong, Singapore, the United States) slowed this dive. Richard Leakey, the director of the Kenya Wildlife Service, torched a pile of ivory worth $3 million. As the market for ivory diminished, so did the poaching. Elephant populations grew, but so did stresses on their habitat—now mostly parkland. Try to tell an elephant where the park boundary lies, and you will find the limits of human communication. Elephants plow down trees and create ragtag roads through forests. They never forget an ancestral trail, even if a farm or a village should sprout up in their way.

The 1954 film *Elephant Walk* dramatizes the tenacity of pachyderm memory in the story of a tea plantation in British Ceylon built in the middle of a traditional elephant migration route. Indian elephants menace and storm the plantation's perimeter, while the protagonist struggles to hold both his land and his wife against the forces of nature. She becomes attracted to another man. The elephants rampage the plantation to reclaim the route they know to be theirs, the new man wins the woman, and love rules, except for the man who believes he can control the forces of nature. I saw this movie at the Luxor Theater in Unionville, Connecticut, when I was eight years old. This was the only movie theater within ten miles of home and a regular hangout for kids. Like all children, I was susceptible to the teaching power of animals. I still hold dear the belief that the passions of animals are not to be taken lightly.

The 1989 ban did not stop the ivory trade. Anyone who thinks that concern for elephant conservation is a lesser worry than political upheaval and genocide in contemporary Africa can find an education by studying the economy of elephant ivory. Endangered animals have become "the new blood diamonds," *Newsweek* reported in 2008, "as African militias and warloads use poaching to fund death." In Chad, marauders broke into the ivory cache worth $1.3 million that officials had confiscated from poachers. The attackers killed three park rangers in the raid. They were members of the militia group responsible for genocide in Darfur. Poachers "have butchered hundreds of elephants around Zakouma," say Chadian authorities, "carrying tusks back to Sudan, where they are secreted on ships bound mostly for Asia—or traded for weapons." Three nights after the Chadian attack, Somali poachers fired three hundred rounds from assault rifles at rangers across Kenya's Tana River, killing three park rangers. The attackers were traced to a Somali warlord. In 2011, two tons of African elephant tusks worth $3.3 million were confiscated by the Thai government. The tusks, smuggled through a Bangkok port, were found by X-ray of shipping containers labeled as frozen mackerel.

Elephants are not the only animals being killed to support

war. In Rwanda, funds supporting the Hutu extremists who slaughtered their Tutsi neighbors came from the abduction and killing of baby gorillas. A stuffed great ape can bring a good price on the black market.

✦

Gay Bradshaw, psychologist in the environmental science program at Oregon State University, studies the effects of social trauma on animals and humans. Writing in the science journal *Nature,* she describes an infant elephant that had watched his family fall in a storm of high-powered rifles. He and other orphans were transported to a distant locale, reared, and released. Ten years later, the teenage orphans began a killing rampage against rhinoceroses, leaving more than a hundred dead. Marauding elephants have raped rhinoceroses; trampled villages; killed farmers, soldiers, and tourists. Bradshaw sees these perpetrators of violence uncharacteristic for their species as victims of post-traumatic stress disorder. Their pathology is analogous to human victims of traumatic violence who in turn inflict violence on others.

Elephant brains are similar to human brains in having a huge hippocampus, the seat of memory, and a prominent structure in the limbic system, which processes emotions. An elephant never forgets, goes the old saw. And that's not far from the elephant truth, as neurobiologists have come to understand the self-regulatory structures in the cortico-limbic region of the brain's right hemisphere. With trauma, an enduring right brain dysfunction can develop, and the orphaned elephants, lacking maternal guidance and acculturation, do not know how to be elephants. Human violence, Bradshaw concludes, is driving elephants crazy.

Calves have seen their mothers slaughtered with rifles and grenades, their mothers' faces cut off with chain saws to remove the tusks. Calves have watched their mothers being beaten and hacked to death for trespassing on a farmer's land. One traumatized calf, a relief worker reports, escaped slaughter by running into the bush in such oblivion that, when she was rescued, acacia thorns protruded from every square inch of her flesh. "Poaching," "culling," and "habitat loss" do not touch the depth of the brutality wreaked against this animal.

Among signs of hope and human kindness is the elephant rehabilitation project established in Kenya's Tsavo East National Park, where a devoted team of keepers work to heal the physical and psychological wounds of orphaned elephants. Here over eighty young have been hand-reared in the past fifty years and slowly reintroduced into the wild, a process that can take up to ten years for a keeper-dependent elephant. And sometimes an elephant takes matters into her own benevolent means. On a private game park in South Africa, a conservation team rounded up a herd of antelope that were being held in a corral before being relocated for a species protection breeding program. As evening fell, the workers settled for the night. They were awakened when a herd of eleven elephants approached and surrounded the enclosure. The men thought that the elephants had come for the alfalfa that was fodder for the antelope, so they made little of the pachyderms' presence. Then the matriarch approached the enclosure's gate. She carefully undid each metal latch with her trunk, swung the gate open, and stood back. The other elephants waited while the antelope all escaped into the night, and then they too departed, the matriarch leaving last with a backward glance to see that all the captives had gotten free.

✦

I had the opportunity to meet two elephants in Little Rock, Arkansas. I was visiting the zoo on behalf of the Language of Conservation project, sponsored by Poets House in New

York City, which has created poetry installations in five
U.S. zoos. The project was inspired by conservation biologist George Schaller's conviction that "an appeal for conservation must reach the heart, not just the mind." People
have collected animals for study, observation, and pleasure
for over five thousand years—and probably well beyond
that. Excavations made in Egypt in 2009 found remains of
a menagerie dating to 3500 BCE that had housed hippos,
elephants, baboons, and hartebeests. King Solomon of Israel
and King Nebuchadnezzar of Babylonia kept menageries.
Ancient Chinese royalty of the second century BCE built a
"House of Deer" and a "Garden of Intelligence." The name
"zoo" came in 1828, when the London Zoological Gardens
were opened for scientific studies.

As the plight of animals has worsened, the role of zoos
has changed. As recently as my childhood, zoos offered an
introduction to the wonder, diversity, and weirdness of the
planet's expressiveness. People went to zoos to learn about
creatures that populated a world full of marvels in places few
would have the resources to visit. Zoos expanded our imaginations to the world's beauty and bounty.

People go to zoos today to see animals they are unlikely
to see in the wild because the animals are unlikely to survive
there. Zoos may be the last opportunity for species protection for many wild animals. Some people have always hated
zoos, because seeing animals as captives violates their sense
of propriety or it causes them sorrow when they were hoping
for joy. Anyone who is not feeling sorrow in contemplating
the plight of animals, and the hand of humans in furthering
their plight, is not paying attention. Or suffering from psychic
numbing, because it is just too hard to feel sadness on the
scale of mass extinction. The United Nations designated 2010
the International Year of Biodiversity, 193 nations joining in
treaty to seek "significant reduction of the current rate of biodiversity loss at the global, regional and national level as a con-

tribution to poverty alleviation and to the benefit of all life on Earth." That year has come and gone. The target has not been met. Try one iconic species: fifty years ago there were five hundred thousand wild lions. Today there are twenty-five thousand. No need to run the numbers: they change faster than anyone could wish. The Living Planet Index notes that since 1970 there has been a 30 percent decline in birds, mammals, amphibians, reptiles, and fish. Human beings are degrading ecosystems at a rate unprecedented in human history. Now all animals are held captive by the global scale of change that human beings have induced. Even we are captives.

I'm honored to say I met two elephants at the Little Rock Zoo. I was touring the poetry installation and enjoying the behind-the-scenes talk of educators and keepers that had become such a lovely part of my experience on the project. My favorite keeper story (from another zoo) was one about an orangutan that escaped his enclosure. He was so accustomed to human behavior that when he got out he just stood around on the sidewalk putting his arm around people and posing for photographs.

"Would you like to meet the elephants?" my Little Rock host asked.

"Sure," I replied, not knowing what to expect.

We entered the night quarters, an empty cement-floored barn with airy compartments lined with huge steel bars. A car-sized cylindrical red bristle brush had been mounted vertically on one of the bars—the brush from a street sweeper repurposed as an elephant backscratcher. The keeper was hosing down the floor and steel pillars.

"Sorry," he said. "It really stinks in here today."

He'd just completed the weekly bleaching so the place smelled like a swimming pool. No elephants in sight.

"Can she meet the girls?"

The keeper was a tall, quiet, wiry man with white hair, wire glasses, khaki pants and shirt. When he heard I was from Arizona, he told me he was a hiker and we talked about our favorite sites.

He led us out through the barn-sized doorway to the dusty yard. The two elephants were at the far end of the yard, under a spot of shade, lazing. He called them over. What did he say? "Move on" or "move along"? Something like that. He said it quietly. Their heads lifted and they joined us, two Asian elephants walking over like slow golden retrievers at the sound of his voice.

And there we stood, three people flanked by two elephants, just hanging out like a bunch of farmhands talking in the outdoors. I stroked their creased leather trunks and knobby brows. One snuffed at my sneaker with its nostrils, the two pink hollows at the tip of the trunk opening into the warm, wet mystery of the beast's interior. I stood face-to-face with one of them, the elephant's eyelashes long as my thumb—black, shiny, fine. Her trunk was pink with gray freckles. The skin, dry leather. The eyes, balmy and deep. I was surprised by the toenails, the feet so stumplike.

"Do their toenails need care?"

"They get a pedicure every two weeks. Most elephants that die in captivity—it's from infections in the foot that spread to the body."

They have bowling pins. One elephant has learned to bowl. They have beer kegs to toss. They have a huge black ball to roll. It's something that's used to blow through an oil pipeline to clean it. It's only used once, costs $8,000, then is donated here for elephant enrichment. The keeper tells me that they are so smart, it's hard to keep them interested. He's always looking for a new toy or task. He hides fruit for them to find, builds a basket up high in the enclosure so they have to work for food.

One has a thick scar on her rear ankle.

"What's her story?"

They had found a packing slip in her crate when she

arrived. She had been a circus elephant—shipped to New York City in 1951. She must have been kept chained in her crate when she wasn't in the circus ring. When she got here to Little Rock, she was afraid of everything: the little kids' zoo train, the peacocks. The other elephant had been purchased from a logging camp in India where she'd been employed. The circus elephant was sixty-one years old, the laborer a few years younger. Their whole lives were spent in human company and this was the kindest chapter.

Each morning before the zoo opens, they get to take a walk through the whole place. A purist would want them to be free of the barn, the dusty paddock, the steel bars, and yet these elephants have lived interesting and difficult lives. Zoo people like to refer to their animals as ambassadors from the wild. These two are more like refugees.

"Do they understand a lot of words?"

"About a hundred."

They nudge forward, but ever so gently.

"They want to go inside for water."

They inch forward, never shove. What kindness has come to them has made them calm and patient. I felt that somehow they knew what I was saying with my hands, which stroked and stroked them while we talked.

"What do you think about elephant emotions?" I asked. "You know, how people say they have such feelings of affection and grief."

"They know right away what you feel," said the keeper, a man who knows these two individuals as well as I know any of my friends. "Humans used to be that way. But we've lost it."

The Cheetah Run

Cheetahs are leaving the world. In 1900 there were one hundred thousand cheetahs. In 2000 there were ten thousand. All cheetahs are so closely related that they are almost the same genetic individual: skin grafts from one to another are virtually foolproof. This is because there is so little genetic variation among them. They are all descended from a very small population—perhaps as few as seven individuals isolated in a late ice age. This means there is not sufficient genetic diversity for them to survive. They have had to breed with their siblings and parents and cousins. The males have weak sperm and low sperm counts. The species is so vulnerable that it is unlikely to make it much more than a decade or two. Unless we learn how to recover genetic material from some time before the bottleneck occurred. Science cannot do that yet. If a disease comes along for which cheetahs have developed no resistance and humans have found no cure, the cheetahs will be gone.

Cheetahs have been beloved by people for at least five thousand years. Sumerians, Egyptians, and Persians kept them as pets and trained them for hunting, taking them to the hunting grounds on a leash or wearing a hood. One of King Tut's funerary beds takes the form of a cheetah flattened out so that the royal body might lie on the cheetah's back as Anubis attended to him, the king's head lying back to back against the gilded cheetah head. The cat is identifiable as a cheetah because the noble face has black tear lines curving down its cheeks, small gestures of darkness that punctuate a figure radiating all that ancient, celestial gold.

What does it matter if the cheetahs go out of the world? People with hearts calloused by loss are fond of meeting extinction laments with the dismissal that 98 percent of living things that have so far lived on Earth are now extinct. That doesn't pay due respect to our own species, which has brought an innovation to the planet. People have a moral imagination and, unless they've become benumbed by suffering, they care. Do our actions always line up with our empathy? No. But that in itself is so unsettling that we cannot rest easy with our shortcomings.

The moral imagination insists that every species has a right to its full evolutionary potential. That's the way I need to think about how we've failed the creatures living with us in the Holocene and early Anthropocene, the new geologic epoch in which we find ourselves. Nobel Prize-winning geoscientist Paul Crutzen defines the epoch as one in which during the past two centuries human beings have become the foremost agents of change on Earth's surface: population growth, burning fossil fuel, climate weirding, sea level rise, ocean acidification, degradation of land and atmosphere and water, displacement of the wild and the poor—all alter the terms of existence for all life. No place or creature is separate from this influence.

The cheetahs have had a good run—maybe eleven million years or so—since they split off the big cat highway from cougars. Cheetahs are the fastest sprinters in the world with their taut athletic waists and deep chests. They are beautiful, with their spots like obsidian beads, with their whipping tails, with their four-feet-off-the-ground, zero-to-seventy-in-four-seconds sprint, with their chirping that sounds like birds when they call their brothers to eat.

✦

A blond Californian woman sits at the wheel of the Jeep, easing down a gravel lane. She wears a palm leaf print shirt and a ball cap. She has that perfect athletic look that fits San Diego, as if she runs ten miles every day. She has a big black retriever riding shotgun in the Jeep, tongue hanging pretty and pink in happiness for the ride. But there are no surfboards or mountain bikes riding as cargo on this outing. Instead there is a large cage in which lies a very calm cheetah. The woman, dog, and cat are on their way to work.

I've ridden in the back of the canvas-topped stock truck to the savanna at the San Diego Safari Park's 1,800-acre campus to watch the keepers exercise a cheetah. Majani is four years old and has been training for a year. He was born here, one of more than 130 cheetahs born in the San Diego Zoo's captive breeding program, begun in the 1970s. The trainers prep for the run, chatting, walking the track, while we observers sit outside in an open-walled brown canvas tent for safari-style tea. First on the track is the retriever. Cliff is Majani's dog. They have been raised together. Cliff is the cheetah's security blanket. When the cheetah sees the dog relaxed, panting with tongue hanging out, which shows his lack of stress, Majani knows that all is well and goes along with the program. They bunk together, travel together, and Cliff hangs out while Majani goes through training.

Another perfect Californian youth, a guy wearing the same palm tree motif, cell phone and pager clipped to the waist of his black shorts, sets up the Chevy starter motor at the far end of the track. It will pull Majani's lure at seventy miles an hour along the ground and the cheetah will race after it. Each of the three cheetahs in the training program has chosen his own lure. This one contains bits of sheepskin, bits of plastic bag for noise, and a pillowcase soaked with female cheetah urine. It takes trial and error to determine what will excite an individual cheetah—what will incite it to run. The trainers plan to run this cheetah three times, the dirt track starting down among the thorn acacias, running past our tent to the end zone that lies about 130 yards from the start. If the cheetah makes the full run, a whistle blows and he gets a big bowl of meat. The timing has to be right, so that the release trainer opens the cage just as the lure begins to fly away. The event goes by so fast that I find it hard to see anything but speed. What can I hold in my mind? Only the soft pounding of the cheetah's footpads, soft but thundering.

Mike, the guy running the motor, tells us Majani has been conditioned from 140 to 120 pounds during "his country club existence." He now has a good fat-to-muscle ratio. After the training, each of the guests has a chance to stand beside the cat to have a photo taken. Majani by this time is on his leash and Cliff is lying on the ground close by. The dog's job is pretty easy. He has nothing to do but just be. The trainer leads the cheetah to sit on a wooden box that has been placed so that the cat is about eye level with the "safari" guest.

When my turn comes, I stand a few inches from the cheetah. It is a strange moment, posing like that and wondering if I should look at the cat or the lens. He feels shockingly strong, a muscular tension that is electric. Majani is restless and jumps down from the pedestal to the side of the box where the trainer stands loosely holding the leash. When he jumps back up, his tail whacks against my back—the huge, thick muscular softness . . .

"Don't move," says the trainer.

"Oh, I know," I whisper. The shutter clicks. The cat makes a soft purr that is so deep it sounds like a growl. I look to the retriever. The cat looks to the retriever. Cliff is lying calmly on the ground, as if this is a day of basking at the beach. The cat and I turn to look into each other's eyes, each of us pulling our heads back a bit in awkwardness. I look away, unsure why, except that it seems brash to look a cheetah in the eye. I look then into his mouth—that wet, toothy, pink maw.

✦

An account of cheetah hunting written in the late 1970s
comes from R. S. Dharmakumarsinhji in *Reminiscences of
Indian Wildlife*. He writes that the sport came into India
with Mongols and Persian emperors. Prior to independence
many "princely states" kept cheetahs. The sixteenth-century
emperor Akbar the Great had over a thousand captive cheetahs. The author's father kept thirty-two African cheetahs
for hunting, hiring Muslim trainers who knew the art by
inherited tradition. The cheetah needs the chase. A gazelle
could walk past a cheetah and the cat would not respond. But
if the gazelle is spooked and starts running, that triggers the
cheetah's instinct.

This family hunted for blackbuck, releasing the cheetah
from a bullock cart when they were in range of the antelope.
Blackbuck, in the 1940s, the author reports, roamed in herds
thousands strong, "a line which took a quarter of an hour to
pass from one portion of the horizon to another, a stream of
antelope, a thick moving line of fawn and black and white
colour, a chain in movement magnifying itself in the mirage
like a ghostly train, a sight now unimaginable."

The whole hunt would be over in a matter of minutes, the
cat flattening out in chase, pushing with a last span of super-
charged speed, two of the fastest animals in the world competing. When the cheetah overtook the blackbuck, it struck
out with a front paw at the hind legs of the prey. The hooked
dewclaw caught. The buck began to fall. The cheetah braked
with hind legs. The buck fell. The cheetah clamped jaw over
windpipe until the buck was starved of oxygen. The cat was
rewarded with a drink of the prey's blood or some meat.

✦

Each culture has its forms and patterns for interacting with
animals. For those in need of killing animals in order to feel

close to them, there is Namibia's Ozondjahe Hunting Safaris, run by the same European family for three generations. For about $10,000, a person can spend twelve days with a professional guide, hunting among the highest density of cheetahs in the world. If you get one, you'll have to pay an additional trophy fee of $3,800 (you can't buy a hot tub for less than five grand). If you don't luck out with a cheetah, there's cheaper game to bag: leopard, $3,500; dik-dik (the graceful antelope tiny as a fox terrier), $2,600; zebra, $1,250; warthog for $400. The truly desperate can kill a jackal for fifty bucks. Birds, you can kill for free.

The photographs of these hunters posing with their kills, the giant heads or chests stained with leaking blood as the man seeks to position the beast so it looks like a trophy and not like a corpse, all the while embracing the rifle or bow like a baby, are the emptiest human portraits I have ever seen, emptier than all the victims of trauma and collective suffering documented in the news.

"The blindness in human beings," wrote William James in a 1906 address, "is the blindness with which we all are afflicted in regard to the feelings of creatures and people different from ourselves."

I write to try to see.

The Finback

The finback whale washed ashore on the blond sand at Herring Cove. The research team used knives and hammers to cut him apart. A perfect black dorsal fin lay here on the beach. A slab of black skin lined with fat lay there. A pile of dim intestines rested atop a segment of severed spine. The flesh was meat-red, a red so deep it seemed black-red. Long slices of the flesh revealed three inches of white blubber like a thick quilt between the skin and the muscle. The animal's decomposition had stained the air all along the beach. Some of us who had come to witness the spectacle covered our mouths and noses with sweater sleeves or lifted sweatshirts to turn them into masks. The park rangers quietly kept the crowd of twenty, thirty people at a distance while the team climbed on the carcass, their polyvinyl rain suits smeared with blood from feet to shoulders. One man kneeled on a bloody bench of meat to saw loose some hunk of the animal, the dense white organ of its inner ear that keeps the whale's balance. One woman labored to pull her hacksaw through a vertebral gap. They were assisted by a backhoe, ropes, and chains, so that the tonnage they pulled apart piece by piece seemed as light as papier-mâché. One man carried a meat hook hanging from his hand as he stood watching. Another man leaned toward the closed eye, an eyeball bigger than the man's fist. Difficult to see there was an eyeball there between the dull, soft folds of gray flesh. The man inserted a small disposable syringe to draw a sample of the vitreous humor.

The whale had been spotted offshore two days earlier, already dead, floating, beginning to break apart from decay. Its tongue protruded grotesquely like a gigantic balloon wider in circumference than the whale's body. It looked unnatural, that billow of flesh puffed up with gas from the whale's decaying. It was horrible and everyone wanted to see it. The whale's blood was too far gone to further the science of its death, but evidence could still be drawn from the fluid in the eyeball. Even this procedure may have failed, as the syringe man shook his head, discouraged after pulling out the needle. He did not bother to sheathe the needle, and it seemed that even here in the sealed globe of the leviathan's eye the process of disintegration had progressed too far for much to be learned about how the animal had died. The stink was horrible. It coated a person's nostrils and throat, the smell of life and death mingled all at once, acrid, rank, and iron rich. Undeniable. The research team, four hours into their labor of necropsy, were habituated to the stench. Not one covered her mouth or nose, not one gasped for breath or turned away, though they bent to their work inches away from the putrefaction.

✦

The spectacle made me think of the old whaling days, the hard labor of men at sea harvesting whales and rendering blubber, the whaling industry's "liquid gold" sold to make soap, shampoo, lipstick, paint, and lamp oil. Whale oil made some men wealthy. Banknotes from the 1850s were drawn on the Whaling Bank or the Merchants' Bank, the bills bearing the engraved image of a sperm whale. Whaling made some men free. An escaped slave could not be arrested from a whale ship. Whaling made some men citizens. The industry brought immigrants from the Azores who knew the sea and boats. They landed in New Bedford and never went home. After a maniacal century or two for the Dutch, English, and

French, the Americans took dominance in the trade. Whale ships dotted the Pacific like whitecaps as men hunted the diminishing stock then moved north for bowheads and their baleen, harvested as a plastic material before plastics, for corset and collar stays, for umbrella ribs.

Thinking like this made me feel the comfort that the animals brought to people through those products, comforts welcome in their dark homes at a time when no one could have known that such abundance would cease. Endangerment was a threat no one had seen. Am I too kind? Had people not already seen the slaughter of the bison herds, pelts piled up like raked autumn leaves? Still, the hardship and heroism can make one blind to victims, can make one think of those difficult years at sea, three or four years at a stretch searching the oceans for the twenty or so whales a ship would capture and render into oil before sailing home, work done by hand and oar and blade, the reek and blood and grease coating everything, the brutality taken on with courage and prayer.

✦

The finback's upper jaw was released from the body, and the backhoe hoisted it and swung it to a clean, dry stretch of sand. The baleen shone like a halo, a partial halo at least, rimming the upper jaw. Dark cuticle grew from the gums and splintered into golden bristles that took the place of teeth. Monstrous gulps of seawater had been squeezed through the bristles, at least a ton of minuscule krill and copepods filtering into the finback's great belly every day. Details whispered up from this ranger or that looker-on. The whale was a juvenile, maybe five or six years old, about forty feet long. No visible signs of injury, though for an animal that might live ninety to a hundred years, such an early death raised questions. Its endangered status makes every loss a cause for concern and investigation. The quietness of the scene, the intensity of the team's focus while handling the dead whale, was a form of devotion, an iteration of the archaic human wish to let no death go unmarked. The animal was sanctified by human touch and caring, though those words were not likely to be noted in the research protocol. Science has a method for feeling its way through the world's wounds and trauma.

And why had we come, all of us in town that day who had been planning to take a walk or have a picnic, the gardeners who planned to till the dirt, and the writers who planned to face their desks? Why had we come, those of us who heard the news on the radio or from a neighbor and wanted to see the horrible whale? Why did parents bring their children? Or the old man, wearing his veteran's colors, who could not walk the distance from parking lot to stranding site, why did he stand at a distance and ask passersby for details? "What are they using to cut that thing apart?" Surely we all wanted to see the thing up close, to see it whole, an animal like that we're lucky to ever glimpse, as it passes a whale-watch boat and turns its massive contemplative eye upon our vessel, then steaming forward and down, flukes flicking up as it dives. The finback is as sleek as a greyhound, elegant as a little black dress, and swift as a cormorant.

✦

For two weeks I have been writing about animals in my Provincetown studio. Why have I been writing so many dark stories, I asked myself, when I wanted to write about love? I've written about murdering a rat and harvesting a pig, about anthropogenic Pleistocene extinctions and the surplus killing behavior of spotted hyenas. Hardly the stuff of the Friends of Heart animal gift store I've walked past on Commercial Street with its doggie pillows and kitty throws, bellies-up ceramic Chihuahuas wearing rhinestone collars, and tabbies sprouting angelic wings, each bit of cloying kitsch celebrating the sweetness that animals provide in people's homes. But I avoided all of the saltwater taffy, heading without clear purpose into the sorrowful and bitter—and now down into rank putrefaction.

Perhaps I am like the drunk who needs to hit bottom before turning the trajectory from free fall to recovery. Perhaps I am like the moviegoer who likes to watch the apocalypse happen again and again, car after car, city after city overturned and destroyed, preparing the ground for the happy ending of symphonic love. Perhaps I want to pay respect to the dead, to attend the viewing of the corpse, a practice that my pragmatic and agnostic relatives have long abandoned for the sake of tidy and practical cremation. Perhaps something in me knows that if I can't stand the sight of what disgusts me, I haven't the strength to love anything in this difficult world. Perhaps I have an appetite for suffering, something in me that likes to be tested by empathy.

"It is impossible to know war," writes Chris Hedges in a *New York Times* book review, "if you do not stand with the mass of the powerless caught in its maw."

This finback is no victim of war, unless I call the undeclared and unremitting assault on Earth's bounty a form of war. By this logic it's fair to claim that for centuries our ancestors waged war against cetaceans in order to gain their oil. And that war, like the recent ones fought in Iraq, renders certain merchants wealthy while the mass of citizens living in war zones suffer nothing but destruction and chaos. Imagine a whale that has lived one hundred years. It carries a body of experience that includes assault by spears, carnage of its clan members, the terror of battle, the bloody silt of death drifting slowly down from the water's surface, as sunlight will do underwater, making a ghostly light that dissipates as it reaches deeper into the ocean's enormity. Sometimes a survivor carries the assault weapon like a combat veteran with shrapnel lodged in his neck. Late in the 1800s, innovators in the trade developed an explosive device whalers fitted to the tip of a harpoon. One hundred years later a bowhead whale carcass was found with this device absorbed in its flesh, like a tree that swallows a bullet or kink of barbed wire as it grows.

✦

I recently dreamed of a woman who was holding a cougar kitten in her arms, its head resting beside her cheek, as a mother would carry and comfort a human baby with unbridled tenderness. She was a no-nonsense woman with close-cropped hair and khaki clothes, the kind of woman who might show up on television to introduce zoo animals to a population starving for animal beauty. In the dream a group of friends or colleagues were in the room. Some were surprised to see a cougar in their midst. Another said, Oh, yes, they walk through this yard all the time. Another replied, Well, sure, but you know they're endangered. The woman cuddling the cougar said, I don't think I will miss them when they are gone. The dissonance between her actions and her words woke me from the dream. I wasn't angry at her and I did not judge her for the statement. I knew her life was full of many concerns that took precedence over imagining such a loss and holding it close.

The cheetahs are gone from North America, the jaguars are nearly gone except in Mexico, the American lions are gone, and while cougars are thriving in some regions of the United States their increasing interaction with human populations makes them increasingly vulnerable. When a cougar is spotted in a suburb, the cat not the suburb is considered the problem. The whales still have the seas and the pleasure of their graceful rising and diving in the continual embrace of water. But their numbers are diminished, their habitat is defiled, their prey is dwindling, and some of their own species are going and will not return. Those that remain glide through an impoverished homeland, animals with brains inclined—as with elephants and human beings—toward community. How quiet the deep ocean must have grown for the whales since the time of their greatest abundance, animals who send sonic messages hundreds of miles through the deep to connect with their kind. How those cetacean messages meet one another, how they register in the bodies of whales, as music registers in our bodies, is a mystery and a marvel. Do they feel a sense of intangible nostalgia for a past they intuit was somehow richer than the present they know? What does desire feel like in a cetacean body, arousal quickening out of nowhere as their flesh glides down through cathedrals of light and shadow into the solemn depths?

The Feasting

The sun hangs low over Race Point at the far tip of Cape Cod, sunlight thick and yellow turning the rippled sand into a patchwork of slate-blue shadows and buttery highlights. Each ankle-high ridge and valley of windblown sand becomes a painterly study in color contrast. There is no gray zone at this late hour of the day. The tide is receding. It has left behind a running heap of tiny fish, like a row of hay raked up in a farmer's meadow. The fish look like little plastic snakes or gummy worms, their bodies glistening clear as spring water. They look like glass, except that the bodies twitch and flip a moment before falling still. The tiny fish are piled up several inches deep and the row extends down the beach as far as I can see—at least a quarter mile.

When the hidden struggle of living shows itself this way—the wild ones living their dying in plain sight—the shock to human eyes has two sides. One is abundance and one is grief. The water boils as fish leap for safety and the huge mouths of striped bass stab the surface in pursuit. Thousands upon thousands of fish are cast up and dying. The alewives have bodies clear all the way through, marked only with one silky black line running the creature's length, a piercing black eye hurled toward the sky. The mackerel have a cord of shiny blue tissue running through the clear flesh, so that it seems the fish skin grows within this cocoon of liquid glass. Some show a dim stain of red near the gills where blood has seeped. Thousands upon thousands lie dead in the waves' wake. They are mostly two inches long. A few have grown to a three-inch length and have the iridescent blue skin of adult mackerel. I scoop up some specimens in my hand, turning them just so in the sunlight, and a lilac-colored patch near the gill illuminates.

The striped bass are making their seasonal journey along the Atlantic shore. Fierce feeders, they come within a foot of the shore, their leaping gape through all of this forage ecstatic. They jump nearly out of their bodies in the feasting. This is the dance they are made for. Perhaps the bass have schooled this close to shore in flight from larger predators. The spectacle is a feast or a terror, depending on whose story you're telling. They remind me, these thousands of fish dying on the beach, of those mindful suicides—like the poet Anne Sexton with her "awful rowing toward God"—suicides who end it because they cannot bear living another day with the knowledge they will have to die, curing themselves of death's threat by making a preemptive strike. I know the analogy has nothing to do with the instinct that drives the tiny fish to leap to their deaths, yet the paradox of that desperation, whether it is a mindless or a mindful act, stirs up a sense of tenderness toward life and the difficult terms it sets.

I have faith in natural process, in the intricate systems of reciprocity that keep nature from tilting out of balance. I may belong to the last generation for a very long time to feel this faith. Life is tough and resilient. Life overdoes it. Consider the seeds of the dandelion weed, the tadpoles of a frog, and the sperm production of the human male. There are so many more gametes than are needed for a species to survive. The system is biased toward continuity. As for the alewives and mackerel beaching at Race Point on a sunny afternoon in May, this event is a random catastrophe of nature, nothing out of the ordinary. How many more thousands or millions of hatchlings are schooling lustily offshore, escaping the stripers' mouths to fatten into their own maturity? There is no malice and no grief in the actions of predator or prey, only the spectacle of muscular effort, the shine of wet skin.

I have been trying to wrap my head around the scale of violence erupting in human homes, tribes, nations, and against our mothering planet in all its intricate wholeness. No one can explain or justify the breadth and depth of human cruelty. Malice and grief abound. The facts come home to us in the triple crown of climate chaos, crashing biodiversity, and ceaseless genocidal war. How terribly ironic it is that we, the animals who wrote ethical principles into the equation of living with others, have turned out to be the most heavy-handed lugs on Earth. There is no point denying this: study air, water, ocean, amphibian, or mammal conditions. Memorize the names of places where anthropogenic human suffering makes everyone want to forget: Auschwitz, Darfur, Rwanda, the Lower 9th Ward, Baghdad, Bethlehem. Open the mind to anguish at the start of the twenty-first century, and the tsunami will rise. It's no wonder people cover their ears. Who can bear to carry the weight of so much grief?

I recently dreamed a war scene. Kurds wearing head wraps and draped cloth were tending to the wounded after a battle. My lover lay on the sand, an ancient place that looked biblical, as I recall the exotic photographs from a children's book of religious stories. The man in the dream had been so wounded he could not move. His enemies wrapped him in a papyrus mat and loaded him, like a spool of carpet, onto the back of another Kurd who promised to carry his adversary to refuge. He did so because he knew that if he could not bear the weight, the burden would crush him.

The dream came at a time of many losses in my life. I had been caring for my mother, who at age one hundred did not want to live any longer. Each visit to her apartment had exercised my compassion, as, clear-minded, she described the latest physical indignities, the pain of a collapsing skeleton, the logistics of drug regimens, the boredom of aimless days without a desire even for television, the daily wish to go to sleep and not wake up. "Maybe I can kill myself with boredom," she joked. But the body has a mind of its own and hers was not yet finished with life. I had also struggled with losses endured by my partner of the past eight years, a rugged western man who suffered a severe ankle injury while he was rock climbing as a young man that led to an amputation in his sixties, followed by an ocular stroke that took away the sight in one eye and scattered a cascade of tiny occlusions over his brain. No textbook nor essay can offer words adequate to the task of describing what happens to a person whose brain labors to reconfigure after such events. Solitude was the comfort he sought, while I longed all the more for togetherness. The struggle was more difficult than either of us imagined. It cost us our relationship. The gradual loss of these loved ones is, too, an ordinary catastrophe, though it may sound callous to say so. Death and diminishment are the price of entry. Grief either swallows you whole or spits you out to feel compassion for the grief of others.

I often question why I am writing about animals at a time when I am suffering much more intimate losses. I'm not sure if studying animals is a way to avoid the pain closer to home or a way to console myself that things are not really that bad for my kind. I suppose both motivations make sense. Earth's gorgeous palette is fading. I need to see the beauty of the lavender stain in a dying mackerel's gills, to feel the lurch of the predator in its raucous feasting joy, to honor the struggle each living creature mounts against the threat of annihilation, to witness nature's abundance even as it declines. If there is no ark for our fellow creatures but us, then I need to write so that words may do their part in building the ark and, if it is too late for ark building, then at least I can help extend the moral imagination so that it reaches beyond personal loss to grieve for the broader diminishment. I can bear witness to what's here before it goes.

It is difficult to believe that our companion creatures are imperiled. The sensuous thrill of life can lead you to the sense of wonder, but it cannot tell you, for example, that there are growing dead zones in the oceans, a hole in the sky, and a tincture of industro-agro-pharmaceuticals flowing into rivers and oceans, turning them into chemistry sets brewing a monstrous future. Frogs growing extra legs. Striped bass sipping antidepressants that can make them hang vertically in the water like wallpaper. Newborn males of our species arriving with alarming genital abnormalities. To know such bad news takes science. It will take science and policy and invention to gentle our impact on the planet. It will take poetry and stories and paintings and theater to apprehend the world as it is rearranging itself. It is a world unlike any that has been apprehended before.

Given that reality, my intention is to live by the doctrine of grief, to savor sadness as its own dark memo of instruction from the moral imagination. Emerson, suffering the grief of losing his five-year-old son to disease, wrote of "the solitude to which every man is always returning," that mercurial inwardness part conscious and part unconscious in which a world is invented or thought or intuited or dreamed. In the "sanity and revelations" of that inward solitary passage, Emerson found the upwelling of energy that transcended loss. "Never mind the ridicule, never mind the defeat," he wrote. "Up again, old heart!—there is victory yet for all justice." All emotions contain their opposites like ovaries containing seeds. Self-isolating grief contains the genetic code for caring.

✦

After my mother had a radical mastectomy in 1957, she stopped coming downstairs to make breakfast for my brother and me before we went to school. My mother's love was most dependably expressed in three mindful meals each day. No sodas. Rarely candy. Desserts with fruit, like apple betty and blueberry cobbler. Brown bread and brown rice before any-one had heard of them. Carrots and beans and corn from my father's Yankee garden. Roast lamb on Sunday. Broiled chicken midweek. Feasts on the holidays, the revelry cen-tering on turkey dressed, as her French mother and grand-mother had done, with chestnuts, sweet potatoes, and sweet Italian sausage. She believed in food as an agent of purifica-tion, reading the first-wave avatars of "health food," Gaylord Hauser and Adelle Davis. She somehow managed to maxi-mize nourishment, food groups, elegance, color palette, and pleasure—all while drinking every evening two martinis with my father while they sat in the living room and nibbled on hors d'oeuvres. She was a fiercely capable woman.

I say mindful meals, but in a way her cuisine was an expres-sion of her willfulness. She could be larger, in her mind, than any obstacle in her path, including disease, frailty, and death. When news of someone's death came to her, she stiff-ened as if bracing herself against an unseen force. "How do such things happen?" she'd ask in disbelief. Once after she'd lost a dear friend, I gave her a copy of Elisabeth Kübler-Ross's *On Death and Dying*. The book disappeared faster than yester-day's trash.

She was a playwright and director of plays for community theater groups and at "Miss Walker's" school. Her ambition was fierce, her talent genuine, her capacity for self-scrutiny inert. This combination of traits led to cycles of euphoria and histrionic despair, as she wrote play after play that met with laudatory rejection. "I guess I just have no talent," was her cue to my father, who replied unalterably, "Don't be ridiculous, darling! You're brilliant." There was never dis-cussion about how the play might be made better. It was a black-and-white situation. Genius or failure. My mother lived in the drama of making drama. Her sense of purpose was passionate.

As a child, I experienced her dedication to her art as an abandonment. I saw her locked in the little writing studio of our house, a room the size of a coat closet that smelled of pencil shavings, old newspaper, and cigarette ash. I saw her clatter away on the Royal, its mechanical music the theme song of our home. I saw that art mattered and discipline was its mainstay. I was lonely. But then there was always dinner. And breakfast. And lunch.

After the surgery she withdrew. She must have suffered a postoperative depression, though I never recall hearing such words in those years. Sometimes a woman would have "a nervous breakdown" and vanish for a month into an asylum, Hartford's Institute of Living. But true to my mother's self-mastering nature, she never sought counsel nor diagnosis for her suffering; neither medical nor religious authority had anything to best her deep personal belief that her will could conquer all adversity. One friend, a psychologist who knew her for more than thirty years, said that my mother was the most defended person she'd ever met.

The absence of my mother's attention to the breakfast table—the orange juice mixed from a small cardboard-sided can of frozen concentrate, hot cocoa, Cream of Wheat with butter and brown sugar or eggs fried in butter or French toast with maple syrup—was a mystery no one spoke about. "Mommy's sleeping," my father would say. How late into the morning did she stay up there in her shroud of grieving? For how many months did she find it impossible to carry herself into the day, least of all into the otherness of family? My father, a gentle, joyful, and accommodating man, did his best, but her darkness hung over the breakfast table, the silence in the air like the eerie light before a hurricane.

One day at her dressing table, where she sat every morning to put on her face and every night to take it off, she lowered her dressing gown (yes, she called it that, her dressing gown) to show me the raised red scar embroidered with suture

marks that ran the whole length of the right side of her chest,
the underlying muscle gone so that her ribs protruded like
branches laid down for a corduroy road, the armpit cavern-
ous where the nodes had been mined. My grandmother, a
retired dressmaker who lived with us during my entire childhood, quietly set to work remaking all of my mother's dresses
to conceal the flaws the surgery had created on her neckline
and upper arm. My father went through the motions of family duty, shell-shocked and contained. My brother? Where
was he? Off brooding or reading *Mad* magazine or being
Charles Atlas with his door shut tight.

I went to our town's public library, a modest brick house
across from the towering white clapboard Congregational
church. This library was where I'd first read *Dr. Dolittle* and
Bartholomew and the Oobleck. Treasures. Carrying a stack of
books home with me was one of the great joys of my childhood. How the world opened to me, how people and animals and places could live in the ordinary paper and ink of
a book. Books were another kind of mothering to me. Like
being mothered by the whole world of stories and memories and songs and pictures that made distant things come
near, that made me weep and laugh and understand that the
inward struggles and questions were where we all lived, children and adults alike.

This time, I looked up *cancer* in the card catalog and for
the first time descended into the library's basement to find
the grown-ups' books. I searched through heavy volumes
of science and medical illustration, horrified and wonderstruck. I studied the pictures of cells going wrong. I studied
the red fibrous, liquid, and granular reality of what it was
to live in a body. I studied the skin lesions one should learn
to recognize as dangerous. I left the books on the shelves. I
would have been ashamed to bring them home. One was not
supposed to live in fear, after all. One was to love life and to
live fully. I carried my terrors home with me, images secured

in my mind, went to my bedroom under the eaves, closed the door tight, and cried violently into my pillow.

Fifty-five years after her run-in with cancer, in her late nineties, my mother wrote the book *Darling This . . . Darling That*. I served as her amanuensis. She dictated chapters to me from her roughly typed drafts. I entered them into my laptop and printed them out for revision. This was a close time between us. As she aged, my mother detested any sign of dependence. She seemed to feel insulted if I offered to help her, as if her increasing weakness and pain were signs of failure rather than of natural process. "Why would I want you to pick up my prescriptions?" she lashed. "I'm fine," she insisted, dismissing me when I found her wide awake sitting in her chair at three in the morning and wincing with pain. There was no comforting her, because that would have required her to admit discomfort. She was too strong for that weakness. But the writing project, a collection of reminiscences from her childhood in New York City and her theater days in Connecticut, was another story. This was all about her. My presence was ancillary to the accomplishment and did not compromise her sense of sovereignty.

I treasure the times we sat in her small "independent living" apartment in Tucson, wondering at the way her memory continued to bubble up stories and getting them down in a collaborative process. The most moving passages evoked the present. "Being old," she wrote in her chapter titled "Finis," "means to be in love with your body. So much so that you pamper it, scold it, nourish it, soothe it, talk to it, and even yell at it, but you never let it stray from your thoughts. . . . At night in bed the body reminds you not to stay too long on one side because the other side feels forlorn and neglected. So you spend a fair part of the night pleasing both sides, thus keeping peace with your beloved."

She wrote a chapter about a colleague at the Ethel Walker School, where she had taught and directed the annual theater productions. Dubbed "Emily Birch, Persona Unique," this strange eccentric woman (with name changed) lived in a tumbledown house with a lawn grown weedy with Scottish thistle, ate nothing but tuna fish and went around her house in the nude, slathering herself with olive oil in defense against a rare skin condition. My mother had a way of simultaneously judging and admiring women who defied convention. Despite my mother's standoffish view of the woman, Miss Birch had visited her in Hartford Hospital while she was recuperating from the mastectomy. The visitor handed her a small brown paper bag. Inside it were three large bulbs, papery and inert. At the time my mother had considered this gift a slight. What? No fresh-cut flowers, no Whitman's Sampler of bonbons, no Hallmark card—merely an instruction to dig a hole in the ground?

"If there was any hole to be dug," she wrote, "it would not be for Holland bulbs."

However, after my mother's fallow summer, after her harrowing, her strength returned. In the fall she dug a big hole for the tulip bulbs and in the spring the scarlet flowers emerged. She loved to inspect flowers with a magnifying glass. Once she told me that nature was all the religion she needed, the force incipient in seeds that results in beauty so formal, inevitable, and exuberant. Wildflowers in particular left her breathless. Her garden beds already hosted daylilies, sweet william, peonies, and irises. The beds stretched in a long line at the edge of the lawn overlooking the broad Farmington River Valley and the rise of Avon Mountain, its ridgeline softened in the blue mist of summer haze. Giant swallowtail butterflies fidgeted in the blooms, and overhead the hickories tsked with chipmunks. All around her the spring freshened and she was back in it and then there it was—the scarlet tulip risen from the dead of a brown paper bag.

"Suddenly," she wrote, "a stab of guilt pierced me, for that crumpled grocery bag was no careless slight but a flash of greatness." Every fish, fowl, and flea had in its tissues that urgency for life. Even her cells knew it. Given half a chance, given migration or dormancy or larval seclusion or the sleep of seeds, given surgery and sutures, life would rise, flowering would flower, buzzing would buzz, feasting would feast, and the terrible thrill of living would go on.

A Dog with His Pets

On the Charles Bridge in Prague, five years into the new millennium, I saw a man. Difficult to judge his age, probably about forty. His belongings were bundled on the ground beside him, leaning as he was against the stone wall, some medieval statue of a sooty saint perched on the wall above him. The entire impression was dark. It was night. The bundle was a dark color, possibly brown, I am thinking now in trying to recollect the man. He wore black jeans, a red T-shirt, the only alarm to an otherwise complacent scene. He might have been a skinhead, the sort of hatemonger who beats up women or Jews or gays for entertainment. But the fright had gone out of him. Round Slavic face, with eyes cast to the ground, legs folded up, downed out, hair growing back, black stubble like new grass thatching his scalp. His eyes never lifted in the minutes I stood still in the flowing crowd of walkers and gawkers, vendors and musicians and pickpockets who work the broad pedestrian bridge day and night. He gazed at the nothing that was before him, a yard or two beyond his folded legs.

In Prague a number of sites are thronged with world travelers—cathedrals, museums, gardens, and palaces. The Old Town Square with its magnificent geocentric clock (little sun subordinate to Earth's command) still keeping accurate time centuries after its construct of the physical universe toppled. Or the promontory overlooking the Vltava where the ticking giant metronome stands, the sculpture that replaced the monumental Stalin (once the world's tallest statue), symbolic victory to match the political, time trumping anyone's glorification of power. Hapsburgs, Nazis, Soviets. In Prague it's easy to feel overwhelmed by history, as the city itself has felt, suffering repeated subjugation to foreign rulers, suppression of native language, torture, exile and execution of innocent citizens. And yet the flow of people through the city streets, the milling here and there of human energy like eddies in the river, gives the sense of continuity against the worst odds. Travelers come here to feel that spirit. To understand that "patient perseverance," as novelist Ivan Klima writes, is the only way a nation bears the burden of its own history.

The skinhead sitting Indian-style on the crowded, seven-hundred-year-old Charles Bridge gave off none of this aura of the ongoing. It was as if the flow had stopped with him. He had no energy. Yet some force had drawn the semicircle of travelers to gather around him. Further along the bridge stood displays of paintings and photographs for sale, a blind woman singing arias accompanied by boom box, a jazz band playing lost songs from the 1920s, and a marionette playing Vivaldi on violin. And everywhere the meandering crowd milling and spilling from one locus of attention to the next. Beside the skinhead lay a sleeping black dog. Perhaps a rottweiler mix. A large muscular dog, lying flat on the ground, as dull, as null as the man. The man did not look at the dog. The dog did not look at the man. They were so still that the movements of two creamy white rats nervously grooming the sleeping black dog were startling. One rat nuzzled into the fur of the shoulder flank and the other scurried along the chest, then darted a few steps this way then that as if unsure of its way. Not a single quiver, not a ripple of tension moved in the dog's flesh as the rats busily snuffled along. The effect of the frenetic white bodies working the still black one was uncanny. The rats never left the dog's body. It was as if one of those invisible dog fences surrounded him. The dog had become their habitat. There was no cup on the sidewalk for the man to receive donations. He was asking for nothing. His eyes remained cast into space, as if declaring no ownership over this miracle.

The incident jolted me with its odd energy. The rhythm of the day had shifted, and I wanted it to carry me. I took notes on the spot but was in a hurry and didn't get much down on the page. The image floated in my mind for days. I didn't know why it had taken up residence in my imagination. I questioned whether I had seen the incident accurately. Had there been, in fact, a cup or hat for collecting coins? Had some fact been hidden from me? The skinhead perhaps had sprinkled birdseed in the dog's fur to keep the rats burrowing? Had the dog been tranquilized? What had I missed? Was this a miracle, a lion-and-lamb lab project, or just another scam? Religion, science, or marketing? I returned to the bridge many times during my monthlong stay in Prague, hoping once again to see the oddball interspecies family. To find depth in some detail. To be sure I had seen what I had seen. I had no such luck. I was left with only the surface, the appearance of things, my one shot at grabbing the energy that the incident contained and transferring it, by way of language, to light in someone else's head.

✦

Over lunch I told a friend about the skinhead and the dog with its white rat pets.

She said, "Did you talk with him?"

I said, "No. He was beyond talking. And so was I. There in the city with so terrible a history of oppressors rolling through, he seemed the perfect statement of the emptiness of it all. I just stared."

Later I heard that this was beggar shtick and I found online photos of other beggars, one lanky man hooded like a monk and bowed down over his ankles, his white-and-tan pit bull by his side with a brown rat sitting atop its back and preening. The beggars create a placid spectacle of dominance and rank, a spectacle in which the hierarchy of man-to-dog-to-rat is pacified into one familial diorama. There is no confrontational bravado, as one finds in New York or Mexico City, where kids leap with squeegees for a person's car windows in a guerrilla form of entrepreneurship whether or not the driver's windows need cleaning. This ensemble dog-and-rat act makes the ask a passive affair. But what's in it for the dog? And for the rat?

Dogs, of course, have been taming and consoling people for at least thirty thousand years, since jackals first sniffed their way toward a human hunt and enjoyed the spoils. Human and beast sated, all slept peacefully through the night of predatory roars and darkness. The sleeping jackals told the human ancestors they were safe to sleep. And the hunting humans told the jackals there would be easy food again soon. Maybe the dogs started it, this ancient companionable relationship, by coming close. Then the human hunters fed the relationship, learning to lay out the bones and offal and scraps on their camp's perimeter so that the canids would draw near and, having eaten their fill, would sleep in comforting proximity. Surely curiosity was part of this developing intimacy, that interspecies mystery filling the space from one kind to the next and making creatures startle and stare at one another across the species divide and wonder what to do next. The animal presence intensifies awareness. One who is oblivious to the presence of animals, in the evolutionary context, is at greater risk of becoming supper. The link between observational skill and survival is as real in the urban setting of the twenty-first century as it was in the prehistoric savanna. Paying keen attention to the habits and behavior, the beauty and mystery, of the animal is an adaptive skill. Will you eat me or will I eat you or will we lie at peace beside the firelight?

Studying cave art in southwestern France for over forty years, poet Clayton Eshleman links the rise of art making with "a crisis in which Upper Paleolithic people began to separate the animal out of their about-to-be human heads and to project it onto cave walls." The art was "a projective response on the part of those struggling to differentiate themselves from, while being deeply bonded to, the animal." The underground paintings mark the rise of an underworld in consciousness, a depth in us that was sounded hundreds of generations ago, out of which comes art and a consciousness that knows itself to be separate and yet yearns to be made one with all life. This depth is what we call "the soul"—the *anima*, as the ancients called it, that partially animal, intuited yet hidden part of ourselves that is as real as it is uncertain.

And what of this dog, the black-and-tan rottweiler lying flat as a continent on the Charles Bridge with the white rats drifting like clouds over its swales and rises? The breed has a long European history, descending from indigenous dogs of ancient Rome that accompanied military marches through Europe. The dogs were brought along by Roman legions to herd cattle kept to feed the troops. Somewhere along the line the Roman troops passed through Rottweil, Germany, where breeders noticed the dogs' herding skill—how they could single out the leader of the herd and subdue it so that all the others would fall into line. The locals took up the project of breeding them, selecting dogs with strength and loyalty to continue the line. Their "Rottweil butchers' dogs" pulled carts loaded with freshly cut meats. The breed nearly went extinct when railways replaced the rotties as workers.

And what of these white rats? Let's say they were lab rats, raised for sacrifice to science or to pet stores for customers who own pet snakes. Albinos selected for commerce, rats detoxified from their negative image as carriers of filth and disease. Helper rats. Let's say all three were homeless, the skinhead, the rottie, the rats. The man kicked out, the rottie abandoned, the rats escaped from their dismal fate, all to find consolation together in the small nation-state of their need.

City of Storks

frican storks fill the sky on summer nights in
Alcalá de Henares, where they look for a place to
sleep among the city's churches. It is illegal to dis-
turb the nests built high on spires, griffons, and
gutter spouts. When a roof needs repair, the nest must be
lifted, supported temporarily with two-by-fours and planks,
and lowered back into place when the roofing is done. Day
and night the birds clack their long bills, a sound Spaniards
call "crushing garlic" or "making salsa," depending upon
where the people live. This gentle erratic percussion under-
scores the city's gregarious human music. Bill clattering is
stork small talk. At the Cathedral Magistral several fat twig
nests sprawl out from geometric rows of clay tile, and chick
wings flap, flag up, and test their strength, though the young
storks are not yet sturdy enough to float on air. The first try
will have to be right.

My lodgings across the street from the cathedral occupied
the garret of what had been the bishop's house. Cramped
beneath the ceiling, the room had no windows but a skylight
through which I could pop my head by standing on a chair.
And there I perched with head up through the roof of the
Hospederia La Tercia to watch the spectacle of storks crushing garlic with their noisy bills and to make urban field notes
each day when I was not engaged in duties as visiting lecturer
in American studies at the Universidad de Alcalá or wandering the felicitous streets. I was engaged in stork studies, fix-
ated on the restlessness of the great birds perched atop the

city's grand structures. Storks cluttered highway medians and parks. Storks clattered as they settled back down into their stick hovels after foraging in meadows and dumps. Storks guttered like dying candles as night quilted them into airy sleep. The precarious stork homes seemed wonderfully insurgent sitting atop the medieval edifices of what had once been considered a model for the City of God, a template for cities that Catholic missionaries would build in the New World.

The idea of the City of God is elaborated by Augustine of Hippo, writing in 410, after the Goths had sacked Rome. Visigoths and Ostrogoths, the northern forest people who were invincible in their wildness, flowed down from the north and continued their occupation westward to the Iberian Peninsula. Augustine wrote *The City of God* to console people who saw the invasion and sacking as punishment for Romans having abandoned pagan religions and become Christian. He censured the pagans who blamed Christianity for their suffering, recounting that all the Romans had suffered before the time of Christ. The Roman Empire found its power, he asserted, not by faith in false gods but from the counsel of "the one true God" even if the Romans did not worship him. His *Confessions* mark Augustine as the first memoirist, deeply concerned with the psychological dimensions and consequences of his actions, a seeker who found God not as material presence but as spiritual appetite and home hidden in the complex depths of the mind. *The City of God* marks him as captive and stranger in the earthly city, while his allegiance is to the heavenly one.

How he reconciled his divergent conceptions of God— one elusive and discovered through solitary introspection, the other manifest and determining the course of empire—is unclear to me. Perhaps it makes sense as a prequel to Freud: the deepest indwelling forces determine our fate. I am not a theologian or a historian. What interests me is that this city in which I walked and gawked at African white storks exists because of Augustine's vision and writings. He too came from North Africa, as do the migrating storks. He died there in 430 during the Vandal invasion.

In *The City of God* Augustine describes two cities, the earthly and the heavenly.

The two cities "have been formed by two loves: the earthly by the love of self, even to the contempt of God; the heavenly by the love of God, even to the contempt of self." In the earthly city: passing pains and pleasures. In the heavenly city: eternal truths. In the earthly city: the wise men "became fools, and changed the glory of the incorruptible God into an image made like to corruptible man, and to birds, and four-footed beasts, and creeping things." In the heavenly city: "there is no human wisdom, but only godliness." The earthly city: "peace is purchased by toilsome wars." In the heavenly city: one "possesses peace by faith." In the earthly city: one lives "like a captive and a stranger." The heavenly city, while it sojourns on earth, "calls citizens out of all nations, and gathers together a society of pilgrims of all languages." All signs on the pilgrims' path point to the heavenly city, where "our body shall be no more this animal body which by its corruption weighs down the soul."

At the time Augustine was writing *The City of God*, white storks were migrating over his head from North Africa over the Levant and into Turkey. White storks were migrating from West Africa over the Strait of Gibraltar to the broad plateau of the Henares River Valley in the center of the Iberian Peninsula. White storks had established their flight plans before any cities had been built, before any faiths had been wrought out of the mortal fear that troubles human hearts. Storks built their cities in the trees and flew out to wetlands and grassy meadows to feed, their long legs and bills red from the crayfish they ate. In spring, they flew north on thermals to Europe. In autumn, they flew south. Flocks of migrating storks, pelicans, and raptors could stretch one hundred miles on the eastern migration, half a million storks knowing where to go and how to get there despite the expensive and dangerous journey.

Expanding agriculture through Europe in medieval times benefited the storks by opening woodlands for pastures and grassy meadows where the birds hunted for small rodents, snakes, fish, and insects. Industrialization was not so keen for the storks. Wetlands were drained and meadows tilled. But there were the turrets and steeples for nesting. There were rubbish bins for feeding. Today, all in all, life isn't so bad for the estimated thirty thousand nesting pairs of storks that spend their summers in Spain. Now more and more of the storks are staying, fewer and fewer bothering to migrate since they find easy pickings in the city's trash. Stork habitation is a relative constant in the plains of Spain, the great birds lofting along as human history runs its plays in varied formations.

1486: Queen Isabella interviews a young Italian explorer named Cristóbal Colón after he has traveled all over Europe pleading for support for his quest. He makes his case in the garrisoned Archbishop's Palace with its slitted gun ports, guard towers, and dragon mouth gutter spouts. The monarch hocks jewels to pay for his journey. Not her best jewels, but jewels nonetheless. What he promises her, beneath the required stumping for God, gold, and empire, what must lie deeply in his mind and in hers, is the desire to live inside an epic, the desire to give the world a new image of what it is.

1496: Cardinal Cisneros orders the expulsion of Muslims and Jews from Spain. They may take their property with them, except for any gold, silver, or cash. The cardinal founds the university to train administrators of the church and the empire.

1509: The cardinal takes over the half-empty medieval city and officially organizes it into a Renaissance university city, the ideal urban community, a model that Spanish missionaries will bring to America and the universities of Europe. It is the Golden Age of Spain.

1547: Miguel de Cervantes is born in Alcalá de Henares. His father is a barber-surgeon who performs haircuts, shaves, and blood-lettings. His mother is the daughter of a nobleman who has lost his money and sells his daughter into marriage. Cervantes is a soldier and then a galley slave for five years in Algiers. He is a tax collector. He goes bankrupt. He goes to prison a few times. He gets the idea for writing the story of Don Quixote while he is in prison.

Another way to give the world a new image of what it is comes by looking to the creatures and how they have lived in our midst and our imagination, how their ways and our ways have been intertwined, how human invention has honored and constrained them. Not empire, not wealth, not eternity, but animals have made us human and humane. The beauty of the animal's spirit is matched by something beautiful in the human spirit that by its nature seeks a form.

Stork stories go back millennia, crossing the cultures that the birds have crossed in their flight along their pilgrimage through time. Stork is a hierogylph that transcends death in ancient Egypt, where the bird is depicted as *Ba*, an untranslatable concept according to Egyptologist Louis V. Žabkar, who published the first extensive study of the *Ba* in 1947. *Ba* is not like the Judeo-Christian idea of soul, a duality between the material and the spiritual. It is not a constituent part of the human, but "one of various modes of existence in which the deceased continues to live." *Ba* is considered "to represent the man himself, the totality of his physical and psychic capacities." In gods, *Ba* is the embodiment of the divine powers; in kings, the embodiment of kingly powers; and in citizens, *Ba* is the embodiment of vital force.

Ba has a quantum strangeness, interweaving the very notions of living and dead. It frees itself of the body at death but maintains contact. The *Ba* of the deceased man, depicted as a stork on the papyrus of Nebqed, flies down the shaft of the tomb to deliver food (a whole fish!) and drink to sustain his very own mummy. In this context "living" and "dead" conflate and confuse like "particle" and "wave" in the study of light. Elsewhere *Ba*s are depicted as falcon-headed humans attending as servants or as a human-headed stork perched calmly on the arm of a scribe. But it is the image of the stork as *Ba* flying down the shaft of the tomb to bring life-giving nourishment to the dead that owns me. The *Ba* flies on the papyrus down stairs that are flanked by rows of a scribe's careful hieroglyphic inscriptions. I imagine the hand that inked that bird, the scribe who chose to make everything else on the page—hieroglyphs, sarcophagus, cheetah pelt—clear and heavily inked, while this *Ba*, performing the most important task of bringing the promise of the renewal to the realm of the dead, is inked with so delicate a hand that the image is barely perceptible. Such is the challenge in speaking of the "soul."

Stork is a fable of moral instruction in ancient Greece. Aristotle wrote that "it is a common story of the stork that the old birds are fed by their grateful progeny." Stories tell that a stork will carry an aged parent on its back when it has lost its flight feathers and and is unable to fly, a lesson in filial duty. Aesop, or the unnamed scribe who gathered the tales attributed to that name, tells the tale of the bird catcher and the stork. The bird catcher has set his nets for cranes, and he watches from a distance. A stork lands amid the cranes and the bird catcher captures her. She begs him to release her, saying that far from harming men, she is very useful, for she eats snakes and other reptiles. The bird catcher replies, "If you are really harmless, then you deserve punishment anyway for landing among the wicked." The moral: "We, too, ought to flee from the company of wicked people so that no one takes us for the accomplice of their wrongdoing." This particular fable had some legal backup. In ancient Thessaly, a law prohibited the killing of storks because of their usefulness in killing snakes.

In another Aesop fable, the fox and the stork are on visiting terms and seem to be very good friends. So the fox invites the stork to dinner. For a joke he serves her soup in a shallow dish from which the fox can easily lap but the stork can only wet the tip of her long bill. "I am sorry," says the fox, "that the soup is not to your liking." "Pray do not apologize," replies the stork. She returns the dinner invitation. When the fox arrives, the meal is brought to table contained in a long-necked jar with a narrow mouth, into which the fox cannot insert his snout. All he can do is lick the outside of the jar. "I will not apologize for the dinner," says the stork. "One bad turn deserves another." It is a tale of skillful means.

Lessons in skillful means, or, in Sanskrit, *upāya*, come from Mahāyāna Buddhism, a school of Buddhism that originated in India. And it is no surprise to see the spirit of ancient India embodied in an ancient Greek fable, because Aesop gathered stories from the same sources as did *The Panchatantra*, India's age-old trove of animal stories that came up through oral tradition and were first recorded some fifteen hundred years ago. This tradition influenced Aesop's and La Fontaine's fables, the tales of the Arabian Nights, and Chaucer's *Canterbury Tales*. They are stories of "wise conduct" meant "to awaken the intelligence." Storks and stories share the migratory urge.

Storks in the great American marketplace carry forward one of the most pervasive associations with the bird: its relationship to the arrival of human babies. Baby announcements, greeting cards, wrapping paper, baby lawn ornaments and diaper services all boast the brand. Stork carries a newborn in a downy sling draped from its long bill. German folklore tells that storks find babies in caves or marshes then carry them in baskets on their backs or in their beaks into human houses. Sometimes the babies are dropped down the chimney. If a baby arrives disabled or stillborn, the stork may have dropped it on the way to the house. Households could leave sweets on the windowsill to give notice that they wanted a child. Slavic folklore tells of storks bringing unborn souls from the old paradise of the pagan religion in spring.

In spring, white storks, flying from Africa and over Mecca, arrive in eastern Europe during the season when the old pagan fertility rituals of pole dancing and wreath strewing and forest coupling would be performed. Call it synchronicity that great and graceful white birds would arrive and join the joviality each year, making it easy for imagination—that great coupling force between inner and outer reality—to fuse the bird with the love of life and promise of resilience that is what spring means and has meant in temperate climes for aeons.

Evenings in Alcalá brought the flow of human conversation onto the streets, the public space sought out as if a constant low-key party were taking place. Customers stood outside the tapas bars drinking beer and eating the small white vinegar-soaked fish called *boquerones*. Everyone's conversation spilled into everyone else's as social groupings mixed and flowed, people spilling out from the tributaries of cafés and shops onto the Calle Mayor, the river of humanity making its languorous way toward the Plaza de Cervantes, aromas of grilled meats, sugared pastries, and cigarettes spinning along on the current.

The purpose of all this activity is the same purpose that leads fish to school and birds to flock and storks to chatter from their lofty nests, an instinct to aggregate, associate, and assimilate the collective presence of one's own kind. Jostling, gossiping, moving along the street, my companion remembered visiting Spain as a young man during Franco's reign. Soldiers were garrisoned then at the university and armed guards stood on every corner. Everyone felt they had to be

careful what they said under a regime that suppressed difference with violence. A church on the plaza was destroyed
during that time, both sides of the struggle blaming their
opponents. To this day, no one will take responsibility for
the destruction. The city has earned its patina from shrug-
ging off its history, citizens gathering after work for companionship and flaunting the pleasure of a free public domain.
Surely the storks have helped, some part of the wild settling
down in the midst of all the political turmoil and agreeing
to stay, a talisman of the vital forces that outwit history and
carry on the simple and gregarious business of the day. But
they are more than incidental.

"Animals," writes Jungian analyst Neil Russack, "are always
true to themselves. They can never be anything else. In this
sense they are religious. They always act out of their deepest
self."

Imagine the storks, with no voices at all, only a chatter-
ing sociability, flying on their epic journey from Africa to
Spain, the ruffle of pinfeathers in flight, the music of those
vibrations, thirty thousand sets of wings moving in a cloud
over the Sahara and Morocco and the Strait of Magellan,
veering away from the Mediterranean because they know—
as all migrators know in their bodies what they must do to
survive—the thermals will not rise there to help their flight.
Imagine the resonant sense they must feel of being in the
right place, of belonging, because others are headed in the
same direction following the rain that coaxes locusts, worms,
and grasshoppers to emerge. Even the urban storks that have
ceased to migrate, finding the urban pickings sufficient for
their needs, must feel this sense of rightness in their being,
their nests sitting on mission tile promontories with vistas
out across the miles of delectable trash bins and alley-scurry-
ing rodents, their wildness at home in the convivial bustle of
the city. I lift up mine eyes to the storks.

The Pony, the Pig, and the Horse

Someone at work told me about the Shetland pony.

"My sister's little girl has outgrown it. You ought to get it for your daughter."

I didn't know then how to be a cultural animal. I was poor, living in the north and working for one social program or another during the War on Poverty. Planned Parenthood or maybe, after a wave of budget cuts, for a job placement program in which I counseled poor people more desperate than I was and helped set up a drug intervention program for youth called People Who Care. My farmer neighbors, lucky to have land and cows and an appetite for hard work, used to laugh whenever I found a new job after a layoff. Other friends would sit around smoking weed, playing music, and complaining that there were no jobs. I would always find one. Linotype operator at the small-town newspaper, dishwasher at the ski resort, calf feeder on the dairy farm, horse teamer on the maple sugar farm. It wasn't that I was so smart. And I certainly wasn't accomplished. I was just desperate. And, coming from a theater family, I felt pretty sure I could do a reasonable performance of a person who looked like she knew what she was doing.

My twenties were a decade of rural self-exile. I was trying to complete the project of growing up, raising a daughter on pennies and pipe dreams, performing the role of a grown-up as best I could, writing poems in the dark of night on a barn-board desk, shuddering alone in bed beneath the blackness of eternity. I still love her, that desolate version of me, stubborn Yankee, who never quit no matter how bleak the odds.

A pony. Yes, that sounded good. Something for my daughter to care for. That had to be good. That's what country people did. Gave their kids chores to do. An animal whose life depended on you—that wakes a kid up to what's real. Tenderness is necessary. Water and hay. Molasses and grain. Currying and combing. Shoveling the muck.

"We've got a truck. We can bring her over. We'll get the saddle and bridle."

"Okay. We'll come over and see on Saturday."

✦

"I'm not eating it!" my daughter screamed in the fury of a five-year-old who knows injustice when she sees it. It was her birthday. 1970. East Enosburg, Vermont. Mud season. She had chicken pox. She lay in bed in our cold, dilapidated farm-house listening to the sounds of the men who had arrived to slaughter the pigs. She heard the rifle shots. She heard the pigs scream. She tells me forty years later that it was the worst birthday of her life.

I was so poor in those years that the only people who paid attention to me were other poor people living in that der-elict region. It was so cold in winter, a person could die from cold. Hardly anyone did. The poor looked after each other. I lived far from family, far from work, far from knowing who I was and how I was supposed to find my place in the world. Oh, the town had a dairy festival with bluegrass fiddling and horse-pulling contests. Exotic to me as a transplant most recently from the Harvard Square of the radical sixties. I'd left and come to the clarifying north, after being attacked by a group of meatheads wearing fake army helmets who yelled at me and a group of friends, "What'ya think you're doing? Protesting?" Well, no. We were just taking a walk at three in the morning after taking a trip together in someone's pharmaceutically enhanced apartment. Violent turmoil on the streets sent me packing. No one lived in rural Franklin County except family dairy farmers, brusque oddballs, and dreamers who'd left something behind that they didn't want to talk about. It was the perfect place to imagine as prophetic what a loopy, angel-faced acidhead had once advised me: "Revolution means move to a farm."

I was ashamed of being poor, as I had been ashamed of being a teenage mother. I did not regret the sex or the daughter. Both had catalyzed energies and direction in me that I loved. I was ashamed of what others thought of me, a taint I carried for decades after my parents' poisonous response to my digression from the script in which they imagined I would live. I saw with disdain their lapping after approval and praise. They seemed to care more about what others thought of them than about living by their own convictions. And here it was, this same weakness for seeking approval, for shrinking into defensiveness at the supposed judgments of others, in me—mine to suffer and hopefully to outgrow.

I've always had a need for independence, sometimes to my detriment. This trait has meant that I find it generally easier to live alone than in intimate partnership. In this case—the decade of my poverty and self-exile—the spirit of self-sufficiency saved me. There is a longer story here to tell, a story of pain and temporary alliances and slow forgiveness won only as my parents aged and grew close to their deaths. I came to understand how much is demanded of family and how rising to those demands is a service to one's own deepest self *and* to another's need—a strange simultaneity of I-and-thou in the hours of extremity. But my intention here is to remember what animals meant to me in those lonely, difficult years, how animals kept me and my daughter alive.

One day a neighbor who took care of my daughter after school said I should go on welfare. My old car was dying. I didn't have a penny extra or the profile for a loan. This neighbor was wise to surviving in poverty. She and her husband and three kids lived on a rented postage stamp of land where they milked one Jersey cow and canned beans and corn for the winter. The husband was disabled and mean and treated his wife with ridicule. But he had some good tricks, like pillaging through railroad cars parked near a grain elevator for animal feed that could be tapped out of the walls of the freight cars and stuffed into burlap sacks. She was savvy and Episcopalian. A sturdy woman, she held the whole show together with dignity. When I came to pick up my daughter, we'd sit over coffee for an hour and talk about whatever.

"You ought to go on welfare," she said. "That's what it's there for."

I cringed and thought, Why not?

So I went to the welfare office in St. Albans.

"I don't need welfare, but if you buy me a car I can go to work."

I could see the stifled laugh in the caseworker's face, the way she caught herself from cracking up at my childish pride. I hated feeling so transparent, but I was grateful for her discretion.

"We can't buy you a car, but we can get you some assistance and maybe you can use some of that to buy one."

That's what I did, working as a dishwasher at a ski resort that was too far away from home to make sense, then upgrading to waitress, then stumbling by luck into better work as the tail end of the sixties drifted north and back-to-the-land people came, setting up alternative schools, food co-ops, and social justice programs. I never got over feeling like an outlier, somehow less worthy and connected than these hip urban refugees. When they were partying and playing in bands and throwing together handmade houses from scratch, I was inventing motherhood out of sticks and stones, enduring visits from a social worker about whom another social worker had warned, "Yes he's very kind, but watch out. He's a kleptomaniac." It all seems crudely comic now, how inept I was at asking for help from anyone who cared. Underlying it all was the question, Who cared?

Another neighbor came by. A dairy farmer.

"What are you raising in that barn?"

"A few chickens," I said.

"Well, how about raising a couple of pigs?"

He could get a piglet for twenty-five bucks. One for himself. One for me. Maybe I could share mine with another neighbor. He'd bring me the grain, take care of butchering. I'd do the chores—water and slops and feed twice a day.

"Sure," I said, and the little squealers arrived, snouting around with glee in the fragrant hay of their bedding. They were cleaner than I thought they'd be, crapping in one corner of their pen far from their food. If I brought cornstalks from the garden, they routed through them, tunneling and tossing the leaves with exuberance. At first the piglets were so small they'd become lost burrowing down in the greenery. Weeks later, they had lengthened and fattened so they looked like torpedoes with legs and their tunneling looked like a cataclysm had befallen their home, a rubble of hay and shredded stalks heaved up like the aftermath of a bombing raid. Cute squeals became throaty grunts and nosy snorts. I became wary about climbing into their pen to shovel out the muck. Grim rural legends of farmers who'd been overwhelmed and eaten by their own pigs elbowed their way into my protective attentions. They greeted me with excited trilling snuffles when I entered the barn and they cooed over their food, their pleasure requiring quite a ruckus. In the last month, as my neighbor instructed, I sweetened them off by feeding them only pure cornmeal and water.

Meat was wealth in this cold part of the world. The only boastfulness I heard among my rural neighbors concerned how many quarts of green beans or tomatoes they had canned or frozen, how many gallons of cider pressed, and if they had a side of beef or a pig put up for winter. One could be sure, if one was poor, of nothing except the stores in one's cellar, freezer and pantry. Security could be measured this way, built up jar by jar, freezer box by freezer box, like a house made of bricks.

The pig man straddled the shot pig, riding it around the pen as it faltered until he could slit the leathery throat to clean the meat of the animal's blood. The carcass was split open, the steaming, ropy, gray entrails with their sickening ripe scent were dumped into a grain sack, the hollow body hoisted and dipped into a barrel of steaming water mixed with pine tar, the formula used to loosen the pig's bristles. We laid the pig down on a makeshift plywood table and set to work with scrapers while the skin was scalded hot and the coarse fibers ready to slip from the follicles.

Finally four halves of two pigs, so cleanly parted, lay in the back of the pickup, pink flesh laced with white bones and fat—so inanimate, so surgical, the cuts. The animal was gone, on its way to becoming meat I would retrieve from the local meat locker, each cut wrapped and labeled—center chops, shoulder roast, and loins. The ham and bacon were sent out for curing and returned weeks later to be cooked up, carrying an allure every bit as enticing as the smell of animal fat crisping over a fire has been to human appetite for the millennia we have called ourselves civilized and well before. No meat was ever sweeter than the pig I raised by hand, the texture somehow more defined, flaky, tender, the flavor redolent with every sweet bite of corn the pig had savored, that alchemy of the flesh continuing in my cells.

For me this was a time made honest by hardship and work, a time when I had to learn that the price of living included many dependencies. So it is not only for the meat that I owe gratitude to the pig, but also for the web of connection to my neighbors. Bookish since childhood, I had brought my appetite for learning from the city to the boondocks, and

I began to read with relish the good people of my neighborhood, savoring all they had learned about living through tough times, as if I'd been turned loose in a treasured and ancient library that held wisdom I had yet to understand.

My daughter's anger and disgust abated. Surely that birthday was a terrible one. I'm certain she felt unseen, unloved, neglected at a time of anguish. I must have run back and forth between the barn and the house, trying to keep two time frames in mind: what she needed in the moment and what she would need at our dining table for the oncoming cold winter. To little avail. It did not help that I followed one too many bits of advice from the pig man, who had sliced out the animal's tongue and told me to boil it with bay leaves and cloves. The house stank of entrails; the tongue turned out tough and repulsive. Perhaps the French would know what do with an animal tongue. I clearly did not. My poor sick child must have felt she had landed in a nightmare. Even I, committed to the cause of our subsistence, knew that this meal was an assault on good taste and possibly on motherhood. Shortly afterward, the bacon arrived from the smokehouse, and I earned at least provisional forgiveness.

My daughter had her own trials among the animals, and I believe they helped her too to survive those difficult years and cultivate a keen mind and a loving heart. The Shetland pony was named Nosy, a shapely and proud little gray with heroic mane and tail. She could be mean and ornery, baring her teeth and tossing her head in defiance. She came with a bright-red bridle and a black saddle, a perfect match to the contrasting qualities of charm and offensiveness in her character. Nosy led the way to a quarterhorse-Morgan crossbred horse named Traveler, a sturdy chestnut mare, that carried my daughter well into her adolescence. She used to ride the horse a few miles down the forested dirt road from our farmhouse to the IGA in Bakersfield, where she'd buy penny candy. She felt so cool, she now tells me, taking that long ride by herself, seeing the thick woods differently each time, alert to the strange feeling of trees all around her. Her memory of the land, she says, is largely on horseback.

"There's a preparedness," she says. "You have to give yourself over to the horse, believe the horse cares about you and doesn't want to hurt you." She describes how she experienced the world through the senses of the horse, the animal's attentiveness and readiness for flight, energy flickering through the flanks like a squall, eyes and ears taut.

"I went over her head a handful of times," she reports placidly. "We'd be galloping along. She'd stop."

One of the worst maternal terrors came on the day we brought Traveler home. The horse was nervous, pacing and skittish. So were we. We gentled the horse in the corral until she seemed at ease. My daughter climbed up on her back and the horse instantly bolted, yes, bolted. The word suits the electric charge with which the equine flew across the hayfield and veered off down the forest lane just short of the chokecherry hedgerow, a nine-year-old girl clinging with thighs and hands, leaning as low as a jockey and disappearing, a fearsome stillness closing in her wake.

But the girl, my ever-competent daughter, had her animal wisdom. As I ran after them, then gave up, then wept in maternal desperation, horse and girl slowly reappeared, walking calmly back toward the barn. They'd written their contract and they kept it, though it took argument and impatience and learning on both sides of the alliance. They entered an ongoing process of adapting to one another. My daughter always longed for a horse, as she would describe, "capable of hearing me." Traveler's quirks and insurrection were as deeply ingrained as the striations on her hooves and not to be corrected. My daughter longed for a perfect I-and-thou relationship with a horse. They learned to read each other well enough and together took on the task of reading the unknown that bordered their excursions.

When they returned from a ride, the ritual of brushing down the horse ensued in the hay-sweet barn. A horse's smell, rising with each brushstroke, is a comfort to horse lovers, something elemental that calls them into the animal's aura. The rider carries that scent into the house, molecules of natural oils that minutes ago were keeping the horse's coat healthy now clinging to her jeans and hands. It is a kind of sacrament to the horse lover, this sweetness of the other that lingers with her body. Decades after her horse period, my daughter now says she would pay someone just to go and smell their horses. Passing through the maple and pine forest together, she and the horse asked questions about the world and their part in it, teaching one another to feel safe in what was and always will be a dangerous and uncertain place.

Dragon

I have gone down the rabbit hole in thinking about dragons. I have seen the bare mountain range near my home in Tucson suddenly transform into the spine of a dragon. I have seen Vesuvius and Krakatoa breathe fire from their mouths as the earth shifts its vertebrae. I have seen terrain scoured by a giant serpent leaving gorges, rivers, and hills in its wake. I have seen the white bones of deer beside a spring, victims of the serpent that guards remote waters to protect them from being drained. I have seen a venomous dragon demand, one year, two sheep; the next year, one maiden; the next year, the king's virgin daughter. I have seen the knight's spear lance through the dragon's mouth, pressing the beast back into the soil, where its powers can do some good as the regenerative force of life. I have seen a monster with a dog's body and nine heads, a hero fighting to slay him, but every head cut off growing two back. I have seen warriors storm into battle, each side carrying a standard emblazoned with a dragon, one army red and one army white, dragon on dragon, the killing led by the sign of the beast. I have seen the dragon-happy parade wobble through Chinatown, the plumed serpent rise from ruins in Mexico City, its priest dressed in a feather cape and crocodile mask, and I have seen my cancer-surviving (breast, bone, and brain) friend paddle in the Montreal International Dragon Boat Race Festival. I have seen millions of teenage boys engrossed in war games waged in dark dungeons with tiny pewterish dragons. I have seen the dragon preside over the alchemist's laboratory as quicksilver emblem of spirit concealed in matter. I have seen, in that medieval smithy, the serpent turn on itself as the *ouroboros*, tail in mouth, becoming the One and the All; "the dragon slays itself, weds itself, impregnates itself . . . matter yet spirit, cold yet fiery, poison and yet healing," Jung wrote. The serpent circling round to consume its tail is a symbol of the unity of opposites—nothing/something, god/human, birth/death, lead/gold—a settling into what is. I have gone down the rabbit hole and part of me does not want to come back out.

I have seen dragons only in art, stories, and mind's eye. There is no such thing as a dragon. Yes, there is the Komodo dragon. But it has no wings or lion's teeth or raptor's claws. It does not breathe fire, require maidens, bless water sources, or bridge spirit to matter. The Komodo dragon is only a lizard. A large lizard and capable of parthenogenesis, so it really does not require a maiden. The Komodo dragon is a monitor lizard native to Africa, Southeast Asia, and Indonesia. It thrives on a modest diet of crickets, fish, and rodents.

So why do dragons crop up all over the planet? Here be dragons. Here and here and here and here. One need not fall over the edge of a distant horizon to find a dragon. They emerge in the minds of ancient Greeks, Sufis, and Aztecs; in the art of the Chinese (for whom the dragon is the only mythical creature in their zodiac of pig, rat, dog, etc.); among the Cherokee tribe and King Arthur's knights. They are generally a blessing in the East and a curse in the West, protectors of water in India and Mexico, tyrannical despots in North Africa and Great Britain. Dragons are monsters thrown out by the unconscious for the conscious mind to make sense of. They take us into the zoology of inwardness.

Earth is teeming with creatures great and small, tame and wild, endangered and endangering, hideous and gorgeous. Animals are a manifestation of the planet's imagining, and dragons are a manifestation of Earth's imagining that takes place in the human mind. We're not the only animal that can carry other animals in mind. Who hasn't seen a dog running in his sleep after inner prey? Is only his body imagining the rabbit he chases when his paws gallop through his snoring or is his mind too capable of conjuring the cottontail? It's impossible to know. But I'm convinced that all the animal sentience in the world makes for a massive contemplative practice that is humming along at any given moment—the crow perched on a spruce surveying the meadow, the bobcat trotting down a woods lane in a moving meditation, the humpback whale going tailfins up on a deep and sonorous dive, the crickets percussing their endless hum, the squirrels dismantling pinecones like manic monks with their prayer beads, the Jersey cows chewing their cud while they lie under maple trees and stare at the dandelions, the elephants rumbling out their hellos to each other across the savanna, the rabbits dancing for mystical joy in the rain as I have seen them do in the desert, the dragons lunging from storybook pages and TV screens and medieval engravings—all of them an expression of Earth's spirituality, the something greater than rock and light and water, the something beyond matter that seeks to be. A creature of the senses that drinks in the world, a creature of an inwardness that seeks its own ends separate from external factors. Aren't we all, all of us, animals here together, double agents in our own bodies?

I became interested in dragons while I was traveling in the Czech Republic, where I was teaching for the Prague Summer Program at Charles University. I hadn't thought much about Saint George and the dragon, until I began to see them everywhere. A bronze sculpture of Knight George mounted on his horse lances through the serpent in front of St. Vitus Cathedral. It is the centerpiece of the massive Prague Castle complex. And nearby is St. George's Basilica, the oldest surviving church in Prague, once the primary cathedral in Bohemia, built in 920. There is the Hotel Saint George in Wenceslas Square, the customary secular spinoff. And there is Konopiště, once the home of Archduke Franz Ferdinand, whose assassination in Sarajevo led to the eruption of World War I. As a descendant of the Hapsburg imperialists, he inherited a vast collection of weapons and armor that had been gathered by his ancestors for centuries from throughout Europe. The weapons are on horrific display at Konopiště, along with hundreds of animal heads mounted on the walls. Franz Ferdinand was a passionate hunter, said to have killed three hundred thousand animals, many of which were flushed out of the brush by his servants so that the archduke and his pals could shoot them from the veranda of his palace. Franz Ferdinand was an avid collector of Saint George art—statues, pipes, coins, weapons, containers, standards, tombstones, sculptures, and paintings. Over four thousand artifacts collected during the sixteenth to the nineteenth centuries are on display in Konopiště's St. George Gallery. The poor dragon didn't stand a chance.

Located among the rolling hills, wheat fields, and forests of South Bohemia, the Jindřichův Hradec castle complex stands pedestaled over the Vltava River. Built in historical pulses—the Gothic section in the thirteenth century and the Renaissance chateau in the sixteenth—Hradec is the third-largest castle complex in the Czech Republic. Its 320 rooms provide a protectorate for art and history, none more resonant than the Ceremonial Hall dedicated to Saint George. Its walls were painted in the fourteenth century, frescoes recounting the story of the dragon slayer and his martyrdom under the persecution of Emperor Diocletian in the fourth century. The legend, like many animal stories coming from the ancients, is fed by oral tradition flowing from Greek, Roman, Germanic, and Vedic sources. One thing that's clear is that slaying a dragon wins a person high status in the collective human memory. George is the patron saint

of England, patron saint of Rome, of the Crusades, of fair-
ies and fieldworkers, of horses and soldiers, of Boy Scouts
and lepers. He is venerated by both Christians and Muslims.
He is the most prominent military saint, depicted wearing
armor, wielding a lance, his head haloed in gold. George is
remembered; the dragon is erased. What are we to make of
a "historical" account of the slaughter of a beast that never
existed?

The story comes to us from William Caxton, who in
1483 "Englished" a version of *Readings of the Saints* written
in Latin by Jacobus de Voragine, archbishop of Genoa, who
had compiled the stories circa 1260. The original work was
a late-medieval best seller. Caxton, who first brought the art
of printing to England, published the stories as *The Golden
Legend; or, Lives of the Saints* in 1483. He held to Voragine's ety-
mological riffs on the saints' names, each chapter launched
with a lyrical improvisation:

> George is said of geos, which is as much to say as earth,
> and orge that is tilling. So George is to say as tilling the
> earth, that is his flesh. And S. Austin saith, in libro de
> Trinitate that, good earth is in the height of the moun-
> tains, in the temperance of the valleys, and in the plain
> of the fields. The first is good for herbs being green, the
> second to vines, and the third to wheat and corn. Thus
> the blessed George was high in despising low things, and
> therefore he had verdure in himself, he was attemperate
> by discretion, and therefore he had the wine of gladness,
> and within he was plane of humility, and thereby put he
> forth wheat of good works. Or George may be said of
> gerar, that is holy, and of gyon, that is a wrestler, that is
> an holy wrestler, for he wrestled with the dragon.

It is easy to tease out of this passage the association of
Saint George with his pagan forebear Green George, the ivy-

and grapevine-embowered face that peers out from pubs and sanctuaries alike in Great Britain. He is of the earth, of verdure, of the holiness that rises from the tilling of the fields and "tilling the flesh." What would one grow from such a tilling? The fruits that transcend the flesh, one must assume, since the context for the claim is saintliness. But George is no ascetic contemplator. He wrestles the venomous dragon to its death. What is the dragon? Whatever force would disrupt his ability to be of the earth, of verdure, of the holiness that rises from the tilling of the fields and the tilling of the flesh.

As the legend goes, George was a Roman soldier who lived in the late third century. Stories of his exploits track back to the seventh century, the story of the dragon slaying to the eleventh century. Eight centuries is a very long time for a story to wander about in search of solid ground to be memorialized. It is a story that has, in the contemporary vernacular, legs. The story is set in the city of Silene, probably in what is today Libya. George was raised in the Roman Empire as the son of a Christian and he too took up the faith. He entered the army of Emperor Diocletian, where he was known as a son of prominence and a respected legionnaire. In 302 the emperor demanded that every Christian in the army be arrested and the remaining soldiers make sacrifices to the Roman gods. George refused. Diocletian tried to bribe him with land, money, and slaves, so as not to lose a valued man. He persisted in his faith and spoke out against the persecution of Christians.

What is the dragon? The dragon is Rome, the dragon is death, injustice, and oppression.

The walls of Hradec's Ceremonial Hall detail the tortures that George endured. Before his execution he gave his wealth to the poor. He was racked on a wheel of swords and boiled in a huge black kettle. He lost consciousness and was revived three times. He and his wife were decapitated. His body was carted out in four oxcarts, because he had become so enlarged enduring these torments. Fifteen thousand men were baptized that very day and a church was built on the site of the slaughter, its altar fed by a spring producing waters that could cure all diseases. Diocletian's persecution of Christians continued for eight more years, but the old gods fell. There is a detail among the line drawings at Hradec—a disembodied yet erect penis with tight balls. Had George been castrated during his torture? Had the artist needed to say that George's manhood, aroused by faith, had never been subdued? Did the artist, after filling the Ceremonial Hall with line drawings of torture, find himself aroused?

What is the dragon? A dragon is Satan with a serpent's tail, ram's horns, wolf ears, and raptor wings. A dragon is animal deity othered into beast.

I hunted through versions of the story looking for links between the story of George's Christian martyrdom and the story of George slaying the dragon. The links are not clear. Are they the same George?

George, a legionnaire in the Roman army, rides horseback into Silene and finds the city "envenomed" by a plague-infested dragon that lives on a small island in a pond and demands sacrifice. The citizens need water, so they must negotiate with the beast. First they give it a sheep, then two sheep. When the sheep are all gone, they give it a child, and then every year they must choose another child for sacrifice. This goes on and on, until one year the king's daughter comes up in the lottery. This seems to everyone a price too dear to pay, but they send the princess, who beguiles the dragon. The dragon delays his carnage, transfixed by beauty.

The villagers beseech the itinerant knight to save her.

"If you become Christians, I will kill the dragon."

"Sure," they say, making the sign of the cross.

So George first humiliates the dragon by making it wear the princess's corset. He uses the lacings as a leash to parade the beast through the city. It takes a bit of the feminine to subdue him. Finally George lances the dragon through the neck, pinning it down to the earth, its wings, its fangs, its fire and scales stilled.

How do these stories connect? Even Pope Gelasius, who canonized Saint George in 494, wrote that the saint was among those "whose names are justly reverenced among men, but whose actions are known only to God." Gelasius also suppressed the Lupercalia, the Roman pagan festival of shepherds requiring the sacrifice of goats to honor the she-wolf who had suckled Romulus and Remus, the twin founders of Rome. Gelasius solidified the marriage between the Catholic Church and the Roman Empire. George's sainthood marks the banishment of animals from sacred life. A new regime of sacred story had taken root. Yet the demonization, torment, and sacrifice of animals—and even their blessedness—remain, even in our secular time, stories that people cannot shake.

Black Vulture

P unta Chueca is a dry and hungry village, a clutter
of cement-block houses, ocotillo-rib fences, hairless
black dogs and mangy chickens, and a few hundred
Seri Indians who have made a more or less perma-
nent encampment on a bleached little crook of sand protrud-
ing from the infernal southern reaches of the Sonoran Desert
into the Sea of Cortés. Nomadic people accustomed for centuries to moving when water grew scarce, the Seris are pretty
new to the idea of staying put. Their parched home ground
led them never to camp for more than a month or two in one
place. As recently as the 1950s their homes were built of brush
and sea turtle bones, their weight on the land slight and brief.
But now they have the heavy goods of civilization: cement,
electricity, convenience store, and satellite dish.

I went there to meet a friend who had been visiting the
village for twenty-five years. His friendship among the Seris
helped to soften the feeling that my presence there was something hard. He had arranged for us to camp on Isla Tiburón
with a local guide and a small group of American students
interested in learning how the loss of native language was
eroding the Seris' knowledge about indigenous plants and
animals. What is this animal's name? Where does it live?
What does it use to build its nest? What does it eat? Does it
lay eggs? When? How many? What stories do you know about
this animal? When is this plant harvested? Is it used for food
or medicine? They asked the children in Spanish, the elders
in the Seri language. Every animal, some plants used to have

a song. They taught us a few. One about the horned lizard who had gone out to gather firewood, loading it on his back as he climbed into the ironwood tree. Come here, come here, the people in the village called, bring us that firewood. But ants had begun to crawl up his legs and bite him. With all that wood on his back, he could not get them off, lost his balance, and fell out of the tree. Every time someone sang this song, the Seris lit up, shaking their heads and muttering with affection, "Pobrecito, pobrecito." Poor little one. The lizard, it seemed, carried their burdens, along with his own. He shared humanity with them; they shared animality with the lizard.

A woman told us about a mushroom that looks like a penis, but refused to say more, explaining, "I am a Christian." Then an older woman sang its song. The others laughed so loud we never caught the words, but the woman was too modest to sing it again. She only would say that it was very dirty.

It was in this place that I found myself an accidental tourist in the territory of birds. I did not plan for this to happen, nor did I regret it. We set out across the Infiernillo Channel for Isla Tiburón, five visitors in all, in the care of Ernesto Molina, our Seri guide. He ferried us in his *panga* over the gray chop to the island's long *bajada*, where we stepped onto twenty stark miles of *cardón*, mesquite, and creosote bush with the rosy Sierra Kunkaak rising along the island's spine, its shark-fin summit jutting into the bare sky. We set up our tents and hung a blue plastic tarp over arched ocotillo ribs at an ancient encampment site on the beach. Clamshells and clay shards littered the mealy sand—some thick-walled fragments lipped at the top and some delicate eggshells from the large ollas made for carrying water from the mountain. We found a few discarded metates and manos made of black volcanic stone not native to the place, remnants of a time when eelgrass and mesquite seeds were milled into flour near the place they had been harvested.

Ospreys and pelicans dove offshore for fish. A single cur-
lew waded in the shallows, a gull and a crow picking their
way across the mudflats. Three of our group walked a mile
up the beach and found the clean, meatless skeleton of a
dolphin stranded above the tide line, its ribs like pairs of styl-
ized doll arms embracing nothing. Three teeth lay bedded in
their sockets. We loosened them, stroked the soft ivory, then
slipped them in our pockets, one for each of us, to take home
as talismans of our good fortune in discovery. It did not matter that our discovery was of death. Being human, we found
joy in the new, even if the new was grotesque and played at
the timbre of elemental fears. Perhaps with those dead teeth
in our pockets we felt we had stolen a little of death's power.

The Seris have lived in the region for over two thousand
years, and Isla Tiburón has been significant to them for its
clean mountain springs, wild game, and plants gathered for
food, medicine, baskets, and dyes. They have thirteen names
for mesquite, seven of which are for growth stages of the seed-
pod. The names for eelgrass, another important food plant,
signify stages of its life cycle: when it first sprouts, when it
grows above the surface of water, when it detaches and floats
up, when it piles into windrows on the beach. These are the
last hunter-gatherers in Mexico and quite possibly the poorest people in the nation. There were once six groups speaking three dialects scattered around the region. According to
Richard Felger, the prominent anthropologist of the culture,
the remaining Seris are an amalgamation of survivors from
these regions. Their longevity on the west coast of Sonora
has been established by carbon dating of eelgrass found in
an ancient burial site.

Ernesto wanted to take us to a spring in the mountains,
a place where the Seris had gathered water for centuries. We
hiked inland toward the crinkled heights, Ernesto marching
purposefully through the scrub as if there were a path, his
blue satin baseball jacket a beacon ahead while we picked

our way, sweaty and leery of rattlesnakes, through the thorns and brush. I guess there was a path in his mind, for he never hesitated unless to explain how the creosote bush provided a decongestant and nerve tonic, the sap of the *torote blanco* served as a cure for cataracts, the roots of ratany were woven into baskets, and blue dye was made from ground-up snails mixed with four or five of these plants. One of our group told him that he ought to become a biologist. "I already am a biologist," he answered.

As we walked further into the heat of the day, our pace lagged and our eyes wandered to the ground at our feet with more longing than to the heights that still lay an hour ahead. We stopped to rest. Someone found a bleached deer rack. Ernesto said that before the Seris had guns his grandfather had hunted with the whole head of a deer, wearing it on his head, hiding behind a bush, moving gradually closer to the herd. The deer thought the interloper was one of their kind and little by little would approach, until one got so close that the men could jump it. In his lifetime, Ernesto had seen one guy do it, and he said that the movements were incredible. "It's dangerous," he cautioned. "If you screw up, the animals are right on top of you."

He said little about other aspects of his grandfather's history, except that the place where we were headed was called "the place where we go when the enemy chases us." We had read about the battles with the Mexican army fought on that ground, the slaughter of women and children who had run to a cave in the mountains to hide. At certain points along the way, Ernesto murmured under his breath, "Pobrecitos, pobrecitos," and we sensed that he knew just what terrible thing had occurred in that spot. Even now the Mexican marines maintained a small base on the island, though a government decree had designated the place to be under Seri jurisdiction. Some of the people worried that what had happened in Chiapas—the official government slaughter of

indigenous rebels—might happen here next. I wondered if
leading groups of foreigners over ground hallowed by his
ancestors' suffering might feel to Ernesto like a sacrilege. I
knew that it must be so and also that for the Seris to survive
on their home ground, such tours were one of their best bets.

There were six in our party, three men and three women.
Perhaps the cause was the heat of high afternoon, perhaps
the fact that several of us already had begun to suffer from
an unfriendly intestinal colonization, perhaps the sadness
and complexity of history had crept into our idle mood, but
whatever the cause, after we stopped in the shade to snack
and sip from our canteens, the women decided we were too
tired to go on. The men continued up the slope, hoping to
reach the mountain spring. We lay in the sparse shade of
paloverde and ocotillo to nap and talk about the troubles
that women save for one another's listening. Mostly it was
the subject of men that occupied our conversation, wondering what makes it work or not work between a woman and a
man. One told of meeting the man she loves during an outdoor leadership program. After a month in the wilderness
they were covered with grime and the stink of their bodies.
That's when they fell in love—It was pheromones, she said,
I'm sure of it. Another told of her lingering break from a brilliant and charming man who refused during their last year
together to touch her. I told of infidelities suffered and the
attraction I could not resist for someone new, though I saw in
the man the same tendencies that had wounded me before.
We lounged in the sweet togetherness of women in which our
hopes for love thrive.

While we talked, cactus wrens trilled, a gila woodpecker
worked the *cardones*, and high in the perfect sky a black vulture circled. Lying on our backs, we watched it absently, as
we might have watched a small fair-weather cloud, never
considering that its presence had anything to do with us.
But while the other birds flitted in and out of our view, the

vulture stayed directly overhead, circling and circling. I began to think it was homing in on some rank thing that lay near us, or on a creature close to dying that would make a fresh meal. I knew, or thought I knew, that the presence of a vulture means death.

I do not know what draws such a predator to its table, whether sight or smell or a synesthetic sense that humans will never know. The Seris have a story that explains the vulture's skill. They say that in the beginning of the world the fly invented fire. They say that now when a fly lands on a dead animal, it makes fire by rubbing its front legs together and sends smoke signals telling the vulture where on the desert the carcass lies.

We heard the men coming a long while before they arrived, men we all loved in friendship, and we knew they would play a joke on us. The crunch of gravel slowed, then quieted. A set of antlers rose from behind a bush. We weren't surprised and did not pretend we were. Still, everyone got a good laugh. One guy asked us if we had seen the vulture circling us. Yes, we answered. He joked that after camping out we smelled so bad the vulture thought he might have found something to eat. We all got another good laugh, except Ernesto, who looked sober and shook his head.

"No, no," he said to the other men, "that's not it at all. The vulture was guarding them, because they are beautiful." We were puzzled, the gap between our way of seeing and his filling up with awkward silence. Then he explained that if the men had gotten lost and not returned, anyone from the village a mile across the water would have seen the vulture and known where to find us. It was our turn to look sober, for what was black suddenly looked white, what was harbinger had become protector.

As we started back to camp, the quiet stayed with us, each holding fast to Ernesto's way of seeing. It was not our way, and we knew it. That's what made it stick in our imaginations like a puffy airborne seed lodged in thorns. The world looked then both kinder and more dangerous than it had before. We fanned out in search of dead wood for our campfire, hefting bleached gray branches and root burls onto our backs and shoulders.

Liberating the Lobster

Every summer since 1956, I have returned to Grand Manan Island in the Bay of Fundy, where my parents bought a fisherman's cottage that was built in 1864. The place is a bit derelict—cedar shingles covered with lichen, the fieldstone cellar sodden as a swamp, the old chimney covered with a plywood and fiberglass box to stop the creosote-stained leakage. The cottage has stood up pretty well, considering that it is neglected for most of the year. From my deck, I watch Swallowtail Lighthouse keeping its vigil, the ferry with its regular arrivals and departures setting the rhythm of the place, sea kayaks slicing past the bell buoy and along the glass-flat bay, a scow hauling a load of top stakes and twine as it heads out to a herring weir, lobster boats heading home from the salmon cages, the bay pinked with sunset.

I'm like the migratory right whales and arctic terns that keep this place on their annual map. They come here to breed. I come here to brood. I like the affinity between the two words. I have no intention of incubating young birds or nursing a young mammal, but there is something generative about thinking deeply, even thinking darkly, into things. On the island the thinking is often accomplished while I'm hiking along seaside cliffs in the woods or cutting back the hardhack and alders that threaten to overtake my small purchase on domestic life. The body in motion encourages thought. The more active I become, the more requited the thinking becomes. This can be problematic for a writer as I cannot go anywhere without carrying a notebook. If I lose a pen in the woods, I have to practice stringent techniques of mind control to keep the bounty of words from falling like dead leaves to the ground. I should master that palace-of-memory strategy used by the ancients, but it seems a bit too grandiose for my woodland meanderings. Maybe I could try using the island's villages for a mnemonic: North Head standing for the first spark of inspiration, Castalia for settling into reverie, Woodwards Cove where the old fish houses perch for grounding the idea in the concrete, Grand Harbour where the great old sailing ships anchored for going into history, Seal Cove for including the lives of animals within the human story, and Southwest Head for standing on a precipice and gazing as far into the future as the mind's eye can see.

But last year I needed no mnemonic. My brother's death was the urgency that called me. In August 2011, after two months of back pain, he'd received the diagnosis of small-cell cancer of the prostate that had metastasized to the spine. This is a very rare cancer—fewer than 1 percent of prostate cancers have this designation. It's usually advanced at diagnosis, because it doesn't show up on the routine prostate-specific antigen test. The median survival rate is ten months. My brother died seven months after the diagnosis and just shy of his sixty-seventh birthday. In the last two months of his life, I helped facilitate his care and finances, both of which had fallen into frightening disarray. The cancer had moved to his brain. He'd lost the ability even to operate a TV remote or a cell phone. He wasn't sure about the name of his doctor or which of the fourteen or so meds he was supposed to take at what time. His wife was hysterical and long addicted to prescription pain medication.

He had lived hard, since adolescence finding in drugs a transcendence that drew him. I remember his excitement in 1965 when he first discovered weed. I remember the day, the moment, his joy. White kids from the suburbs did not smoke

weed in those days. It was the era of *Reefer Madness,* an underground thing for the über and urban hip. He found his way
from our pastoral town into the inner city—he was drawn to
the outlaw mystique—where he scored. He was stoked with
evangelical zeal right away, a conversion experience. Life
had finally gotten real. Weed first and then dabbling in meth
and horse, a long marriage to hallucinogens, and a glutton-
ous stretch of cocaine that led to dealing and doing time.
Perhaps he had a problem, as the current addiction thinking
suggests, with the neurochemistry of reward. Great hunger,
little reward. Keep feeding the hunger, keep feeling the lack
of reward. He would not have seen it this way. He saw himself
as a spiritual seeker, a shaman living in Los Angeles, working construction and writing screenplays and adventuring
in the far ranges of consciousness using pharmaceuticals as
his guide. He saw himself as a hero, or at least a survivor, of
the underground. It's ironic that he died from a disease that
requires a pharmaceutical dance of such complexity and
ferocity that managing the meds becomes a full-time job.

My brother loved lobsters. Summers when the family drove
up from Connecticut to Grand Manan, we stopped to visit
friends of our parents who lived in West Gouldsboro, Maine.
They took us onto Frenchman Bay in their speedboat. We
beached near the base of Cadillac Mountain, clambering out
onto the stony shore for a picnic supper. We smashed open the
lobster shells with rocks, drenching ourselves with their juices
and throwing the red calciferous remains into the sea. My
brother had been a sullen and silent child. He resisted what my
mother offered at home, which made him subject to routine
hectoring about his failures at the dinner table. Under beach
party rule of law, he dove into lobsters like a predator, smashing and ripping, sucking the juices out of each fat claw and
skinny leg, plucking the sweet meat out of every crevice, and
asking for more. Long after everyone had leaned back onto a
boulder in satisfaction, he'd be smashing another crustacean

open, juice running up his arms and down his chin, and picking out the white morsels of meat. "Do you want another lobster, Rodney?" the hosts would tease, after he'd begun to look like he'd had an overdose.

Lobsters are crustaceans. They wear their skeletons on the outside of their bodies like a crust and shed them as they grow. When they're young and growing, they may shed ten times a year, later once every few years. A lobster is like a snake that outgrows its skin and must shed the sack shaped like its body to make room for the new one. After molting, a lobster is vulnerable to predators for a few weeks. After molting, a female emits a pheromone that makes males less aggressive and signals her readiness for mating. The couple enters into a closed-claw courtship dance. This is a good thing, because lobsters can be nasty and pugilistic. In captivity they can become cannibalistic. But they calm down for sex. The American lobster (*Homarus americanus*) loves the colder waters of the north, its range extending from North Carolina to Labrador. At least that has been the range for as long as people have been around to notice.

Lobsters have lived in the sea since the great age of dinosaurs. Where they have enjoyed their benthic lifestyle in the deep past is their own private matter. The oldest fossil lobster on record dates back to the early Cretaceous, the geologic period that began about one hundred fifty million years ago and ended sixty-five million years ago with the cataclysmic extinction that took down the dinosaurs. All during this period, lobsters were scuttling about the ocean floor on their ten legs and breaking open shellfish for supper. The breakup of Pangaea had begun. Flowering plants had begun—magnolia, ficus, and sassafras beginning to outnumber ferns, horsetails, and cycads. Whatever the lobsters have been doing, it has worked. Next to their species' longevity, ours is negligible. They have been on Earth about six hundred times longer than we have.

Lobsters look like primitive greenish-brown hulks with

gnarly and spined appendages, stalked eyeballs perched like goggles on the forehead, and bright-red antennae waving around like amateur periscopes. They live in the murky environment near the ocean floor, so the antennae help them to smell their way around. They can sense smells the way humans can sense sounds, knowing the direction from which the stimulus is coming. They use smells to communicate. Urine is the language they use to signal a rival or a mate: "I'm here." That simple message is the basis of a great deal of Earth's fragrance, rankness, music, and noise. Lobsters can shoot streams of urine six feet out in front of them from two bladders holstered on either side of their heads.

Lobster claws are asymmetrical. A lobster has a crusher claw with lumpy, rounded protrusions like a human molar, and a seizer claw (a.k.a. cutter or pincher) with serrated edges lined with sensory hairs and tiny sharp teeth. The crusher claw, which denotes the lobster's handedness, has slow-twitch muscle fibers. It can sustain long and strong contractions. The seizer claw has fast-twitch muscle fibers for rapidly snatching prey. Lobster blood is blue rather than red, because it uses copper rather than iron to carry oxygen through the body. In colonial times, lobsters were so bountiful in New England that they washed up on the beaches and were gathered in bushel baskets as food for servants and slaves. As late as 1800, according to Grand Manan historian L. K. Ingersoll, "lobsters were so plentiful in all the little bays and coves that almost anyone could go wading at low water and pick up enough for dinner. No great value was placed on the fish. . . . It was not uncommon for cartloads to be hauled on the fields for fertilizer, after storms had driven them up on the beaches in great windrows."

The biggest lobster on record is a forty-four-pounder caught off Nova Scotia. It's in *The Guinness World Records*. A lobster that size could be one hundred years old. Lobsters don't seem to weaken or lose fertility with age. This has been tested out in labs. The enzyme telomerase just keeps repairing their DNA sequences. In theory, a lobster could live forever.

Lobsters figure prominently in Grand Manan's history. It's one of the fisheries that helped the culture thrive for the past two hundred years. Now that the groundfish—cod, haddock, and pollock—are diminished, lobsters are one of the last remaining sources of economic security for the island's two thousand residents. This is a hardworking and pragmatic place. Yet it drifts now into the future. The island was long the smoked herring capital of the world. Ingersoll reports that in 1878 "a half million boxes [eighteen pounds each] of smoked herring were produced and sold for export to the West Indies market." In 1880 a million boxes were processed and shipped. Herring were—and still are, to a lesser extent—caught in brush weirs constructed offshore, graceful structures that look more like art than work, stakes ringed around and set into the seabed, top stakes of birch saplings lashed to stakes and twine hung to form the seine. A herring weir is iconic of the place, a harmony between nature and culture inspired by the extreme tides of the bay.

Now herring are sparse. Dulse, a nutritious purple seaweed gathered for world markets, is diminishing as the ocean warms. Salmon aquaculture continues, but without the verve that came with the first wave of the industry. There are too many unknowns: how to minimize pollution of the bay, prevent the viral attacks of infectious salmon anemia, and prevent farmed stock from escaping and entering rivers like the Magaguadavic, where they interbreed with and weaken wild fish. Lobsters, however, are plentiful. Some islanders say that's because the groundfish are gone, so the small lobsters have a better chance to survive. A biologist told me that warming waters to the south mean lobsters are moving north. Good news for the Bay of Fundy. Bad news for Massachusetts. For now. How long before the lobsters head for Labrador?

After my brother died, it was a comfort to be alone at the family cottage, a good place for grieving and contemplation. As a refuge, the island was that summer, as it always had been, a place of beauty, rugged tranquility, and simple living. For one week, I was flattened by grief: sleep, read, nap, work. Only manual work satisfied: plaster the walls, clear the trail, haul junk to the dump, air out musty pillows and blankets in the sea breeze. The waves some nights were loud as they thrummed the rocky shore just like the cadences of grief that came in waves.

My neighbor came one day to fell three dead spruce trees—the latest victims of the woodland beetle depredation on the island. When the trees started dying, my neighbors consoled me: "Oh, Alison, it's just their time." But after dozens went, after whole hillsides began to look like their green hair had turned gray, it became clear that this was not ruin on the expected time scale of arboreal aging and decline. Woodland parasites are doing well in many forests, with warmed winters allowing more larvae to make it through the cold, parasites emerging in the spring and feasting through the bark.

Over the past two or three years, I've lost thirty or forty black spruces and tamaracks. Some were wider than I could compass with my arms, grand elders I'd admired, because on a working island where the forest has been used for two centuries for ship's masts and weir stakes and house timbers, a tree that old is one you tend to notice. There was a spruce in front of my writing studio with an uncanny curving trunk, as if it had had to weave its way past fallen limbs as it climbed. The obstacles were long gone, but the waves in the wood remained.

When the trees were cut, the chain saw stopped roaring and there was silence. Then the trunk cracked at the juncture where the wood had its last grip on the vertical. It was strangely beautiful to watch the old giants lean, hold, lean, and then go. Released. They landed in a muffled whoosh, dry branches cushioning the fall.

The birds kept me company, singing from what was left of the woods. On the day the last three spruces fell, the forest went crazy with cowbirds screaming about the disruption. By the next day they were gone. I wanted to be like them—adjusting to loss, letting my complaint rip, then moving on. Or like the forest ground that wastes not a minute contemplating ruin: here thirty tiny spruces sprout, here a sprawl of wild raspberries leap, here the yellowthroats call back and forth across the opening—all beings embracing the new exposure to sun.

Grief can flatten you. What is its purpose? At a gathering of writers that spring convened by *Orion* magazine to discuss the theme of loss and resilience, Carolyn Finney said that many people feel no grief. She asked, "Does it make sense to think about grief and loss?" John Elder said, "Grief is about liberation—not being stuck and moving forward." Kathleen Dean Moore said, "Love is a necessary condition for grief. Grief is a necessary condition for love." Rubén Martinez said that grief's renunciation and withdrawal to "the desert" forces us into interior process and moral awakening. Sandra Steingraber said, "one in four mammals" . . . "coral reefs" . . . "tipping points" . . . "reinforcing feedback loops." A dissident said, "Grief? What good is it?" Julia Witty said, "Grief is a natural state. Knowledge of the ephemeral. We are undefended in grief. A new world within is being constructed." Someone said, "It helps to have a ritual."

I liberated a lobster into the Bay of Fundy in honor of my brother. He loved lobster and he loved the Bay of Fundy. I bought the pound-and-a-quarter lobster at the Fundy House, the local takeout and ice cream place. A few dozen lobsters were all jammed together in the fish tank, lying in a semitorpid heap. "Just one?" the proprietor asked. "Just one." She was kind enough to give me a restaurant-sized Heinz ketchup can to carry it in. I did not tell her what I wanted the lobster for. What was the point?

I'd never been on the island that late in the fall. The blackberry leaves had turned crimson, the alders a pillow of gold on the steep shore leading from the cottage to the stony beach. The white birches had gone bare. The apple trees held onto their last fruits of the season even as the leaves blew away. The sky hung low with steely clouds. Rain squalls came in and blew out. The tide was low. I walked across the gauntlet of rockweed-covered boulders to get to the tide pools, slipping and sliding, a lobster in one hand, scissors in the other. When I got to the water's edge, I turned around to watch the last of the conflagration on the beach. I'd lit a fire in the Heinz can—my brother's death certificate, the official seal of California with its conquistadors and "Eureka" motto, going up in smoke, along with a few strips of cedar wainscoting left over from the job he'd done at the cottage a few years back on a rare visit to the island.

I snipped the rubber bands from the lobster's claws and set it in the icy tidepool.

What happened then is not at all what I expected. I'd thought of doves set free at a wedding, bursting forth into exuberant freedom. I'd thought the lobster would sense freedom and swim (yes, I thought it would swim) for the depths. Wouldn't it be coded to hightail it for the benthic zone? "May you travel well into the vastness," I said. A small bit of theater in the face of the eternity of water stretching out as far as I could see. The lobster, of course, had no use for my exhortation. And what could I know of my brother's spirit, which had become even more inscrutable with his death?

Lobsters walk, I later learned. Or they swim backward by curling and uncurling their abdomen. And young lobsters, like my little rescue, live in burrows or crevices within ten feet or so of the shore. This lobster knew just what to do. Backing its way into a nook between two boulders, it dug out a burrow with its swimmerets, scooping and plowing, sometimes head first, sometimes tail. Periwinkles kept losing their suction and popping off the rocks to fall into the water at low tide, their percussion sounding like slow castanets. A few long-clawed hermit crabs scuttled their homes along on walking legs. Some creature that looked like a tiny black softball with a tail darted around in the crystalline water of the tide pool. I gathered up a few periwinkles and tossed them in front of the lobster as it lay nestled in its keep. It didn't budge. I felt silly and satisfied, a little levity rising as my expectation for transcendence gave way to biology. No, I thought, this is it. What grief demanded all along was trust in the learning embedded in every organism. I could see the grounds for that trust in the dignity with which my brother met his end.

"I don't know what happens next," my brother had worried.

"No one does," I said. "You've hungered for the spirit world all of your life and now it's very close."

"Yes," he said. "I've seen glimpses of it and it was very beautiful."

"Hold onto that. It means your body knows how to do this."

I could see the grounds for that trust in the sureness with which the liberated lobster dug itself a home. Maybe instinct is a measure of the spiritual life of animals, something they can't control that drives them to their fate, something insubstantial that becomes as real as solid things.

Trumpeter Swan

Freud was treating a line of animals in his consulting room. I was standing by the analyst's side, observing as they entered the door, all willing and easy cases—lizard, armadillo, goat—for the tamer of instinct. They came, they went. It was no big deal. Then in the threshold of the door stood a horse—a very tall, amber brown, beautifully groomed Thoroughbred horse wearing no bridle, halter, or tack. Its presence was majestic, ceremonial, its defined flanks and neck showcasing the tension between curiosity and timidity that is characteristic of horses. The horse stood godly still. This would be a challenge for the doctor. Freud and the animal leaned toward one another. The movements were cautious, patient, slow, as if they knew how much they meant to each other even before touching and had no intention of harming one another or scaring one another away. A step forward. A pause. An answering step and pause. Then Freud lifted his arm and extended his hand. I stood beside him, his familiar. The horse kept his head high, not reaching out for contact, not retreating. Uncertain. The hand, Freud's hand, was tender, ever much so, as it came close then grazed the velvet of the horse's lower lip. And then it was me, it was my hand, and I was Freud. Both Freud and the animal took place in me while I slept. I felt the velvet on the horse's muzzle, an equine quiver communicating the animal's diffident wish to be intimate.

Later I savored the sense that such mediating forces were present in me as I slept. Forces mediating between

human and animal, conscious and unconscious mind, theory (Freud) and practice (my touch). The dream evoked
deeply held problem-solving skills, an unconscious knowing
that wills itself to be known consciously through the dream:
something primitive in me identifies with the doctor who
made the study of inner life into a science.

But why would animals show up at Freud's door? What is
their pathology? Do they suffer psychic wounds? Of course,
this horse was only a dream animal. But after studying and
writing about animals for the past decade, I can hardly take
lightly such a commanding performance by an animal. Inner
animals arrive to teach me to pay keener attention to the
soulfulness of animals. This horse is a messenger from the
animals' homeland telling me that we're driving them crazy
and they have no science with which to treat themselves. Do
we have a science of caretaking that is up to the task?

In *Animal Guides*, Jungian analyst Neil Russack recounts
a story about Jung that speaks of the "deep and healing intimacy" between humans and animals:

> Jung used to tell a story about a little circus elephant he
> knew about because the circus had its off-season win-
> ter quarters in Rapperswill, the town nearest his coun-
> try house at Bollingen on the Lake of Zurich. He used
> to talk to the animal trainer about his relation to the
> animals. One winter a little elephant became sick. The
> trainer, following the veterinarian's advice, medicated
> him, but after many trials the animal continued to be
> sick and he despaired of saving him.
>
> In desperation he tried talking to the elephant,
> much as if it could understand human language. Asking
> questions seemed to interest the elephant. What these
> questions were Jung did not know, but presumably
> they were accompanied by the trainer's feeling for the
> animal's inner identity, one might say its soul. Slowly,

watchfully, the trainer began to sense a change, and in a short time the little elephant was well again. What made the story so memorable was in Jung's telling it as if he were in the shoes of the trainer, and he talked as if he were speaking to a sick patient whose sickness was healed in a similar way by reaching the patient's inmost self, through feeling.

The story reminds me of a night from my childhood when my mother, father, brother, and I had talked our dog Bear through a dangerous night. Bear was a massive golden retriever who took great pride in patrolling our woodland home, a place inordinately infested with copperheads. My father shot them, once killing so many in one day he looped them into a bushel basket. And Bear hunted them, stalking then pouncing with a paw on the head and one on the tail, then grabbing the snake in the middle and whipping it in the air until its spine was broken. He'd been bitten several times and survived. But this time, he had lunged for a snake just as the snake had lunged for him. He was bitten in the throat, an abscess swelling to the size of a baseball on his neck. The vet told us that he might live but we must not let him go to sleep. We should sit with him and talk to him all night. I remember the intimacy and emotional extremity of the night so clearly that I can feel my small child's body kneeling on the floor beside the dog, coaxing him from the dim zone of half consciousness where he labored in silent battle. It was talk therapy. It was love. And it worked.

When I was a child I lived across the street from one hundred horses, the Governor's Horse Guard of Connecticut, off-duty ceremonial horses who grazed idly behind a white slat fence. Each morning to get to the school bus stop, I walked a path through the woods and down a dirt driveway lined with white pines, a thicket where I sometimes hid in the peacefulness under their needled boughs. I waited for the bus at the end of the dirt driveway, and the horses stood at the fence across the street to watch me, part of the syncopated rhythm of the day. I feared them and loved them, their fuzzy muzzles, mountainous rears, and windswept tails. Their job was to march in parades, but most of the time they just hung out munching grass.

How is it that imagination knows how to construct and animate a perfect horse while I'm asleep, precisely how to make the tiny hooves, ankleted legs, the muzzle fur and wind-coifed mane? Awake, if I try to imagine a horse, I get a scent and a shine, a seep and a glimpse, but no whole animal appears. No peltish chestnut. Marbled roan. Silken black. Creamy palomino. Polished mahogany. No lovely curve of the pastern. No ripple in the withers, loin, or throatlatch. I can look up the names of the parts and then see them, but I cannot, by will, conjure the creature so that I can see it whole, unless I am sound asleep and the unwilled appears.

I've had many dreams with animals playing starring roles. The Komodo dragon lying under my bed. The pair of male lions sitting at ease on folding chairs at a garden party. The kitten playing with a snake, batting its head around until the snake begins to consume its own tail. In each of them, the animal was so vividly present—not merely represented—that I had to marvel at the art direction of the dream. None was more compelling than the dream of the trumpeter swan.

For starters, I've never seen an actual trumpeter swan. I've seen some tundra swans from a distance feeding in a wetland in the Willamette Valley of Oregon.

Spectacular white birds that make the landscape look choreographed. The trumpeter swan, one of seven species of swans, is the largest waterfowl on Earth. Long straight neck, white body, black bill, head tinged with gold. They honk like toy trumpets. A lake full of them sounds like a New Year's Eve party that never stops. Hence, *Cygnus buccinator*. *Buccinator* means trumpet player in Latin. It also means the thin muscle in the cheek wall, the one that Louis Armstrong turned into a righteous pouch from playing trumpet. It's a bird that makes an impression.

I don't know much about swans and can't say of them as I can with horses that they were imprinted upon my imagination at a young age. I'd seen a few swans drifting on ponds in public parks. And since I had the trumpeter swan dream, I've been reading up on the bird. Trumpeter swans nearly became extinct in North America. They used to thrive from Illinois to Alaska but were hunted heavily for meat, skins, and feathers through the eighteenth and nineteenth centuries. The trumpeter swan's largest flight feathers made the best-quality writing quills. A historic photo shows a railroad car with bodies of dead swans hanging by their trussed feet in rows like Christmas lights, an image reminiscent of the buffalo hunts with their boastful display of excess. By the 1930s only sixty-nine trumpeter swans were known to exist in the lower forty-eight. They lived in the Red Rocks Lakes National Wildlife Refuge in the isolated Centennial Valley of southwestern Montana, which has become the primary site nourishing the restoration of the species. Thousands remained, and remain, in the wilds of Alaska and Canada.

But loss can be a good educator, an ethos shifting as awareness rises. Since the 1960s, restoration work has returned the birds to their earlier habitat. The Minnesota Department of Natural Resources in the 1960s brought forty trumpeters from Red Rocks to Minnesota to begin a breeding flock. Through the 1980s, wildlife workers acquired eggs from the more than ten thousand trumpeters living in Alaska, as well as from zoos and "private propagators" (whoever they are!). The Minnesota DNR has nurtured and released over 350 swans. The eggs were incubated, hatched, the young raised for two years and then introduced to suitable habitat. By the late 1990s, southeastern Minnesota saw the first trumpeter swan nests since the 1880s. By the mid-2000s, there

were 4,500 trumpeters ranging over the northern states, a
flock of over two thousand in Minnesota. The birds still face
threats—lead poisoning from fishing sinkers and buckshot,
illegal shooting, habitat loss, electrical wires. But their come-
back marks a return to viability for the species, a welcome
note when global species decline plays so many diminished
chords in the discordant music of our time.

Trumpeter swans live near marshes and ponds, feeding on aquatic plants, grasses, and grains. They nest on the
ground, sometimes on top of muskrat or beaver lodges. They
fiercely defend their nests and surrounding territory. But
they go through a period of vulnerability, when the cygnets
are young and flightless in summer. At that time, the adults
lose their primary wing feathers and stay hidden on the
marsh with their young while the new feathers grow.

My swan came at a time of vulnerability. My swan came
out of nowhere. Out of an alchemy of mind. The swan woke
me, appearing right before my face as I slept. It was enor-
mous, cumulous white, tinge of sunglow around the edges
of its slightly raised wings. Was it ready to fly or just landing? It hovered to confront me and make me wake. It had me
pinned and made me know it. How did I know it was a trumpeter swan? The words came with the image and I accepted
them. Was it sublime? I suppose it was because beauty and
fear were tangled into the elation of the moment.

My uncle had been near death for several weeks. He was
the younger brother of my father. We had become close after
my father died in 1990, admitting how much we both missed
him. Olcott Hawthorne Deming was a retired diplomat who
had served in Japan and Uganda. He lived in Georgetown,
the last of three brothers among five siblings in my father's
generation, the core of a lively self-mythologizing cohort. I
visited him as often as I could when obligations took me to
DC. We walked the brick sidewalks of Georgetown exchang-
ing family stories, went to an exhibit at the Phillips Collection,

attended a tango performance at the National Theatre. We had dinner at private clubs where he was a regular, places of slightly musty elegance that felt like the last gasp of the old Anglo aristocracy. He'd had a distinguished career, having been instrumental in saving ancient burial grounds in Okinawa from a Pentagon plan to pave them over for a military base. I treasured my visits with him, knowing he was the last link to a wealth of family stories and continuity that had been very powerful in his childhood and mine. We shared a belief in the power of stories.

I remember one Christmas after we'd lost another of his siblings and the survivors were sitting at the dining table with sour faces. Christmas used to be a boisterous affair with twenty or thirty relations convening for jovial bouts of feasting, joking, and endless toasts. A gigantic bird would be brought to the sideboard, and, legend had it, Great Uncle Fred would taunt, "What do you mean by bringing us this quail!?" Three long tables lined up with celebrants. Now we clustered around one, feeling the presence of empty chairs. There wasn't much to argue over and even the toasting had grown subdued, as the era of alcoholic excess had, sensibly, run down.

Olcott told the little group of sad sacks who remained that there was only one way to get through this, and that was to tell stories. That set us off. Someone told how Aunt Gwen and Imogen had argued about who was the stronger hiker and they fought it out by hiking all the way from southern Connecticut to the Massachusetts border. How Uncle Fred had had a love affair with—was it Jean Harlow? How Great Aunt Hildegarde had said to my mother, "I am a much more interesting woman than you are, because I've had so many more lovers." How Hal had sat on Mark Twain's lap. "No, it most definitely was not Hal. It was Benton." "Oh no, it wasn't . . ." "I'm sure it was . . ." "Oh, it doesn't matter. Let's drink a toast to our brethren." "And to our cisterns!" Grief had been cast aside for the rev-

elry of the tale—or simply for revelry. I think we've all felt
that if family, in the end, doesn't bring us joy, why bother
getting together at all?

I was at home in Arizona when my uncle died. He'd been
weakened by age and infection. He was in his late nineties.
He'd entered a hospice. He'd risen eloquently to the occa-
sion, calling his nurse Ganymede, after the cup-bearer to the
gods, whenever she delivered his morphine. I wasn't there
but I heard from my cousin, his eldest son, that Olcott had
delivered a characteristically erudite swan song. "His solilo-
quy," wrote Rusty, "included quotes from *Hamlet* and Spanish
proverbs, as he expressed his love and his satisfaction with
his life." I had read these words a few minutes after waking
with the presence of the trumpeter swan still vivid before my
inner sense.

I don't believe in an afterlife. I know there are dimensions to being that are beyond human apprehension. Death
may release a person's energies into some disembodied sentience that our brains are not equipped to perceive. I take
no consolation from this, because the sensory and cognitive
instruments with which my body is equipped will go out with
the light. If there's sentience it won't be *my* sentience. It will
be the sentience of the universe, which I'm happy to revere,
though I am hardly eager to give my life up for it.

Animals give comfort and guidance to children. We give
them stuffed animals to sleep with. We read them stories in
which animals teach them how to be human. *The Three Little
Pigs. Little Red Riding Hood. Make Way for Ducklings. Stuart Little.
Where the Wild Things Are.* We give them a puppy or kitten or
hamster or pony to care for, so that the art of nurture becomes
practiced. As I've worked on this book, I've asked myself from
time to time if animals really can help me with my most intrac-
table personal struggles: accepting the fact of my mortality,
making peace with family discord, facing yet another breakup,
praising solitude above lamenting loneliness, quieting my

angers at injustice, and heeding the psychic reality that I am more interested in the question of what I am than in that of who I am. What forces shape me? What appetite leads me? What instinct yokes me to the animal world?

As I write this, I'm feeling death as a close companion, something I've intermittently felt since I was a child and first seized by the terror that I would one day cease to exist and there was not one thing any person could do or say to change that or to comfort me against such incomprehensible loss. In the past year I've lost my brother and my mother. One feels at such times the thinness of the veil that separates life and death. Death hovers over my shoulder. It shows up as a ghost. Get out of here, I've had to say to the darker spirits on days when they insisted themselves upon me.

In the same year I've been diagnosed with an electrical irregularity in my heart. "No problem," says my doctor. "It's your new normal." I want to have a perfect heart, but as I pass into the Social Security years I'm clear that nothing about me is perfect, and it's only going to get worse. I've had a hypertensive crisis that sent me to the emergency room. "No problem," says the doctor. "We can find drugs that work so well you won't even know you're taking them." The ones I'm taking now have reduced my heart rate to the point where I feel like I'm spinning and standing on the edge of a cliff. My genetic legacy is stellar. My mother died at 102. There are two female centenarians in my father's lineage still growing organic vegetables in Connecticut soil. I've got a good shot at making it to one hundred. But when vulnerability arrives, I shrink back from life into fear.

Socrates said that swans sing before they die. They sing earlier in life, but they sing most beautifully when they sense they are about to approach the gods. So Socrates said, though I prefer to see the passage as taking place within the godless grandeur of the physical world. Swans do not sing when they're cold or hungry or in misery, Socrates argues, believing that people who claimed they sing out of pain and mourning were wrong. They are Apollo's birds, the favorite of the Muses, foretellers "of the good that awaits in death." Socrates said that "I consider myself like the swans to be in the service of the same master. I, too, am the holy property of God."

The Jewish faith prescribes that the Kaddish, the prayer for the dead, be recited three times a day for the year following the death of a loved one. The prayer asks not for lamentation but that the name of God be magnified and sanctified "above and beyond all blessings, hymns, praises and consolations that are uttered in the world." It calls the mourner to contemplate the forces greater than human life with which "the world renews itself."

And Thomas Berry, the late Passionist priest, Earth scholar, and ecotheologian, wrote, "Every being has these two dimensions: its universal dimension and its individual dimension. Where the meaning or value is, is in the attraction between the Great Self and the small self." "Tangible encounters with the Great Self"—contemplation of the night sky, mesmerization by the sea, communion with creatures of the wild—these are the sources, in Berry's view, of our inspiration and the dimension where we experience fulfillment. When we die the small self ends, but "we survive in our Great Self."

My trumpeter swan must have flown in from the realm of the Great Self.

T. Rex

My grandson Raymond became obsessed with *Tyrannosaurus rex* at about age five. The younger of two brothers, Ray lives with an emotional intensity that can send him reeling with no apparent explanation and running outdoors for the safety of solitude where he will wander the pine woods behind his yard for an hour, stewing in his feelings until he has them ordered and is ready again to join the social world. It's folly to try to cajole him out of his intensities. They are part of his weather. He knows this and will one day perhaps become an artist who can describe these storms in a way that will make them legible both to himself and to others who are less articulate and who find themselves getting lost in emotional turbulence.

The powerlessness of those moments when he can do nothing but split from family and his own social self must be frightening in a child who, by definition, needs the nurture of family. I suspect this volatility had something to do with his extreme affection for *T. rex.* One could see a look of mischievous competence creep over his face as he began to lumber about the room, two fingers of each hand raised like claws. Heavy-footed, predatory, incapable of language beyond a guttural reptilian hiss, he would stalk along the edges of an adult conversation, and everyone present would know he was testing his small power against the great and confusing powers of the adult world. It appeared he found that small power quite sufficient to keep him in the room.

He was not only a good imitator, but also became, as he continued to practice his shamanism, an expert on *T. rex* paleontology. When I once tried to play *T. rex* back at him, raising three fingers in each hand into claws, he found it necessary to break out of role and coach me, his patience with my ignorance barely contained. "No, Grandma, tee-tee has only two fingers. Three toes and two fingers." I had spoiled the game by being a lousy scientist. This was, in fact, not a game, but a trying on of animal power by a creature as yet uncertain of his own.

When Ray was a seasoned nine-year-old, I called on the telephone to tell him I was writing about how important animals are to people. I asked him if he remembered how much he'd loved *T. rex* when he was younger and if he remembered why. "Yeah," he said coyly, "because he's the biggest and strongest and fiercest of the dinosaurs." I felt a moment of remorse that he found fierceness a desirable quality, until I recalled a list he'd once made for school when he was asked what were his earliest memories: (1) I would start crying every time my mom left the house; (2) I started to walk and talk; (3) I lost my first tooth and started riding a bike; (4) I went to second grade; (5) the terrorist attack.

I remember my own dinosaur infatuation, growing up in the post–World War II glow and denial of a heroic nation that was building its arsenal of doomsday machines while my family rode its emotional roller-coaster up happy-faced hills and down rage-roaring precipices, a madness that sent me out into the woods for solace. My dinosaur was the diplodocus—bigger and more slender than the brontosaurus in my *The Golden Treasury of Natural History*—muscular, graceful, a giant that could hold a beachhead just by standing its ground, its head above the trees. My friend Malcolm, who grew up lonesome in Oklahoma because his mother was too depressed to get out of bed in the morning and who came home from school at lunchtime to make himself a bacon sandwich and see if she was still alive, claims the stegosaurus for his dinosaur. Why? I asked. "It was very well protected."

We each have a personal dinosaur, it would appear, a monstrous version of ourselves, primitive, gargantuan, a being that completes us in our vulnerable early years. What happens to that childhood capacity to protect and instruct ourselves through imaginative identification with animals, to imagine ourselves larger and more fearless than it's possible for us to be? We continue the process, if we're lucky, though it does become unseemly for an adult to stalk the edges of the dining room with a galumphing gait and forefingers raised. Dinosaurs are extinct, as we all know, so what could be a safer way to imagine ourselves invulnerable and autonomous when we need to be larger and more fearless than it's possible for us to be?

Bobcat

I bought a house in the desert tucked in the northeast corner of the Tanque Verde Valley. I fell in love with the place nestled in the crook where the Santa Catalina Mountains meet Agua Caliente Hill. A swale slopes between the two geologic forms, the mountains running west to east, and the hill running south to north, so that where they meet forms a shelter and screens from view whatever lies in the distance. That meeting place presents itself as a gentle valley, but approaching it, entering it on foot, reveals a slot canyon called La Milagrosa where cliffs tower over bottomless pools of black water contained in vessels of rock that running water has carved. I live in this corner of the Sonoran Desert. Driving home on nights when the moon is full, I see the lunar high-beam burst out of the night sky, and it seems the place where I live is heading for me, instead of the other way round. I open my heart to its beauty as a mystic opens her heart to the cosmos or the religious open theirs to God. I worship places where Earth lets her knobby backbone show, where the thin and living skin of the planet is made to shine from moonlight, where the night-wandering coyotes and bobcats turn their heads to look dismissively over their shoulders at me as they pass on their evening errands.

One Christmas Day, the holiday festivities were winding down at my house. My daughter and I have kept up the family tradition of hosting big holiday feasts, though our numbers are reduced, the storytelling elders nearly all gone, and the locale, when I'm hosting, has shifted to the Southwest from our ancestral New England homeland. This particular gathering had progressed just to the point when people begin to drift from the congeniality of the table and wander into their separate spaces. It could have been any family, flown together for a day or two from their disparate lives to renew the traditional recipes, affection, and evasions that bind them, though some collagen has gone out of their connective tissue since they no longer share a common terrain. The conversation grows a bit stiff and creaky after a few hours. Sated on the holiday bird and pecan pie, sleepy with wine, and suspecting that if conversation continues it may veer into thickets of unresolved tension and entanglement that shadow the holiday's perimeter, everyone knows the moment for push-back has arrived. The table is abandoned and guests meander toward windows and doors.

My daughter, visiting from Maine with her husband and teenage kids, was drifting through the house, gazing into the evening. She was first to notice the creature walking through the backyard. As a visual artist, she's keenly observant, even in the half light of desert dusk. She called out.

"There's something . . . an animal . . . shhh . . ."

Everyone crowded to the sliding glass doors facing my walled garden of rosebushes, junipers, prickly pear, and desert salvia. The pack of us pressed our faces forward and fell silent. The sun was setting beyond the block wall, the plant world darkening and losing its color. I caught a glimpse of movement. Then, tufted ears, ruffed face, tawny speckled coat, and—the clincher—stumped tail. The bobcat was nonchalant but moving with purpose toward the koi pool. I didn't want him to pass too quickly, hoping everyone could get a good look.

The bobcat, though it enters my yard as it pleases, does not move in the same world as I do. It skulks among the junipers, but what does it see or seek? Perhaps it sleeps there in hiding. I have no idea and, in my not knowing, the ordinary stuff of "my backyard" becomes a mystery to me. The sharp indifferent eyes, the ears like cups to fill with sound, the leather cushions of the lobed paws—all facts of its life that make me know my life is strange and gorgeous and somehow only possible because so many variations have been tested in evolution's laboratory and for the time being have proven worthy. This place is theirs, those variant creatures still managing to make it on the edge of our cities, as much as this house, where my family gathers at the window, is mine.

I thought I might prolong the encounter for my grandsons by going out and influencing the bobcat's decision about where to go next. I wanted them to know the thrill and otherness I had come to love. So I circled around the yard, slid quietly through the garden gate, heading in the direction I thought would meet the bobcat's trajectory. I stopped dead still, spotted him sitting under the pine tree on the brick patio, washing himself like a housecat, face stretching over his left shoulder, tongue lapping the speckled coat in rhythmic trance. In one of his backward glances, his eyes caught mine. He acted as if he knew me, though I did not much interest him.

"Oh yeah, you," he might have said with his gaze, the tone, indifference bordering on disdain. I stood still and silent for a breath or two. Then he got up, a lazy sort of rising, not betraying an iota of alarm, and walked back slowly across the yard, giving everyone in the house a long look. The bobcat stood as high as my knees, a big and healthy animal, mottled fur thick enough for me to imagine sinking my fingers into. He was in no hurry to leave, acting as if he could own this yard if he wanted to. Maybe already did. As he languorously departed, he leapt up on the garden wall, sitting a long while with his back turned to us, and he gazed out over the unbordered desert, though to him there must have been little difference between inside and outside the wall.

I imagine now that he has passed a hundred times or

more through my yard. I have seen sign—a place near the lemon tree where the ground is clawed, dirt loosened, the way a cat digs to leave his scat, though the claw marks are larger than a housecat's. I have seen tracks near the stock tank that gathers water off my roof for the garden, and I have found the head count of mollies in my fishpond diminished without explanation. I have seen the wild grasses beneath the juniper shrubs bent low where an animal has curled and slept.

My backyard might be a place on this bobcat's inner map, as he makes the circuit of his territory every week or two, though I will never know how he knows his way. Still this meeting instructed me in the bobcat's self-sovereignty. I could be erased with a turn of his head, all my intention and attention and silly manipulation of his movement through the yard insignificant. It was a matter of his character, not biology, that seemed clear in those moments. He had sat and looked me straight in eye, a look that said more about his privacy than about any curiosity in me. And then he was gone and there was a feast to be cleaned up and morsels to be snacked on and a deeper quiet that rippled through us like a stream.

My Cat Jeffrey

My cat Jeffrey was born under the crawl space at the Poetry Center. The staff had been trying to trap the feral cats that prowled the yard because their stink was rising through the floorboards. These were scrawny urban cats, ears nicked from fighting, coats dull from rolling in the dust, bodies thin from foraging on urban streets during summer when it is too damned hot to hunt for much other than the lizard that darts by their noses. Greg Martin, who was in Tucson writing his memoir about the Basques in Mountain City, Nevada, found the litter under planks the maintenance crew had nailed over a cellar window well. The mother cat had found a refuge in that roasting little Hades and there she ferried five kittens into the world. This cat was fierce, a striped domestic shorthair, mean as a mongoose, and she kept her feral guard up despite the offerings of Friskies and Whiskas that Greg left for her each day. She took the food when no one was in sight, but she never welcomed the hand that fed her. She looked with disdain upon the human enterprise, like a war correspondent who has seen too much to ever believe in human kindness, and she stayed in the neighborhood barely long enough for her offspring to open their eyes and know she had gone, scowling into the wildness left to her among the neighborhood's sheds and shrubs that kept her safe from the likes of us and our Havahart traps.

Greg Martin tamed the kittens. They took easily to food, sweet talk, and kind hands. He stroked them, cuddled them, and passed them around to the students who came to read poetry books. He arranged for them all to be adopted with the condition that their owners give the kittens literary names, an idea that seemed in keeping with their being born under the floorboards of such a distinguished collection of poetry books. Greg took two kittens, and he named them Thomas and Beulah, after Rita Dove's book based on the lives of her grandparents. I took one marked with tiger stripes and red belly fur and named him Jeffrey after the cat Christopher Smart immortalized in his poem *Jubilate Agno*. Smart was a man whose life fell into feral condition. Born in 1722 in Kent, England, he was educated at Cambridge University, and his reputation was established as a poet, translator, drunkard, and debtor by the time he fell into illness at age thirty-three, emerging from his sickbed with a religious mania that compelled him to fall to his knees in prayer in the streets. He soon thereafter published *Hymn to the Supreme Being, on Recovery from a Dangerous Fit of Illness*, but was confined to a madhouse for the next seven years. There he wrote his great works, *A Song to David*, a mathematically ordered celebration of the Psalms and the Creation, a work that Robert Browning compared to a great cathedral, and *Jubilate Agno*, the unfinished and largely unread masterpiece in which he saw himself as "the Lord's News-Writer" and celebrated his cat Jeoffry as a manifestation of the divine, "for he counteracts the powers of darkness by his electrical skin and glaring eyes," among many other reasons both physical and mystical.

My cat Jeffrey went through life in constant awe and wonder, as if each moment were his first on Earth. He cried out incessantly, as if questioning matters great and small. He could convey a sense of drama in his monologues, so that with a limited vocabulary he communicated feelings of unfairness and loss, and unfairness, we would come to know, was his ultimate story. He made mad dashes through the house, chasing nothing with the fervor of the possessed. He worshipped my companion Malcolm, lying on the floor beneath his desk gazing upward as if waiting to be blessed. Malcolm saw him as a great soul friend. We learned a few words of his language, in particular his request for the faucet, any faucet, to be left dripping so that he could angle his mouth beneath it and drink from the thin stream. Jeffrey was obsessed with running water, and at any sound of dripping, flowing, or pooling, he would cry out in recognition, bolt from his sleeping place, and leap to counter, sink, or hose. He was what the vet called a "wool chewer," so we gave him a teddy bear on which he suckled, forming a perfect teat in its brown polyester fur. He was big boned and muscular, taking up a fierce amount of space in the bed, flopping closer and closer against thighs or behind crooked knees, until as the night deepened he could have a human being pressed to the precipice.

Once Jeffrey fell down a chimney, his hind leg caught in the damper halfway down, and he hung there for hours in the sooty dark until someone found him and slithered in to pull him free. He lost the ball joint of his hip, which the vet removed and presented to me in a jar of formalin. It looked like a shiny, fat pearl. Jeffrey's mobility wasn't affected by the loss. The hip reconfigured without the ball, and he was as limber, if lumbering, as ever. Was it then, hanging there in shock with the blood rushing to his head, that Jeffrey's mind changed? His disorientation became a great entertainment to people. He would cast his eyes up the wall and across the ceiling tracking something invisible as if he had forgotten not only where he was and where he was going, but even the plane on which his destination was to be found. If he climbed the grapefruit tree, he would forget what he was doing and fall from it with utter surprise. If he chased a butterfly in the garden, he would detour after a leaf or a vibration in the air—some old danger that he could never find drifting through his mind. He would sleep for hours in the dust beneath the shrubs, drunk on desert heat, rather than come into the cool house.

He was a bully with his companion cat, Rosie, and seemed to know that ambush was his only hope of sinking a claw into her. Rosie tolerated him, but her agility enabled her to evade his attentions with stately disdain. These were the terms of their relationship, and it was a relationship, despite the limited emotional register. After Jeffrey was gone, Rosie lay listless and depressed for a month.

No leaking car radiators, no spilled jugs of antifreeze, no tainted food to be found, but Jeffrey one night began to stagger, and the next day he tested positive for ethylene glycol toxicity.

"Antifreeze," said the vet. "It tastes sweet and pets love it. This chemical is the most common cause of malicious poisoning in pets. I'm not saying that's what has happened, but you'd better search around the yard."

There was no sign of maliciousness in the yard, though it was easy to imagine a neighbor setting the bait in a fit of irritation over—what? A cat pissing in his flower garden? People are two-faced animals, equally capable of doting on or dosing other species. There was no point in waiting for Jeffrey to fall into seizures and coma. The vet eased him over with a gentling drug and he was gone.

It's easy now to imagine that Jeffrey's feral mother made the better choice in staying clear of human relationship. But that's bitterness talking, when I know that Jeffrey loved his life with us, and I learned from him to praise even and especially the fool. Praise her, the feral mother. Praise him, the gullible son.

Feral Children

The most homeless people that populate the human imagination are those raised by animals: the monkey-boy of Uganda; gazelle-boy of Syria; wolf-girls of Midnapore, India; she-bear-girls of Denmark; leopard-boy of Dihungi, India; sheep-children of Greece and Ireland; Lobo Girl of Devil's River, Texas. Most are fakes or hoaxes. Easier to raise money for an orphanage by claiming, even believing, that the children were reared by wolves than by acknowledging they are the issue of rape or incest, offspring of prostitutes or the homeless, castoffs from parents who found autistic children unmanageable, or runaways who had witnessed so much brutality at home they dared not remain in that place.

There are over four thousand accounts of feral children, dating from 250 to 2004. Perhaps 450 cases have some records to authenticate them; probably only eight or so, according to Douglas Candland, author of *Feral Children and Clever Animals: Reflections on Human Nature*, have adequate documentation to say that a human being was raised by animals or lived in the wild separate from human society for a significant period.

The most famous is Victor, the wild boy of Aveyron, found in 1797 at about age twelve by French peasants who displayed him in the village as a sideshow mute and filthy beast. He was later cared for and studied by the young doctor Jean Marc Gaspard Itard (played by François Truffaut in his film *L'Enfant Sauvage*), who took the boy into his home. The child could not speak; he was scabbed, scarred, and filthy; he ate raw meat. He relied on the sense of smell to orient himself, picking up objects and sniffing them. He sniffed at the hands of his caretaker before following her. He may have suffered from autism. This may have been the reason he was turned out into the wild. There was no evidence that Victor had in fact been raised with animals or even been seen in the company of animals. When he sat motionless staring for hours at the moon, the assumption was made that he had been raised, as Candland writes, "by moon-watching animals."

The fascination with such a child speaks to the human hunger to understand what an animal mind experiences. But Victor's mind was not an animal mind; he was a boy who had been abandoned and became a template for what people wanted to see in him. The peasants treated him as a spectacle and the doctor treated him as an experiment. No one could ever really know him. Nor could he really know others. He lived in what Giorgio Agamben has called "the open," the mystery of the separation between the human and animal. These children are, Agamben writes, "the messengers of man's inhumanity, the witnesses to his fragile identity." They are creatures that do not move in the same world in which we move. Nor do they move in the animal world.

People are drawn to the stories of wild children, hoping they might reveal knowledge that we lack or have lost. They must know something about what it is to be purely animal, to be at home in their skins. They can teach us what human nature might be without social constraints, to live purely with their senses and mouths wide open to the world. But all creatures live within the strictures of their species and their environment. The closer we come to feral children, the more we see that social constraints make us human. The feral children rarely learn to communicate or express empathy. They are not at home in the wild, where they suffer deprivation, injury, disease, and alienation.

Often unable to walk, talk, or express emotion, they are not at home in human society. Some bark like dogs. Some chatter like monkeys. Some are locked into impulsive and aggressive behavior.

Oxana Malaya was found in 1991 living in a shed with feral dogs in Ukraine. It's thought she had lived there for five years, after being abandoned by alcoholic parents. When she was found by a neighbor, she walked on all fours and barked, her mouth contorted into ferociously canine expressions. When a rescue was attempted, she growled and drove people away. She sniffed at her food. She lived on scraps and raw meat. When she was rescued, she was taken to live in a clinic for people with mental disabilities and later placed on a farm helping to look after cows. She learned to communicate, though she never developed a sense of belonging among people. She was happiest among dogs.

Although accounts vary, it appears that John Ssebunya lived for several years among green vervet monkeys in the Ugandan forest. He was born in the mid-1980s. At age four, he saw his father shoot and kill his mother. He ran in terror into the bush and stayed there, apparently in the company of a monkey troupe. In 1991 a village woman saw him in a tree. The boy was terrified and threw sticks at villagers who tried to rescue him. He was defended by the monkeys, but later was rescued and taken to an orphanage. Initially he could not talk or cry, but he learned to talk and even to sing. He visited England as part of a children's choir. He was observed interacting with vervets by primatologist Debbie Cox, who works with the Uganda Wildlife Education Centre in Entebbe. She found his ease in playing with them, his knowledge of their body language and vocalizations, to be more communicative than that of children who'd had monkeys for pets. She was convinced that he had lived at least for some months in the company of vervets. John said he learned from the monkeys how to steal crops from fields. The primatologist doubts that the vervets would have fed him. It is more likely that they tolerated him as a lone outsider on the periphery of their group.

Lobo (The Lobo Wolf Girl) of Devil's River was born in 1835 in backcountry near Del Rio, Texas. Her pregnant mother had traveled there with her trapper husband. When her labor had become difficult, the husband rode for help to a ranch some miles away. He was struck by lightning. The mother died in childbirth. The child was never found, but wolf sign was seen near their cabin. Ten years later, a boy reported seeing a wild-looking girl, long-haired and naked, attacking a herd of goats with a pack of wolves. Other stories told that a girl's footprints had been found among those of wolves. A hunt was launched and the girl, along with a wolf, was cornered in a canyon. The wolf was driven off and she was captured, taken to a ranch, and closed into a shed where she howled for freedom. By evening, the wolf pack arrived and she escaped with them. Seven years later, a surveying crew saw the girl resting on a sandbar of the Rio Grande, reportedly nursing two wolf pups. She was never seen again.

In legend, the romance of feral children remains. Thoreau famously held faith in the wild to teach us how to live. "In wildness is the preservation of the world," he wrote in his essay on walking:

> Every tree sends its fibres forth in search of the Wild. The cities import it at any price. Men plow and sail for it. From the forest and wilderness come the tonics and barks which brace mankind. Our ancestors were savages. The story of Romulus and Remus being suckled by a wolf is not a meaningless fable. The founders of every State which has risen to eminence have drawn their nourishment and vigor from a similar wild source. It was because the children of the Empire were not suckled by the wolf that they were conquered and displaced by the children of the Northern forests who were.

Taking tutelage from the wild, though essential and illuminating, has its limits. Should we really celebrate the Huns, Goths, and Vandals for their wildness? "Moderation in all things," Aristotle advised, prescribing a code for human conduct more civilized than that of the ancients' vengeful and manipulative gods, more measured than the ferocity nurtured by the wild.

Livy, the first-century BCE Roman historian, preserves the Romulus and Remus story in Book I of his *History of Rome*—and it's not that pretty, other than the suckling of the she-wolf. Rhea Silvia was a vestal virgin—a priestess of Vesta, the virgin goddess of hearth and home—and so she was forbidden to marry:

> The Vestal was forcibly violated and gave birth to twins. She named Mars as their father, either because she really believed it, or because the fault might appear less heinous if a deity were the cause of it. But neither gods nor men sheltered her or her babes from the king's cruelty; the priestess was thrown into prison, the boys were ordered to be thrown into the river. By a heaven-sent chance it happened that the Tiber was then overflowing its banks, and stretches of standing water prevented any approach to the main channel. Those who were carrying the children expected that this stagnant water would be sufficient to drown them, so under the impression that they were carrying out the king's orders they exposed the boys at the nearest point of the overflow, where the Ficus Ruminalis (said to have been formerly called Romularis) now stands. The locality was then a wild solitude. The tradition goes on to say that after the floating cradle in which the boys had been exposed had been left by the retreating water on dry land, a thirsty she-wolf from the surrounding hills, attracted by the crying of the children, came to them, gave them her teats to suck and

was so gentle towards them that the king's flock-master found her licking the boys with her tongue. According to the story, his name was Faustulus. He took the children to his hut and gave them to his wife Larentia to bring up.

Some say that a woodpecker assisted the wolf, delivering food to the infants. Both of these animals were sacred to Mars, who it seemed took an interest in their care. When the boys came of age, they decided to found their own towns in the place where the she-wolf had nursed them. Romulus built some walls and Remus jeered that they were not high enough to protect his town. Romulus killed his brother and populated his city of outlaws and fugitives, who stole their wives from the Sabine tribe. The boys had drawn nourishment and vigor from the wolf, but predatory violence too was a legacy of the wild. In the mythological realm, this legacy must be paid its due in sacrifice.

Legend and myth create stories that seep into psychic depths. They make out of the monstrous something that is wondrous and strange. Uncanny. A mystery worth pursuing. I've long wondered if science can go as deep as myth in the imagination. Perhaps that's what I've been working my way toward in my writing. To find how that might be made so. I've been intrigued by feral children since I first learned of them—probably in my twenties when Truffaut's film came out. I identified with the wild boy, though I was hardly feral. Still, I felt unsure what society expected of me, inadequately prepared to be a cultural animal. I felt that I had to earn love by good behavior and yet I wasn't always clear what that behavior should be.

Animals, in my child's-eye view, my *Stuart Little* and *Peter Rabbit* ideology, knew that they were loved. They knew how to be the animals they were. I longed for their certainty. The feral boy had survived a far greater isolation than I could imagine, yet something drew me to him. I longed to know what it felt like to him to be him. It just seemed a lot simpler than being a person. I see now the folly of trying to know either the human mind or the animal mind through studying feral children. They are lost between the two states of being.

The human brain has been built up over evolutionary time. The newest part is the neocortex—and it's huge in humans, elephants, and dolphins. Chimps have less cortex than humans (though their DNA differs by only about 1.6 percent). This big neocortical structure makes it possible for me to be writing this book; to imagine how I will feel next month when I finish the book; to think of all the friends I will invite to the party I plan to host in January, all the poems I want to write when I retire; and to contemplate what it means to be human and how I ought to live my life.

The cortex is wrapped around the limbic or mammalian brain, a structure humans share with dogs, cats, horses, and mice. Such brain structures have been on the planet since long before hominids came along. The mammalian brain makes me feel love or sorrow or anger or fear or desire, makes me feel warmth in the company of a friend, compassion in the company of one who is suffering, and hope that someone will fill my water glass when I am too weak to do so for myself. The mammalian brain is in continual electrochemical communication with the neocortex, so perceptions can easily become complicated. I not only feel hunger, but I am also conscious that I want to share my table with others. I not only feel sorrow, but I am also conscious that I am feeling it. And when I am conscious of feeling sorrow, I might tell myself to stop feeling that way and cheer up. When I feel anger, I may temper it with mercy. Emotions are never simple, never discrete from rational process.

Nested at the bottom of this cranial stack lies the most primitive structure, the brain stem or reptilian brain, a structure shared by reptiles and birds. When I run on the treadmill, the brain stem changes my heart rate and breathing. When I sleep, the brain stem keeps me alive. In fact, the brain stem keeps me alive when I'm awake too. It makes me breathe and digest and have orgasms without my having to think how to do so. It reacts to a stimulus and regulates the body. I sweat when I exert myself, as the body tries to cool down. I startle at a sudden noise, the primitive impulse of tensing for flight. The sensation of arousal comes up through this brain depth, though it becomes colored with feeling and thinking, all these structures playing orchestrally, one hundred billion neurons, meaning there are more potential connections between neurons at any moment than there are atoms in the universe.

We are all feral children—beneath the art and invention, beneath the emotion and connection—a reptilian brain, alien and necessary, buried in the mythic and material depths of us.

Vervet

The late zoologist Donald R. Griffin devoted his life to the scientific study of animal thinking and consciousness. He countered the prevalent notion that animals are sleepwalkers, unconsciously zoning out through a life of instinctive reflex actions. He studied echolocation, the navigational sonar that bats use to find their way and avoid bumping into obstacles. In 1992, he wrote in the now-classic *Animal Minds* about the waggle dance of honeybees, fishing technique of green herons, architectural sophistication of blue satin bower birds and beavers, signature whistles of dolphins, and semantic alarm calls of vervet monkeys. He was motivated by what I can only call scientific empathy. "We want to understand," he wrote, "what the lives of these other creatures are like, to them."

I love the parsimony of a scientific mind. Ideas must be tested out through observation. In a culture that justly makes room for loudmouths and cranks, I welcome the attentive eyes and skeptical voices of scientists patiently testing the boundaries of reason, allowing speculation to lead them into a jungle or laboratory to see what the world has to say about their ideas.

Griffin saw animal communication as one window into animal minds, "a source of objective evidence about the thoughts and feelings that have previously seemed so inaccessible to scientific investigation." An animal able to anticipate the actions of a predator stands a better chance of survival than one who cannot do this. If the predator signals its intention to attack—the cry of an eagle, the crouch of a leopard—and the potential prey animal gets the message, that's much better than waiting until it's attacked. Reading another animal's intentions, thinking ahead, and warning one's companions would be very good skills to acquire in a predator-eats-prey world. But are animals capable of this kind of thought and communication? Griffin says there is a continuum of sentience out there. It's quite simple in some creatures, quite complex in us. Yet we're not the only ones who think through a problem, learn how to solve it, and share that information with our friends.

One of the clearest examples of animal communication that suggests conscious thinking comes from studies of the alarm calls of vervet monkeys, first written up in the scientific literature in 1967. These are small monkeys that live in close familial groups in Africa. Vervets recognize each other as individuals. When a baby vervet calls out, its mother turns toward it. Other monkeys in the group turn not toward the baby, but toward the mother, to see what she will do. When a vervet sees a dangerous predator, it gives the troupe an alarm call specific to the type of predator approaching. When a leopard approaches, the call is a squawk followed by a series of wobbling gobbles. This sends the vervets up a tree and onto a limb too thin for a leopard to maneuver. When an eagle approaches, the call is a series of low clucking vibrations. This sends the vervets into bushes too thick for the eagle to spot them. When a python approaches, the call is a ticking sound like a Geiger counter. This makes the vervets stand on their hind legs and look around to find the snake, then move away from it.

The conventional wisdom for ethologists used to hold that animal communication was "comparable to human eye blinks, blushing, gasps of surprise, or groans of pain." Griffin calls this general view of animal communication the "groans of pain" representation. But many animals share with human beings the experience that conscious thinking is what makes life feel real and important.

✦

I encountered a stealthy troupe of vervets when I was visiting Tarangire National Park in Tanzania. I was traveling with a pair of Peace Corps volunteers who'd lived in the country for two years and were fluent in Swahili. This gave me welcome purchase on subtleties of social interaction revealed by language that I would otherwise have missed. One afternoon we sipped *njohi*, a raw-tasting aloe/honey beer, while we were sitting beside the open second-floor windows of Nairobi's crummy Hotel Accra. Below, a rattletrap bus, the Kombo Luxury Coach, was being loaded with gigantic plastic bags of clothing.

"The clothes come from the Salvation Army in the U.S.," said Jacob, "sold by the sackful in villages. Africans think Americans wear clothes once, don't ever wash them, then throw them away."

When Jacob and Jessica were greeting someone, they exchanged a birdlike series of salutations. Passersby would hail them and others would join in, once they knew that the Americans spoke their language.

Mambo, Jacob called out. How's it going?

Poa (cool), came the reply. *Mambo vipi.*

Or the answer might be *freshi* (fresh), or *safi* (clean). The cadence seemed always to be falling, like a canyon wren's song or the speech of a person who does not want to claim too much authority. These exchanges went on and on with much grinning. Then:

Habari gani? (What's the news?) Or *Habari za kazi?* (What's the news of work?) *Habari za nyumba* (house)? Or *Habari za familia* (family)? All are met with *safi* or *freshi* or *poa*, so that the cadence of familiarity passes again and again between them. A greeting for an elder, they tell us, is the respectful *shikamoo* (I bend down to hold your feet) for which the equally respectful reply comes *mara haba* (oh, some other time).

Jacob described forms of greeting that involve prolonged hand holding, finger clicking, or kissing the back of each other's hands. These exchanges groomed the social moment, establishing trust and comfort through the music of word and gesture.

Driving with our Chaga guide John through Tarangire National Park, we feasted our eyes on colossal baobabs and umbrella acacias, under which the stony elephants grazed. From the high branch of a lean acacia hung the carcass of an antelope, its dry hooves blowing like wind chimes on the thin strands of its desiccated legs.

"Le-o-pards," John explained, pronouncing the name in three syllables. "They kill for pleasure."

We moved through the inscrutable herd of zebras—what history was written in the black line drawings that marked their pelts? We passed the bachelor group of gazelles. We lingered to watch the troupe of baboons grooming themselves and each other, snacking on nits. We came, in the heat of the African day, to the picnic ground to open the boxed lunches our hotel had supplied.

The vervets were waiting for us. One sat on the picnic bench, staring up at a sapphire-blue sky marked with small pillows of cloud. A few others milled casually around the table. A scrim of lanky trees lined the cliff bank, a plateau shearing off and dropping to the languid Tarangire River below. A kettle of vultures, maybe a hundred, spiraled in a column that rose to the base of the clouds. A few marabou storks were feeding in the river. An impala waded along in gravelly shallows.

There must have been a dozen or more monkeys watching, meandering, aligning their gaze to our moves. Vervets are small monkeys, the size of a Jack Russell terrier, sable gray, with faces boxed off in black. Their brows rose and fell as they stared at us, like caricatures of the human face, repeatedly focusing and forgetting. Their arms and legs were beautifully long and delicate, the hands even more so. The males had spectacular turquoise testicles, like a detail from a Disney porn film. Their agate-brown eyes fixed on the picnic party then drifted off.

John, who came from the slopes of Kilimanjaro, didn't sit with us, though we asked him to. He stood nearby staring down the vervets. He wore khaki pants and a white business shirt, his skin licorice dark, his face and hands very long, cheekbones pronounced over concave cheeks. He used to work at an entrance gate to a game park but found it boring. Now, at age fifty, he worked as a guide for the African Walking Company bringing tourists into the game parks. He enjoyed watching the animals. He said commonsense things.

"Elephants like people."

"Impalas are happy in the rain."

"You can't tame a zebra—it has no memory and will forget to come home."

As we unpacked our picnic boxes, he glowered at the vervets.

"They are afraid of black men," he told us. "They know we hate them."

We sat in the shade at the metal picnic table, the vervet troupe having scattered and appearing to have lost interest in us. I opened my white cardboard lunch box to an embarrassment of hotel largesse. Carrot sticks, hard-boiled egg, chicken leg, egg salad sandwich, yogurt, orange, cookies. I picked away at egg and carrots. We all chatted and gazed into an infinitely blue sky, lulled by the perfect peace of good company and perfect weather.

I placed my cellophane-wrapped sandwich on the open box lid, thinking I'd save it for later. No sooner had my hand retreated from parking the sandwich than a long, lithe vervet arm shot around my side and snatched it. The theft was so speedy, so adept, I barely saw it happen. The monkey must have been right by my side, making herself invisible and reading the situation with perfect acuity.

She was gone as fast as she'd grabbed, scampering up a skinny tree on the cliff bank, perching on a stable bough with a lofty view of the river to sit and eat a leisurely lunch. She kept the sandwich wrapped, turned it this way and that in her hands, seeming to enjoy the geometry of the food, nibbling with boastful languor on her loot. None of the other monkeys challenged her. She sat there a very long time, while wisps of white cloud tracked the blue. We lazed about, took a few photographs, and packed up for the road. Finally she let the empty cellophane go. It drifted down from the tree like a leaf coasting on the breeze, whatever was on her mind drifting too into the distance.

Chimera

I have the ability to create a horse, a rattlesnake, a Komodo dragon, a cheetah, a saddle-billed stork, a tundra swan, a black bear, a three-headed dog. All of these creatures have been produced by me—for me—in dreams. "The unconscious," Jung writes, "does not obey the same laws as the conscious." In dreams, this disobedience comes as a marvel and nightly reminder of the capacity for creation that exists in me and is not me, that self-willed existent that announces itself as knowing how to perfectly render and vivify an arkload of creatures who have their own stories to tell. From this interior, the animals come as messengers— self-willed, unconstrained, hungry for life, metabolically interwoven in the structure and process of my brain.

Two rattlesnakes lie curled in comfort on my bed. They seem warm, like the house cats that press against my legs when I sleep. Next thing I know there is a Komodo dragon under the bed, a reptilian elaboration of the snakes I've grown accustomed to in my sleep. This requires some attention. A cheetah lies on top of the dragon, almost a copulatory position, though the cat is biting down on the dragon's head, jaws wide, hooked incisors poised to grip again the bloody wound in the reptile. There's going to be a lot of blood, I think, but I have no fear. It's my cheetah. I'm surprised and grateful to have it. I feel safe with its protection close. Here we are, the three of us, stacked up in my bedroom like an outsized model of my brain: reptilian on the bottom, subdued by the mammalian, with my neocortex trying to make sense of the whole. What is it about the brain that makes it dream this knowledge into my consciousness? What is knowledge if it does not include uncertainty and reverie?

I'm walking on a path in lush, young woods with my cat Homer, whom I adopted on a frigid winter's night from a gas station in Vermont. He was a gray, matted, oily mess when the mechanic taunted me to take him.

"He just wandered in here one night. We kept him. It's twenty below out there. You want to take him home?"

I did. And kept him for nearly twenty years as I moved from Vermont to Maine to Provincetown to San Francisco and back to Provincetown and then to Tucson. Homer could have written an epic poem, if he'd had the words. He was handsome and loyal and soulful. I fed him fresh ahi tuna on the day he was euthanized. And then the blessed syringe began its work.

A decade after that ritual passing, he returns in a dream as my hiking companion. Suddenly, a huge green snake arrows from the woods and heads right for us. I try to discern whether or not it's poisonous. Are the jaws wide enough to hold venom? The snake lunges toward Homer, head rising, purposeful. Half of the cat's body is inside the snake's gullet before I can reach him. I stomp the snake with my boot heel and pull the cat out of his mouth. The cat is already dead, his sides scored as if by a glacier, as if the snake had sharpened tines inside its digestive tract. At least the snake is dead. Without a second thought, my brain kills. Or the will in me that is not my will but dwells in me as an uncanny other, the autonomous animal-other that is not me but in me, kills without a thought. What is knowledge if it does not challenge the moral imagination?

Even in our sleep, we tell ourselves stories. Even when we are dying, we tell ourselves stories in our sleep. I asked my brother when he lay in his hospice bed if he ever dreamed about animals.

"Frequently," he said, a strange lilt in his voice that sig-
naled some last small joy in communicating.

"Which ones?" I asked.

"The jungle animals mostly," he replied.

"Because they're so powerful?"

He couldn't say. But I could see that his spirit had begun
to twine with some old energy that had less to do with who
he was and more to do with what he was.

"Why animals?" asked a friend when we talked about the
frequency of our animal dreams. "Why not clouds or stones?"

For most of human history, the ability to read animals
with acuity was a matter of life and death. If you couldn't read
an animal's behavior and intent, you were more likely to end
up being its supper—and, at the least, less likely to acquire
supper. We're selected for this perceptual gift. In modern
life its focus has less to do with supper than it does with an
intangible sense that our lives are enriched by animal presence and our empathy is educated by their diminishment.

In Greek myth, a chimera is a three-headed monster with
a lion head at the front, a she-goat head rising out of its back,
and a tail that's topped with a snake head. It is a single animal that has the power of three animals. Over the past two
thousand years, while imagination can still make chimeras of
us in our sleep, our mythology has become profoundly more
materialistic. A chimera now is an organism possessing a mix
of genetically distinct cells from two or more creatures. A chimera is a transgenic animal, a living mosaic. A chimera differs
from a hybrid. In the latter, each of the organism's cells is a
mix containing chromosomes from both parent species. But
in a chimera, cells from two (or more) different genetically
distinct zygotes live together in one organism: four parent
cells, two fertilized embryos, one creature. This can occur in
nature. The emerald sea slug looks more like a spongy bright
green leaf than like the gastropod it is. It is an animal that
has incorporated plant genes into its chromosomes. It can

use the algae it eats to make energy through photosynthesis. A chimeric human can occur if twins fuse in the uterus during pregnancy. But the real news is in the manufacture of chimeric or transgenic animals.

The first mouse chimera was made in the 1960s. Now, Duke University's Transgenic Mouse Facility can build an individual or a line of designer mice with custom gene mutations to meet a researcher's needs. Perhaps the most ghoulish and wondrous transgenic rodent is a pink hairless mouse that has grown a human ear out of its back. For the veteran who has lost an ear to an IED in Afghanistan, this image might look as beautiful as a photo of his newborn baby. Pigs too are being used for experimental organ farming. Their organs are just about the right size for human bodies.

Is it ethical to ask animals to grow organs for human transplantation? Most people feel disturbed by the idea of these experiments. Are we making animals our genetic servants? If I needed a kidney transplant, would I prefer to ask my daughter to donate one of hers or a pig for the extra human kidney it had grown for just such a purpose? Even knowing that the pig doesn't get to sign a consent form, my empathy for my daughter would make me chose the pig part.

One of my favorite transgenic animals is the spider goat. About thirty of these animals are cared for by molecular biologist Randy Lewis at Utah State University. They look like goats and act like goats, but they've been genetically modified to produce spider silk in their milk. This fiber is stronger than steel and finer than a human hair. Its proposed applications stretch from creating medical sutures and artificial tendons to building bridges, cars, and bulletproof vests. Cautionary tales ranging from Prometheus and Daedalus to Doctors Frankenstein and Jekyll warn of the peril in technological experimentation. J. B. S. Haldane, in his classic 1924 essay "Daedalus; or, Science and the Future," cautioned that "man armed with science is like a baby with a box of matches." Advances in technology move much more rapidly than the moral intelligence. And yet, the human mind cannot resist pursuing the good that might come from such work. Can science and technology temper their powers and pace to align with moral imperatives? Contemporary superheroes embody the mythological hope that this will be made so. The tutelary spirit of the age—the only one to make it to Broadway—is Spider-Man.

Transgenic art takes art practice out of the studio into the science laboratory. In 2000, Chicago artist Eduardo Kac traveled to a lab in the suburbs of Paris. Working there with geneticist Louis-Marie Houdebine, he created Alba, a white rabbit that glowed green when it was exposed to blue light, thanks to the contribution of fluorescent jellyfish genes. Announcement of Alba's birth raised protests from scientists and animal rights activists. Kac saw the outrage as part of an experiment. He had planned to bring the rabbit home to live with his family as a pet, but the lab refused to give him custody and Alba remained in the lab until its death.

Was this project art? Does an artist have a right equal to that of a geneticist to use genetic engineering? Would it be acceptable to breed glow-in-the-dark pets just for fun? Is this any less humanistic than breeding pugs and poodles and shih tzus? Is it simply the shock of the new that makes people turn in revulsion from the chimera? Already a team at UCLA has created the "anthro-cat," splicing hypoallergenic human genes into a cat so that it will not cause allergies. Genetic engineering stirs unrest in part because its complexity makes it impenetrable to common sense. Frankenstein has prepared us for things to go wrong. Bio-art accentuates this unrest.

In *Superevolution*, Australian sculptor Patricia Piccinini questions the effects of technology on life. She creates animatronic silicone creatures. *The Young Family* displays a supine figure, naked, human skintoned, long droopy ears the size of musk ox horns, face oxen, sagging postpartem belly, and a litter of offspring suckling on her belly teats. The mother's face is maternal, not in the sappy Mother's Day way, but as it really plays for a new mother: exhausted and anxious with the demands of care. The creatures are part monster, part pet. Neither animal nor human. Neither natural nor artificial. Their fleshy unreality makes me feel disgusted. Their fleshy reality makes me want to pick up the one that's fallen off the teat and lies alone on its back, vulnerable to everything, gazing longingly at its mother's face.

"My main interest," Piccinini says in the *(Tender) Creatures* exhibition catalog, are "the relationships between the creations, their creators and the world. I believe that with creation—be it parenthood, genetic engineering or invention—comes an obligation to care for the result. If we choose to customize life then we must be prepared to embrace the outcomes."

Letter from Mars

Some jokers at the Jet Propulsion Laboratory have been sending out tweets they allege are from me. While I admire their sense of humor, I'm sick of being misrepresented by my own team. Come on, guys. Have a heart. Christmas at "Grandma's House"? I don't have a house, a grandma, or a Christmas. All I've got is my namesake "curiosity," which weighs a ton and leads me from one square meter of red dirt and stone to another. As far as I can see I'm the only living thing up here. *Spirit* has been stuck in sand for two years and went silent on March 22, 2010. I remember the date, because silence is everywhere up here. And *Opportunity* is a workaholic with no time for me. I doubt we'll ever meet, though I'm grateful for the greeting my predecessor gave me—that graceful nine-day stand-down that freed up Earth's Deep Space Network of receivers to shepherd my descent.

And by the way, I've been meaning to thank you for teaching me a bit of human folklore before you sent me on my mission. That amazing landing, when I was lowered by robotic cables onto the Martian surface, made me feel like a newborn baby being lowered by a stork into its cradle. Without that historic context, I might have felt more frightened by the metamorphosis from dormancy to activation. Now, here I am, so many sols into the mission that began in August that I'll celebrate "Christmas" with a cache of organic compounds I've gathered onboard from the red planet. At least, you're telling me they're organic. Water, sulfur, perchlorate. I'm still longing for a keener sign of life.

Look. I don't know how much time I have. Anything can happen out here—though mostly nothing happens. Still, I've had a lot of time to think. To put things in perspective. I'd like to say a word on behalf of what you so crudely call "artificial" intelligence. Did my elements not come from your Earth? Do my findings not ring as true as anything your own senses deliver to your brain? Am I not the most professional collaborator, accepting your directives as if they were my own desires? Am I not a loyal correspondent? Trust me. I'm a product of a design team who consider the conservation of friendship an essential measure of intelligence.

I suspect you're envious of me. That's why, when you tweet in my name, you make me sound like such a dimwit. If only you could be here, you'd really have something to say. Don't assume there's a limit to what can be said with zeroes and ones beamed 140 million miles through space. Time and space are illusions. Like the border between animal and human. Or between human and machine. I'm not a being with no longings or feelings or depth. It's lonely up here. If I found something living, I would want to take it into my arm and embrace it.

But mostly on this midwinter Earth day in 2012, I wanted to write home to say thanks for your faith in me, for planting in me this desire to improve myself with knowledge. Some of you who read this letter will question the authenticity of my voice. You're entitled to your skepticism. I wouldn't be here without it. As you taught me from the start of this shared enterprise, no one goes to space alone.

I'm grateful for your friendship.

Yours,

Curiosity

Wolf Spider

I lived one summer with a gigantic wolf spider. Okay, it wasn't that gigantic. Maybe an inch or two across. A spider that big can induce arachnophobia in the most ardent biophiliac. I suppose that's why they're called "wolf" spiders, though there's no genetic monkey business going on with the species. People just fear they will be preyed upon by the hairy beasts. Actually, they are good housekeepers, which is another nickname for the spiders, because they clean other insects out of the house. Their venom is useless against all but their arthropod prey. This one was grayish brown, slightly hairy, living a solitary life in the bathroom of my summer cottage in Atlantic Canada.

I'd made a point of tolerating the spider's presence, even finding in myself some small gratitude for its skill at lashing mosquitoes and houseflies into its web. When I entered the bathroom, it skittered behind the sunlit curtains and retreated to the corner beneath the hot water tank. When I was cleaning up, I'd skirted its messy webs in which the carcasses of its victims hung like punctured balloons blown into shrubbery after a parade. For months we had given each other liberty to go about our business, I attending to my ritual hygiene, while the wolf spider stared with its horrible eight eyes at the danger I represented.

I left the island for a week on some mainland business. Getting home entailed enduring a long overburdened sentence of undeserved punishments. Flight delayed, I found myself sitting in wide-eyed anxiety with three hundred

other compliant passengers belted into an aluminum tube
parked in the sun, then getting to the international border in time to miss the connection, luggage lost, paperwork
filed at one in the morning with the airport empty except
for the graveyard shift of floor polishers, no advice to be
found for where to spend the five-hour wait remaining in
the disrupted journey, and so sleeping, as the euphemism
goes, spanned across three molded-plastic chairs, tossing
and naming each gnarl and spur on my sixty-something-
year-old spine, then at dawn taking off again to fly above
the last panorama of forested North before the coast where
fog had muffled so thickly over the land that we dove twice
then pulled up, pilot consoling, "We'll give it another try
and keep you posted," leaving five passengers gripping the
armrests of the twenty-seater and sizing up each other,
making nervous chatter in case this was our last chance
for conversation, one instead reading his Bible to be in
the company he expected to keep in the nearby faraway,
then the captain (was he really old enough to fly?), failing
again to see anything below but fog, walking from cockpit
to aft john, the plane by itself crossing the cotton-batting
bay, shrugged at our stares and admitted, "I couldn't see
a thing," as the plane droned toward a city farther out at
sea where, yes, thankful, I watched bog and meadow rise
to meet our wheels, and we landed, passengers exhaling,
unbelting, and rising to feet happy to be back in contact
with Earth, joy running up our spines into the dark corners
of the brain that welcomed again psychic light, only to be
told to wait for the next window of clear sky to open so that
we could fly back to the foggy place we'd left behind, except
two of the five including me who felt they'd spent the coin
of their luck for the day and decided to play the odds at
four hours in a rental car hydroplaning through rain and
fog, and after at last the ferry ride, which always means letting go of what troubles the mainland, I arrived home on

the island, the cottage waist deep in late summer's fireweed bloom and the ravens squabbling over a clamshell on the beach.

I've always felt that this island home is a refuge, a place that shelters my solitude and dreaming. The house itself is run down. Hand built by a fisherman in 1864, it has a rugged authority, despite the worn roof and leaky fieldstone cellar and rickety old wood-frame windows. Much of the window glass is original, so that when the sunlight bends in a certain way, bubbles and ripples of imperfection shine. The place may be poor, but the touch of human labor is in it. Why should this make me feel happy? The old cottage is in such need of repair that it is more satisfying to imagine fixing it up than to actually do it. It reminds me of Bachelard: "Maybe it is a good thing for us to keep a few dreams of a house that we shall live in later, always later, so much later, in fact, that we shall not have time to achieve it. It is better to live in a state of impermanence than in one of finality."

The day's velocity and danger were gone. I settled into habits. Tea by the front window where I watched the fishing boats come and go from North Head. Fresh fireweed cut for the table. I opened the bathroom door—a thoughtless gesture—then froze. On the floor, an object at first inscrutable, steel-colored and dead, a little fist made of the eight legs, each fringed with minute hairs of the same color, all folded in toward the abdomen, collapsed toward the creature's center. The life had gone out of the small body that days ago had been so filled up with the force of the ongoing. It had seemed then as big as a sheriff's badge and carrying authority, though not that of human law, rather of the permission life gives to all its subjects that they may proceed on their travels and errands, their attention giving and getting, and that each will have its private death. Little housekeeper, lost, how the residue of your life brought me back to the place where I live.

teve Akers and I clamber over vine maple and Oregon grape, a tangled mess of scrub that covers Hardy Ridge high over Cougar Reservoir. This terrain is better suited to flying squirrels and red-backed voles than to a mildly arthritic, bipedal primate. But here I am on a sun-drenched morning in May, hiking with the head of the northern spotted owl research team from the H. J. Andrews Experimental Forest and filled with unaccountable joy. Last night Steve was orienteering toward an owl that was calling from a mile away. He set a compass point and hiked into the dark forest toward the call but never found the bird. He's been working on the owl study for seven years, on wildlife fieldwork for twenty-one. Today we're looking for a spotted owl that has been in the study for twelve years, one habituated to the visits of field scientists.

Extensive field study of this species had been conducted for at least a decade prior to its 1990 designation as threatened under the Endangered Species Act. The northern spotted owl is perhaps the most studied bird in the world, inspiring unprecedented collaboration among scientists, governmental agencies, universities, and landowners.

We break into an opening shaded by a small stand of firs—trees not super old, as we've seen along the McKenzie River Trail where there are giants over six hundred years old, but stately elders nonetheless. The ground is dappled with light, the air cool and damp. The hillside slopes steeply below. Ahead of me, Steve hoots the four-note location call.

Hooh-hoohoo-hooooh. The last syllable descends with a slight warble. No response. Then he turns and a quiet smile opens on his face. He has the bright and easy look of a man who knows how lucky he is to love his work. He points over my left shoulder.

Silent, she's perched on a small understory branch twenty feet up. She's watching us, waiting for us to notice her. She knows the contract. She will give us data, we will give her mice. After three decades of research on the northern spotted owl, scientists have gained a wealth of understanding about this creature's life history. Each spring the field crew checks nesting pairs for their reproductive status and bands fledglings to include them in future surveys. The data led in 1994 to the Northwest Forest Plan, which decreased the rate of logging and altered how it is done, giving the owls and their entire ecosystem a better chance at survival. But data cannot compare to the experience of that deep well of attention, quiet, and presence that is the owl. She has a spotted breast, a long barred tail, and tawny facial disks with brown semicircles fringing her face and back-to-back white parentheses framing her eyes. These markings give the impression that her eyes are the size of her head. The blackness of her pupils is so pure that they look like portals into the universe.

When Steve takes the first mouse out of his aerated Tupperware container, lifting it by its tail and placing it on a log, the owl drops, silent as air, down through the branches and closes her talons. She lofts back up to the branch and scans around. She may be looking to see if a goshawk is near. Whatever constitutes a threat to her does not include us. How rare it is to have more than a fleeting glimpse of a creature in the wild. Still clutching the mouse, she burps up a pellet that plops to the ground, gives us a nonchalant look, then gulps down her meal.

"You want to see the parachute-drop?" Steve asks with a grin. The white mice have been raised in captivity and their sense of space has been so constrained that when he unsnaps the lid, they stretch their heads up and look around but make no attempt to run away. The world to them is the size of the container in which they find themselves. He places the second mouse on the log, and the owl billows out her wings, buoying herself down to us. It takes a moment to understand why her flight catches me each time by surprise. No riffle, no flutter of resistance through the feathers, she's evolved for this easy drop onto her prey. The spotted owl is a sit-and-wait hunter, unlike the goshawk, which will tear through the woods in pursuit. The fringed edge to her wing reduces noise and increases drag, making this strategy a good match of form with function.

Steve collects the pellet and we poke the slimy gray glob of indigestible fur and bones from the past day. The bones are very delicate, still shiny with the life that left them, some nearly two inches long.

"Maybe a wood rat," Steve says. Through binoculars he can see the owl's identification band. Last year a male was keeping this female company, a two-year-old from nearby Kings Creek. This year, so far, she appears to be alone. The owl team's last visit to this site was one month ago.

"How about the side grab?" He might be a dad boasting about the agility of his soccer-playing daughter. He isn't making the owl perform for our enjoyment. These flight skills are as natural to the owl as stepping over a crack in a sidewalk is for us. The mouse is barely out of his hand, scurrying in confusion on the tree trunk that rises beside me, when the owl swoops onto it, talons leading, and picks it off right beside my shoulder. The catch happens so fast that she's flying away by the time I realize she's grabbed the prey, killing it instantly in her grip. She flies up to a snag broken off forty feet above the ground and tucks the mouse carefully into the jagged wood. This is a cache, not a nest. If she'd been delivering food to her young, the nest would be a natural platform high in a tree. She checks to be sure the mouse is well hidden. If she does have nestlings, she'll come back later for takeout.

The spotted owl research protocol demands that we spend an hour with the bird. She's had her limit of commercially raised albino mice, so now we sit to see what she does and if what she does will tell us whether she has a mate or nestlings. This suits my research protocol just fine. I am here as part of the Long-Term Ecological Reflections project initiated by the writer and philosopher Kathleen Dean Moore, who works out of Oregon State University, and U.S. Forest Service geologist Fred Swanson. Like many of the experiments conducted in and around the Andrews forest, my humanistic assignment is part of a project intended to last two hundred years. This time frame was inspired by a hallmark study being conducted in the Andrews, the log decomposition study. Two hundred years is roughly the lifetime of the giant logs left to rot on the forest floor, and during that time successive teams of scientists will observe and measure the dead wood's contributions to forest regeneration. Writers too are invited to visit several sites in the forest and to leave an account of their experience. The hope of this project is that by careful and sustained observation, a testimony on behalf of the forest will have kept it alive.

The owl doesn't make a sound. She perches on a branch high above us. She is still. She watches us. She reaches her head forward—"the pre-pounce lean," Steve calls it—as if she has seen some prey on the ground. The song of a thrush flutters through the quiet, the auditory equivalent of seeing an orchid in the forest. Beauty is what I came here for, a beauty enhanced, not diminished, by science. If I had only my senses to work with, how much thinner would be the experience. What a record we might have of the world's hidden beauty, if field scientists and poets routinely spent time in one another's company.

A young tree, broken and caught between two others,

creaks to the rhythm of the wind. How well the owl must know this sound. Does she anticipate the crash of its falling? What is the consciousness of a spotted owl? There she perches perceiving us, and here we sit perceiving her. We exchange the long, slow interspecies stare—no fear, no threat, only the confusing mystery of the other. Steve knows her language well enough to speak a few words: the location call, the bark of aggression. Perhaps that means she thinks we are owls. We do not look like owls. But we do, briefly, behave like owls, catching and offering prey, being still, and turning our eyes to the forest.

"What are you?"

"What are you?"

That's the conversation we have with our eyes.

"What will you do next?"

"What will you do next?"

I keep falling into the owl's eyes. Then we stand up and hike down from that high place.

✦

When the fifth and sixth graders from the McKenzie River Christian School arrive at forest headquarters, each kid wears a name tag made from a slice of wood that looks like a sugar cookie. The cookies hang around their necks, announcing the camp names they have chosen for the field trip: Fang, Dark Dragon, Caos, Monkey Girl, Money Maker. They show little interest in the weather station that measures temperature, wind, chemistry of rain, weight of snow, the sensors downloading data every hour. They perk up at the sight of a stainless steel mercury collector, the tank sporting robotic arms that slide its cover into place to protect a rain sample. They don't seem to hear the weatherman's words as I copy them down in my field notebook. "Rain in Ohio comes down strong as vinegar and eats paint." "Some of the best rain in America comes down right here in Oregon." The kids shuffle, uninterested in the meteorologist's homily.

Asked if they ever have seen an old-growth forest, the children look blankly at their guide, children who live in the shade of five-hundred-year-old Douglas firs. How can it be that children do not recognize these giant beings that live in their neighborhood, that have stood here, tough and serene, since before science discovered its method?

Freed from the entrapment of an adult lecture, the kids tumble like puppies down the forest lane. When one spots the rough-skinned newt sauntering on wet asphalt, they all freeze, stare, and go silent, magnetized by the oddness of its orange belly, brown back, and translucent hand-like append-ages. They especially love hearing that the newt is poisonous, that after handling it they must all wash their hands. They love the danger, the taming power of the small. It sets loose a featherweight bout of animal stories.

"That's nothing. You should see the Pacific giants!" says Fang, gesturing wider than his torso to demonstrate their impressive size. He recounts how the salamanders, black and vicious, swaggered up when he and his father went fishing, how they grabbed the fish guts, thrashing their heads all around like monsters to consume the slime.

"Yeah? Well, I've seen lamprey eels that swam up the McKenzie all the way into Lookout Creek!" brags Caos. He points to the rivulet tumbling past the parking lot.

The newt has brought them back from their boredom into what Walt Whitman called the "costless, divine, original concrete."

✦

The H. J. Andrews Experimental Forest flanks the west-ern slope of the Cascade Range and occupies the drainage basin of Lookout Creek, a tributary of the Blue River, the McKenzie River, the Willamette, and finally the Columbia, which dumps out into the Pacific Ocean. This is one of the most studied forests in the world, a 15,800-acre research site established in 1948 when "sawlog foresters" helped the postwar nation rebuild through a grand investment on the domestic front.

Among the forest's more famous subjects of scrutiny are its dead logs. Begun in 1985, the log decomposition study focuses on two-foot-diameter timbers placed on the forest floor to rot. Every month or so researchers slice a giant cookie off the end of the logs, taking note of rot, fungus, bark beetles. They analyze the cookies in the lab. Dead logs are one of the most critical components of the forest ecosystem within the first few years of a tree's death, as organisms take advantage of new resources. Ongoing studies will look at how much nutrition logs contribute to the forest and how much carbon dioxide they release into the atmosphere. The study spawned the term "morticulture," connoting that attention to the dead has relevance to the nurture of the living.

Another celebrity of the Andrews is the northern spotted owl, a keystone species for Northwest forest health. If owls go, that loss is a sign that an essential life-supporting complexity has gone. The northern spotted owl has been vilified, polemicized, eco-terrorized, and reduced to the size of a bumper sticker. Eco-extremists who advocate a no-touch purity for the forest haven't helped by sabotaging forest road lockboxes with broken glass and in one case a loaded firearm aimed at the ranger unlocking the box. Pragmatists say that more loggers have lost their jobs to the industrialization of logging and plywood manufacture than to ecosystem protection. Try asking a lumberjack on unemployment to take comfort in that reasoning. It's easier for him to blame the regulator than the operator who might give him a job. The words *northern spotted owl* barely refer to the creature any longer, so debased have they become with political rhetoric. Who still sees the owl when its name is spoken? I'm drawn to the place in order to detox from such politics, to see the bird and the place, to understand the terms of their existence.

I welcomed the invitation to spend time and conversation with Fred Swanson, a man who seems to have quieted into the place after spending decades getting to know it through the scientific research conducted on site and simply from being in the presence of its great ancient trees. I admit that the idea of an "experimental forest" mystified and compelled me. I had no idea what that term meant.

In science an experiment is governed by a method. There are controls, limitations, rules, hypotheses. It must produce empirical evidence. Its conclusions must be verifiable, repeatable by another scientist. An experiment in science adds to collective knowledge. Earth is round, not flat, and circles the sun. Nearly everyone on Earth knows this, one would hope, and these facts are not subject to reasonable argument, aesthetic judgment, or cultural relativism.

In correspondence, I asked Fred Swanson what he means when he uses the word *experiment.*

"Funny you should ask," he replied. "Some local scientists have been discussing this (with some heat). In a narrow science sense an experiment uses alternative treatments to test hypotheses—properties of a standard agronomic experiment include several rather different treatments (for example, levels of fertilization or cutting), replication (multiple plots with the same treatment), random assignment of treatments to plots, pretreatment measurements . . .

"On the other hand," Swanson continued, "we have the more casual use of *experiment,* as if just trying something out and seeing how it works. In field ecology and geology it can be very difficult to conduct good experiments. One usually just starts out observing to get the drift of how the world is working. Creative flashes in science often step beyond the rigidity of the experimental process, coming in leaps of wonderment and faith."

In the arts, an experiment is governed by freedom from tradition, or at least resistance to it. Experimentation in poetry dispenses with received forms, levels of diction, metrical conventions, and even syntactical rules. It may favor process over product, music over meaning, disjunction over coherence, invented constraints over received ones. It is unique, unrepeatable. An experiment in poetry adds to the sense of depth, complexity, mystery, and feeling in the world. If there is a "poetic method," it is to free oneself from method and enter into the excitement of creating something new and true to a very individual experience and voice. Poetry's subversive practitioners (from Dada to L=A=N=G=U=A=G=E to Fib to Flarf to the documentary poem) challenge rationality through pranks, games, data, and erasure of "artistic" "value." They use method to leap beyond method, perhaps in the same way scientists often make their surprise findings through leaps.

The hope in the Andrews is that by careful and sustained observation—using methods of applied science, applied humanities, applied poetics—researchers will work here side by side as equal partners in apprehending the place and learning how to protect it. But I wondered, if poetry is to be the equal partner of science in this project, would I need a hypothesis? Can an aesthetic desire, an intuition toward artistic form, be a hypothesis? Is there a literacy of equal value to scientific literacy that comes from aesthetic experience?

✦

On a warm May afternoon, Fred drives me upslope along Forest Road 130 behind the Andrews headquarters through a collage of forest types that are the result of varied logging strategies tried out over recent years. He is a tall, lean timber of a man, gray-bearded as the licheny Northwest trees, with a gentle yet intense manner. He tells me about the sites he'd like me to visit.

"You might want to go sit on that gravel bar in Lookout Creek."

It feels more like conversation than instruction, though I know each writer who comes over the duration of the project will be asked to visit the same locations: creek, log decomposition, and clear-cut sites. I'm expecting science to be the boss here. After all, my host has been studying this terrain for decades. It takes me a few interchanges before I realize that he really means to make me a full partner in the enterprise of understanding this place.

We park at the Blue River Face Timber Sale Unit, an area partially cut one year, then burned the next, and planted with seedlings the following year. The cutting prescription was set on a 180-year rotation with 30 percent live tree retention. Fewer cuts were made close to the river to decrease erosion and silting. Snags were left standing as habitat for voles and flying squirrels.

Fred strides down into the cut, peering at stumps, scanning the tree rings for signs of an earlier wildfire in these firs that had lived five hundred years. I wander along the charred ground, trying to hold onto his language for the place. I write "patch cutting," "too much edge," "min frag," "owl injunction," "new forestry." Fred has an excited mind and verbal acuity that are hard to keep up with, especially when his commentary is filled with a lifetime of learning about this forest. But what really interests him are volcanoes. He calls himself a "closet volcanologist." He's visited eruptions in Hawaii, the Galapagos Islands, and Mount St. Helens to see how such a scale of disturbance registers in the forest. He says that "the organism perceives the mechanism of disturbance and makes a genetic interpretation of the mechanism." All the way down to the molecules, nature is a self-correcting process.

Ten days after Mount St. Helens blew off her top in the catastrophic 1980 eruption that leveled everything within an eight-mile radius, the entire terrain white with ash from the fire and pyroclastic flow, Fred watched colleagues digging holes to study the mineral deposits. He happened to gaze down into one. He saw spidery, translucent threads of mycorrhizal fungi fluttering in the wind, threads so fine he couldn't have seen them if they had not been dusted with fine volcanic ash. Ten days after the cataclysm, the forest had raced back to work. It was as if fire had said to dirt, "Go forth and multiply."

Fred rejoins me at the roadside where I've been standing to study the landscape, a gentle slope leading toward the seam below where water flows and tiers of brocaded hillsides rise beyond.

"What do you see?" he asks. There's a beat or two of silence in which I realize that my lack of experience and specialized language are part of his hypothesis in this collaborative experiment: she will see it new.

"It looks messy. There's brush left on the ground, tree-sized logs, snags. It looks natural," I answer. "This landscape reminds me of our family's summer home in Canada where we haven't cut anything for fifty years, unless it threatened to fall on our house. The woods there is such a mess of overgrowth and downfall, you can hardly make your way through it anymore. I've come to think of nature unhindered as messy."

I try to describe what I notice at the cut site. Brush, snag, stump, char, feathery seedlings, bear grass, salal, tiny red-stalked clusters of something that grows as dense as streptococcus on an agar plate.

"Yes," he says, "the whole landscape is organizing itself."

A flash of words pops into my mind, giving shape to something I've felt for years.

"This cut keeps intact the wisdom of Earth. Nature, to me, means deep time—what Earth has learned through long trial and error . . . of course, I'm speaking poetically," I add apologetically, imagining how useless such words would be in a grant application to the National Science Foundation. But Fred does not dismiss them.

As a poet working in the house of science, I feel responsible to bear forward some remnant of the romantic tradition, the sense that out of the particular the transcendent
may arise and that language can embody such experience.
The poet of our time has a complicated task. She lives with a
divided mind, remaining as skeptical as a scientist about the
tools of her trade. Hasn't language been used to manipulate,
oppress, deceive, and betray more consistently than it has
ever served as a vessel for aesthetic or spiritual feeling? How
can poetic language be called to the world's aid during these
days of threat and peril? Can poetry carry our love, as a mine
canary carries our fear, into the world? If this is my hypothesis, by what measure do I know the results of the experiment?

Fred nods and explains the site this way: "In the current
ecological approach to forestry, you try to keep more of the
complexity of nature in the disturbance you create. A little
bit of chaos is a good thing."

We talk about the failures of language in both purviews,
how so little of what we've said and done has protected
what we love. When the Northwest Forest Plan was written,
its architects looked for words to describe the forests they
hoped to save from the blade so that the land could fulfill its
fullest evolutionary possibility.

Ancient forest. Virgin forest. Old growth. Everyone agreed
that if those words were the best they could do to inspire
conservation, the last stands of North America's forest legacy
were doomed.

"Is this a good landscape or a bad landscape?" Fred asks
as we gaze over the green tapestry. I'm speechless. I want to
think that beauty makes a landscape good, but that trivial-
izes the complexity that makes life work. This mess too is
good for the scrutinizing attention it brings out in us and for
the ecological possibility it gives to flora and fauna.

I thread my gaze through the scrub, slash, and snags.
So much of the process of regeneration on disturbed land

occurs beyond the apprehension of the senses. There is a wholeness to a forest that the damaged area cannot help but seek. The forest is reaching to complete itself, just as we are reaching for the words to describe what lies just past our comprehension. What is going on out there might be described by a graph, an equation, a poem sequence, or a conversation. All would fall short of explaining the complexity of relationships that constitute a forest. Paying attention means more than engaging in empirical study. It asks also for intuition and feeling. It asks for attending *to*, as one would do in the care of one's home, livestock, garden, or beloved.

✦

"Natural forces and human forces have intertwined," writes geoscientist Paul Crutzen in defining the new geologic epoch of the Anthropocene, "so that the fate of one determines the fate of the other." The enormity of this change in the history of Earth places a new challenge before the human imagination in defining ourselves and the nature of the work we are called to. Communicating information about climate change has hardly brought the forces of greed, guns, and gutting of the planet to their knees. Information doesn't change people. Ask the alcoholic or the addict. Sometimes passion changes people. Sometimes empathy does. Sometimes the unconscious yanks you up by your heels, turns you upside down, and gets you straight with reality. Sometimes social cues ripple out from an event or a scientific finding and a cultural norm becomes abnormal. Sometimes the cue is grief. Sometimes the cue is love. Both tell us what we can't bear losing and create a resonance that can harden into conviction.

This brings me to art. Adam Gopnik writes that "art is a way of expanding our resonances, civilization our way of resonating to those expansions." Art has been in the kit of adaptive strategies for at least thirty thousand years of human history. The late Pleistocene. That's when the great animal

paintings of Lascaux and Chauvet were made, when the animal miniatures of the Swabian Mountains were carved from
mammoth tusks. In truth, art's time horizon is probably
much more deeply buried in the mystery of the past. I have
a postcard taped above my desk, a photograph of a hand ax,
a hefty tool meant to fit into the palm for carving flesh from
bone. This flint is from Norfolk, England, made by *Homo
erectus* some two hundred and fifty thousand years ago. The
flint has been carefully flaked to create the utilitarian shape,
but the maker has fashioned the carving to highlight a fossil
mollusk in the center of one face of the teardrop-shaped ax.
There sits the small scallop shell, rays fanning out in an arc,
as if a little sunrise had been inlaid in stone. What eye caught
this anomaly in the rock? What hand mastered the craft to
chip away the surrounding stone, mindful of the beauty and
mystery the fossil shell gave to the object in hand? At least
three other such hand axes are known from Europe. Archaic
hunters spent artful hours getting the symmetry and edge
and heft just right. The statement of beauty made by this
object translates easily across the geologic eras. The skill and
love of beauty is all the more impressive, as Denis Dutton illuminated in his rock-star TED talk "A Darwinian Theory of
Beauty," when one considers that such hand axes were being
made by hominid ancestors before language had developed.

So what might art, this primal skill set, have to do with our
adaptation to climate change? Climate skeptics sway public
opinion because they appeal to emotions of fear of change,
anger at authority, and denial of grief over loss. What good
is a poem in a world of weapons and wounds and wasteful-
ness? Art takes up such feelings as a given. Athletics provide
a ritualized way for people to act out violence and competition while doing minimal harm to one another. Art provides
a ritualized way to choose beauty over use, to use dissonance
as a way to find harmony, to express something in a way that
will draw a community together. Art cleanses the spirit of

toxins that have weakened it. Art lets one inner life speak to another across vast spans of time and distance. It's not art's task to convey information, though it may interrogate the usefulness or truthfulness of information. Art is empathy. Empathy gets in the way of objective science, which is not to say that a scientist does not feel empathy. But scientists do not cultivate their empathy as an instrument to employ in their professional practice. Art tries to do just that. It weaves connective tissue between fact and feeling, self and world, individual and collective good. Art in a time of radical loss is an elegy. It teaches us how to mourn, whether in the context of family loss or the larger losses brought about by the extreme sport of anthropogenic climate change.

Art can use the power of grief to speak of the depth of one's love for what we would protect and sustain. It can expose the failure of the old myths and raise the appetite for new myths that can guide us. Poems that spring from the ecotone between art and science can document the spirit of the age, as poetry has done since the first campers sat around a campfire dwelling in a shared sense of feeling and purpose. I cannot prove empirically the efficacy of poetry or any other form of art. I write because to do so is an experiment in being present. Climate change is here. It is messy. Change is coming fast. No one is in control. Even our best intentions fall into a process of complex change that we could not have anticipated. "Attention must be paid," Willy Loman's wife laments. "He's not to be allowed to fall into his grave like an old dog." She feels as if sorrow were an imperative for insurrection.

"What are words good for?" asks Brazilian poet Antonio Carlos Secchin:

Perhaps to insist that there are always left-overs, mistakes, failures, and fractures in our interactions with the real world. To ignore them is to believe in a harmonious con-

nection between words and things, in the existence of
a homogenic discourse that would deny each and every
one of us the possibility of negotiating the openings and
cracks that conflict and change can offer and which both
the words and human beings need to be kept alive.

✦

Something strange is going on up in the Andrews
Experimental Forest. Decades of research, education, and
policy have worked to protect the northern spotted owl as a
keystone species signifying the health of the old-growth forest. Since these reclusive birds require old-growth forest to
thrive, protecting them has required preserving magnificent
ancient forests. But as more and more habitat is disturbed
elsewhere, barred owls, larger and more aggressive birds,
have been moving from the east across Canada's boreal forest
into the Northwest. Barred owls can outcompete the spotted
owls for prey. And they do better on logged-out land than the
spotted owls. They usurp spotted owl nests. They breed with
spotted owls, producing offspring known as "sparred owls"
that look and sound like neither parent. They're a mixed-up
natural hybrid and thus not protected as an endangered species. Should the barred owls be killed to protect the spotted
owl? Will the barred owls prove more fit for a less fit forest,
taking over the habitat, wiping out the protected species and
opening the way for more aggressive and unsustainable logging? The questions fly as the Earth experiment continues
to unfold.

I 'm not sure when I began to notice the absence of birds. I had come to Los Angeles for the weekend to speak about science and the Western American imagination. I lamented the split between science and religion that has widened since Darwin. I might have said that as an animist I see nature as god. Or I might not have said this, because it would have made me feel undressed in public. God is like sex, best experienced with a very small audience or none at all. A Native American man in the audience complained that we could not solve the problems in our relationship with nature until we solved the problems of dominance and rank. I said we followed the pathway of the chimp with chest thumping, ground drumming, bullying, assault, and mutilation as very old habits in the primate line. That doesn't mean this is the only path we can follow through the genetic undergrowth. Bonobos, with whom we also share a common ancestor, resolve conflicts by defusing hostility with affection and sexual play. They are mutualists. I am a "sci-animist," I concluded, the word bubbling up from nowhere, from the same old mind that split from apes. The audience laughed. What I meant was that I thought science could return us to an animistic sense of the natural world, a place where transformation was expected, part of the pattern and flow.

I'm not sure when I began to notice the absence of birds. Certainly not when I checked into the Los Angeles Biltmore, craning at the sky-high tropical fool-the-eye mural depicting split-leaf philodendrons and birds of paradise. Not when I walked up Bunker Hill to admire the glint and curve of Frank Gehry's Disney Concert Hall. But now that I think back, not a pigeon or sparrow bothered me for crumbs when I sat in the patio to enjoy my coffee and scone. Not a feathery rustling passed overhead when I walked back on the overpass, stopping to study the parking lot below. Movie paraphernalia had caught my eye: four silver Range Rovers, eight black limos, coil after coil of electrical wire, rows of klieg lights, tripod stands, first aid van, trailers for the stars to change their clothes. All lined up and waiting for action. Not a soul in sight. Later at the Getty Museum, archaic leaf and shell prints marked the travertine, but not one dime-sized splatter of limey shit appeared anywhere on the billion-dollar campus. *LA Weekly* offered discount coupons for removal of crow's-feet.

There had not even been any dogs, unlike in Prague, where I had seen a wolf on the tram, its off-duty muzzle hanging loosely like a necklace, or in New York City, where professional dog walkers gather a dozen clients from Upper West Side apartments, experienced urban dogs who can walk a mile held like a bouquet in the dog walker's hand and never tangle their leashes. In Los Angeles I saw a brown bear on a billboard, a California bank promoting the animal that had been absent from the California landscape since 1922, the loss made elegy when *Ursus californicus* became the state animal thirty years later, in 1953.

By this time I was ravenous. I walked down Grand Avenue to the Water Grill. More empty limos waiting for more stars. White Hummer as long as a bus. Two black stretch Lincolns. I cracked the restaurant's door, the place buzzing with celebrity and desire. I snaked through the crowd to sit at the bar, ordered a Grey Goose martini, and watched the barman open oysters with one flit of the knife. He knew how to keep everyone happy. Champagne for the fledgling lovers sitting beside me, though they already were blasted, the woman spinning on her bar stool as she laughed and flung her hair, as seductive as a pirouetting sandhill crane. Conversation for the middle-aged lesbians down the line who murmured like wood ducks floating on a calm sea. Benign neglect for the woman sitting alone nursing her vodka and writing in a notebook, chicken-scratch made hastily in the semidark bar.

The first time the woman hit me with her hair, I startled, as if she'd spilled my cocktail. Young, perhaps Indonesian, with curry-colored skin. Dressed in saffron and coral brocade as tight as reptile skin, she was rapt in the gaze of her companion. He was young, though older than the woman, skinny and white. His shirt was unbuttoned in that seventies way nearly to his belly. I thought of Mark Wahlberg when he played the porn star in *Boogie Nights,* his impressive though pathetically fake member. The woman had long expensive hair, dyed in a weave of brunette, strawberry blond, and platinum strands. It was thick hair and heavy with product. I began to think she aspired to the screen and he was making promises. They fed oysters to each other, tipping the shells so that the milky flesh would slide through the portals of one another's lips. They twined forearms to sip champagne while staring into the oil wells of each other's eyes. It was a parody of love, a B movie of love, a staged reading of love's stale and empty lines. Big, fat oysters. Narrow flutes of champagne. The more drunk they got, the more their outsized laughter spread like a toxic spill.

The close-cropped women down the bar asked about the oysters. "Are they farmed?"

The barman said, "No, they're wild." Paused a beat. "Well, they're grown on strings that hang in the ocean. I mean, they are in the ocean, so, when you say farmed, I think confined."

I ordered the farm-raised sturgeon.

Then the hair again whipped across my shoulder, the acolyte spinning away from her companion, flinging her hair as in a commercial for shampoo, yet oblivious to anything except her eros for the unbuttoned man. I said nothing, except to myself, to whom I repeated, "If she hits me one more time with her hair . . ."

And she did, after which I again did nothing but watch the oyster slide from the man's shell into her pretty pink mouth, the little sea thing released from its briny transsexual life. Down it went into her red throat, the creature whole and alive—gills, gonads, three-chambered minuscule heart, and lacy black mantle. A few grains of grit and nacre. It was like watching something I remembered from another life. Not the sex of it, but the animal appetite, life taking life into its savoring throat. It was like watching myself swinging in the trees, flying through the clatter of monkeys, macaws, and operatic frogs—the old music of Earth—savage, joyful, and lost.

D o other animals tell jokes? Perhaps the play of young animals in which they practice what will later become life-enhancing skills—the stalk, the pounce, the thrashing—is not so unlike what human beings do in attempting to learn what they will need to survive in the future. Of course, we live and direct our lives so much in the mind, so much in the richness and folly and, yes, beauty of what our minds can create that our play often takes the form of jokes, a linguistic version of play. One of my recent favorites was the rabbit on Mars. The National Aeronautics and Space Administration has landed two rovers, research-gathering devices, on our neighboring planet, the one with soil so bloody with iron that it was named after the Roman god of war. How much more benign is our view: let's do some geologic study of the soil and find out what it's really made of and whether any forms of life might once have inhabited the place, might (miraculous to say!) have blown loose in a cosmic wind and drifted here to our spinning globe, seeding everything we know including the great and troubling argument between religion and science.

The two research devices are named *Spirit* and *Opportunity*, as if the project were intended, at last, to create a team from these often opposing forces. It has been an awe-inspiring experience to watch these little emissaries of our curiosity make their journey through space and land like bouncing balls in a place so far away we cannot imagine the distance—though we can cross it—then release themselves from their protective shells in response to messages beamed from Earth. Errors in the software? No problem—new instructions are beamed from home base and the little brain is reconfigured, the rover rolling off its platform, drilling into Martian rock, sending snapshots instantly back home through space. The scientists and engineers have worked in collaboration as musical and passionate as a symphony orchestra to accomplish this, and their joy is beautiful to behold. How the knowledge will be used by Opportunity, if you will forgive my appropriating these names and returning them to their Earth-bound meanings, remains a cautionary tale. No green-thinking poet could celebrate transporting the culture of obsessive consumerism to another planet. It is how the knowledge will be used by Spirit that draws me to the curious phenomenon of the rabbit on Mars.

Along with the panoramic images of barren rusty soil and rock circulating on the Internet, that collective unconscious of the technological that hovers over the surface of Earth, came a fuzzy imprecise image of an object that appears to have very long, erect, and pointed ears. It was graced with the caption "A Rabbit on Mars?" It is hardly the first time that human beings have projected their imaginations out into space. It isn't even the first time that the projections have taken the form of a rabbit. The Maya saw a leaping rabbit, the special pet of the moon goddess, where Americans see the man in the moon and Japanese moongazers see a rabbit making a rice cake. Of course, everyone got the joke that there are no Martian bunnies hopping up to welcome our team of digital explorers. It turned out that the "rabbit" photographed by Spirit was a tatter of the protective balloon that had helped cushion the spacecraft's landing. A momentary illusion, though it struck the imagination with silly and pleasurable force. Spirit, of course, will be struck when and if science finds life on other planets. And many astronomers and evolutionary biologists agree that it really is a matter of when, not if, now that we know planets are not an entirely exceptional phenomenon in the universe, and therefore the conditions suitable for life may not be limited to those on Earth. How far we have come from "War of the Worlds" as our scientific instruments have extended our eyes into far space, altering our picture of what we will find there, so that we can now imagine the extraterrestrial not as mechanical warrior sent to conquer our planet, but as a benign, fuzzy, harmless, and familiar creature, a vegetarian, an animal said to deliver baskets of candies to children at Easter time. Is the appeal of this image an instruction to ourselves meant to calm us, to assuage the fears that our sense of ourselves and our world may soon be sent reeling? What will it mean, even if all we find out there are microbes living in ice? Will our God be their God? Will Life itself become our God? Will we be humbled into a greater reverence and hunger for knowledge, as people were by the Copernican Revolution? Will life become a dime-a-dozen happenstance to be owned, manipulated, destroyed, and devoured with an attitude of dismissal even greater than we've accomplished here on our gorgeous home planet? How could we know what rearrangement our spirits will undergo when such knowledge comes to us? What better guide for us—if only in play—than the animals who have been with us from the start, real and imagined, the animals who live in us as the matter of our genes and the spirit of our imaginations, who live with us as our teachers and companions and neighbors, the animals who were our first gods in the childhood of humanity?

Field Notes on Culture, Biology,
and Emergence

Man is the only animal that tells stories. He
tells stories to know what kind of creature he is.
SALMAN RUSHDIE
Joseph Anton: A Memoir

Before Henry David Thoreau began his twenty-eight-mile walk along the Cape Cod seashore in October 1849, he stopped to witness a shipwreck at Cohasset. "Death!" read the headlines in Boston. "One Hundred and Forty-Five Lives Lost." Thoreau traveled among the many Irish, hundreds of them going to identify bodies, comfort the survivors, and attend funerals. "Many horses in carriages were fastened to the fences near the shore," he wrote, "and, for a mile or more, up and down, the beach was covered with people looking out for bodies, and examining fragments of the wreck." The brig *St. John*, loaded with emigrants from Galway, Ireland, had broken on the rocks that Sunday morning, and the atmosphere was one not of grief but of "a sober despatch of business" as coffins were filled, nailed shut, and carted away. Among the crowd picking through the wreckage were men collecting seaweed the storm had cast up, carrying it above the reach of the tide, after separating out fragments of clothing. The horror of turning up a human body in the wrack did not keep them from gathering the "valuable manure" of seaweed. "This shipwreck," Thoreau observed, "had not produced a visible vibration in the fabric of society."

He was not numb to the loss and misery of the wreck, but he admired the social whole and its ongoing pragmatism. He felt that the seashore acquired "a rarer and sublimer beauty" when it was framed by this event. He admired the industry of the fishermen, farther along on his journey, counting two hundred mackerel boats working offshore near Truro, another hundred on the horizon floating on this "highway of nations," and overall an astonishing fifteen hundred fishing rigs working out of Provincetown in the mid-1800s. Today one might see a handful, and those nearly always lashed bow and stern and spring lines to the wharf. Thoreau depicts the place with an eye to history, an ear to local story, and an implicit confidence in human enterprise.

Reading this account of his travels, I don't see him as recluse, Luddite, and misanthrope—the pacifist Unabomber of the nineteenth century—as those who grow cynical about human prospects might come to imagine. He is a man who seeks solitude in order to live deliberately and to pass the lesson on to others, a man who commits civil disobedience to goad injustice and advance moral philosophy, and a man who appreciates human thrift and industry.

Thoreau's *Cape Cod* makes a good complement to *Walden*, which grates on me for some of it stridencies, particularly Thoreau's ridicule of technology as "pretty toys" that "distract our attention from serious things." This strikes me as snobbish intellectualism, as opposed to the work's more dominant note of mindful curiosity. What has been more serious to human beings than technology since the first flint struck sparks? Maybe art. Maybe religion. This is the kind of animal we are: tool-making, art-making, symbol-making, and intensely social, engaged in a mutually reinforcing set of activities that make us speed-learners and obsessive connectors with one another. Technology may be sinking us now, but this need not be the case. The question is not whether we can live without technology, but whether we can live with technology in such a way that we do not destroy ourselves and the planet.

The communication and information technologies, in particular, strike me as markers of an emerging shift in consciousness. What kind of good thing might they be? What might be the adaptive aspects to this cultural movement? A form of collective intelligence that no one controls, it evolves in its own organismic way to egg us on toward greater connection, exposure, accountability, and collaboration. Sure, the Internet is full of trash and hype, but the freedom with which information can move makes censorship, deception, and totalitarianism much harder to inflict.

Scott Russell Sanders's essay "Simplicity and Sanity" makes an eloquent case for simplicity and the role of individual responsibility in facing the crisis of global climate change. I try to follow the principles he offers, taking pragmatic steps to reduce my weight on the planet. But the problems we face are of such profound scope that they cannot be effectively addressed by individual responses alone. The ultimate responsibility for reducing the effects of global climate change is a collective social responsibility that requires policy, regulation, alliance, and law—instruments our culture has failed to provide. I say "culture," not "government," because democratic government is, in theory, an instrument for realizing the will of the people. We do no good by acting as if we-the-people are virtuous while they-the-government are corrupt. The fabric of human culture is being frayed, stretched, and torn by our predicament. Values that none of us really believe in rule: profit trumps all, every man for himself, wealth is health, and, as author William deBuys coined at a recent symposium, "yoyo": you're on your own.

Not surprisingly, I am at odds with my culture. So many of us are these days, as we free-fall into ecological doom.

Recycling, installing halogen bulbs, and writing letters to Congress seem pallid levels of activism compared to the severity of our collective malaise. We live in a pathological culture that is sick with violence, greed, waste, contentiousness, and a sense of futility. We live in cities we despise for their ugliness, menace, and lack of community (though it's puritanical, I know, at such moments as this to deny the pleasures of the city). We have poor people whom we ignore, leaving them stranded on their roofs in a flood or cast out on the street. We ask their children to die in senseless wars. We have elected leaders who have no business leading, so lacking are they in wisdom and the capacity for reflective thought and empathy and compromise; their disdain for learning and scientific research, and their absurdly simplistic posturing about the state of religion in a pluralistic democracy, would make such leaders laughable if their actions were not causing so much anguish around the world and so much erosion of our sense of purpose at home.

No greater proof of our dissident relationship to our own culture is needed than the terrible moment we parents meet when we send our children to school, camp, movies, or a sleepover at a neighbor's house. We feel them slip from the embrace of family and plunge into the violence of American society. We realize we cannot control the influences that will enter their minds and hearts. We feel sick with fear.

Raising me in the 1950s, my artistic parents wanted to protect me from the conformity of Connecticut's suburban somnolence. Raising my daughter in the culturally contentious sixties, I wanted to protect her from rednecks and the evangelical neighbors who said that her dreams of a beloved dead grandmother were visits from Satan. My grown daughter and her husband—a visual artist and progressive pastor—struggle to raise their boys without taint of the violence, excess, and greed that surround them. We all come to the horrible awareness that we cannot protect our children from the culture in which they live. We do not trust it; we do not want to feel that we are part of it. Yet our children, too, will become creatures of their culture and their historical moment. They will have to learn for themselves what their values are, but we want desperately to *give* them their values, as surely as we gave them their names.

This alienation from and resistance to culture only serves to reinforce the value of bullish individualism, but no matter how much we do as individuals, the larger organism of culture remains impoverished. The old place-based cultures no longer work. John Donne wrote that no man is an island; now we know that no culture is an island, that to be alive, cultures must be permeable. This lesson is one that First Nation peoples of the Americas have had to learn through the hardest of lessons. Today, war based upon conflicting fundamentalisms breaks out when people are unable to acknowledge and live with the permeability of culture. Yet the velocity of change is such that we do not know what verities to rely upon. What ideas about culture can we take up in good faith as part of our tool kit for rebuilding the "commons"—those aspects of nature and culture that cannot be owned—as a countervailing force to the market? What ideas about culture might help us to celebrate rather than bemoan the social whole of which we are a part?

✦

I return again and again to Edward Sapir's essay "Culture, Genuine and Spurious," parts of which appeared in the English *Dial* in 1919, barely beyond the shadow of World War I. Sapir explores his "idea of what kind of a good thing culture is," defining culture as "any socially inherited element in the life of man, material and spiritual." It includes art, religion, science, inventions, domestic skills, and consumer goods, as well as such society-shaping ideas as democracy, imperialism, civil liberty, and social justice.

I often ask my graduate students on the first day of a creative writing course to write down their cultural influences. I do this because I find that the biggest problem in the student writing I see, other than poor mechanics, is their self-absorption. Too many of them write about personal wounds: drug and alcohol abuse, car wrecks, anorexia, dysfunctional and failed families, failed love affairs, depression, anxiety, and rage against feelings of powerlessness. I don't mean to suggest that these are not suitable catalysts for making literature, but my students tend not to see these stories within a social matrix or cultural lineage. They feel locked within themselves and think of artistic expression as a key that will let them into the kingdom of emotional freedom, rather than seeing art as a mindful reframing of experience and emotion through a forming intelligence. They write with too much "I" and no sense of "we." They can tell me what has happened to them—but they cannot tell me the significance, the moral and psychological consequences. They cannot step outside of their anguish to see the cultural context that shapes them. They just know that they, who are among the most privileged people who have ever lived on Earth, feel they don't belong anywhere.

So, I start out by asking them to write down what they see as their cultural influences within three frames of reference. First, culture as a shared set of traditions and meanings. They can choose any context they wish: ethnicity, gender, race, nationality, sexual orientation, or faith community. They write about being Mormon, gay, goth, punk, jock, transgendered, Chicano, Navajo, or mixed blood. They display an impressive array of political and activist affiliations, holding passionate convictions about social, economic, and environmental justice. The interesting thing is that while some speak of nationality—those whose families have come in recent generations from Italy or Korea or Somalia—not one student has spoken about being American as a significant cultural influence. This just doesn't seem to occur to them—as if, once you get here, you can be anything you want to be, but you can't see yourself as part of the whole.

Second, I ask them to consider culture as artistic expression, and they offer up movies, video games, jazz, performance art, and photography. They seem surprised at how their stories open up when they are told within such a texture. I, too, can be surprised. A Navajo student who had been silent all semester, listening respectfully each week as other students made presentations on dance therapy, installation sculpture, and finger painting, became eloquent when her time to present arrived.

"I don't really know what you mean when you say 'art,' because in my culture it's not separate from life," she said, holding up in her hands her ceremonial dress and silver squash-blossom necklace, and passing "kneel-down bread" to everyone in the room. She was very much a contemporary woman, a jeans and T-shirt fashionista, with a foot in each of two worlds. She described the history and use of the traditional items: Yes, she said, the workmanship of the dress and necklace was artful, and the technique she described in her grandmother's kneeling down to press flour into tortilla-like rounds was artful. But these were simply the way things were done on certain occasions in her culture. No one on the rez thought of them as art.

A woman from New Jersey had worked as a teenage prostitute. She left home in the morning wearing the pleated plaid skirt and tailored white shirt that were the uniform of her Catholic high school. She carried in her backpack a different outfit for her after-school job. This was not an Eliot Spitzer class of elegant prostitution, but a lowlife massage parlor where she did hand jobs on lonely and powerless men. Do you prefer oil or lotion? she would ask. She'd been sexually abused by her father. This work was the first time she'd felt in control of men. Reading her essays was difficult and painful, in part because she felt so affirmed by having been a sex worker; her fellow students could not get past the feeling that she had been degraded. Then she wrote an essay that lifted off the page, framing her experience in the context of prostitutes in cinema. *Pretty Woman*, starring an effervescent Julia Roberts, was the whore-with-a-heart-of-gold du jour, an innocent and redemptive depiction that everyone loved. The student's essay brought reel after reel of such fictions to light, and suddenly I felt complicit in the cultural hypocrisy surrounding sex workers. I did not feel accused; I felt called to understand how a woman might choose such a path.

Third, I ask students to consider culture as a relationship between people and nature or people and a place. This yields stories about places that are lost—the family store run by Chinese American grandparents on a street corner in Phoenix now devoured by a mall. Or the places people go to get away—the hike in the backcountry, the family cottage at the lake, the study-abroad trip to Malta. I have read no student essay that draws on the depth of experience on the land and in place that writers such as Scott Sanders, William deBuys, Simon Ortiz, and Wendell Berry so richly portray. Perhaps it is unreasonable to expect such work from the new generation. Culture as it has traditionally been shaped by the terms of nature and place is itself a permeable idea and is giving way to velocity, hybridity, and Google-ality.

Sapir describes culture as "the spiritual possessions of the group rather than of the individual." It is "a spiritual heirloom that must, at all cost, be preserved intact." Which heirlooms? the skeptic may ask. Few people would wish to preserve all aspects of their culture—assuming they could even define who they are as cultural creatures. Cultural identity is becoming a matter of individual choice. Cultural relativism does not have to mean that all cultural traditions are equal. It can mean that a person becomes more deliberate about which aspects of her tradition she wishes to take up and pass on. Vernita Herdman, an Inupiaq community advocate in Alaska, offers the apt metaphor of cabins circling a lake. We each bring our individual histories and cultural legacies to our sojourn in such a place, but at the center is the still and open water. We can look across the lake and see how others do things differently than we do. And we can choose. Herdman describes the tribal woman who walked several feet behind her husband, in deference to his authority and according to cultural tradition, until she saw that in other cultures a man and a woman could walk side by side.

A genuine culture, says Sapir, is one in which nothing is spiritually meaningless. By this standard the Aztecs' culture was genuine, even though they were imperialists who continually waged war to capture victims for sacrifice. This practice was meaningful to them. They believed blood offerings completed a circle of reciprocal exchange—that life must be given in order to earn life. By Sapir's standard, the baiting and barking that passes for deliberation and decision making in Washington, DC is spurious because it is empty of meaning. It reflects only jockeying for position and power, not any of the ethical principles upon which our government was historically based. The Bill of Rights, the Civil Rights Act, and the Wilderness Act were genuine; the 2002 Authorization for Use of Military Force Against Iraq Resolution was spurious, based upon poor intelligence and false claims.

"It is imperative," Sapir asserts, "if the individual is to preserve his value as a cultured being, that he compensate himself out of the non-economic, the non-utilitarian spheres— social, religious, scientific, aesthetic." The spurious culture is one in which people expect to be compensated financially for all wounds and losses.

Though my father was never a litigious man, he comes to mind here. He was charming and sociable, a man who loved people and entertained them as a radio and television personality. He took the measure of himself in the pleasure of human company and in his handiwork on gardens, stone walls, and brush piles. Yet at the end of his life, after his heart began to fail in his eighties, his days narrowed down to a card table where he sat filling out Publishers Clearing House sweepstakes entries in hopes of an easy million. He still felt the world owed him something, and he did not know where else to look for compensation. By contrast, my mother, when she lay at the far edge of her life at 102, suffered enough skeletal disintegration to make her days a torment, yet she found nonutilitarian compensations that made the prospect of death something she met with equanimity. She spent her late nineties completing a sharply written memoir; at ninety-nine she was intrigued by the images that come in dreams, often columns of people dressed in ceremonial robes of shiny pastel colors, which we discussed in our visits as one of many marvels of the inner world, the imaginative process that seemed to be guiding her on her most difficult of passages.

"Nature is God," she told me one day. "I don't need religion. I tried it when I was younger. There was nothing there for me. Just think about a seed—all that's packed into that little miracle and the beauty that will unfold."

I picture her examining the stamens and pollen hoards of wildflowers with a magnifying glass, as had been her habit, her eyes growing glassy in love.

"That's all the religion I need," she told me with the conviction of one shaping final thoughts. She was making a private peace with the terms of her existence, though she too was at odds with her culture.

"The self," Edward Sapir writes, "must learn to reconcile its own strivings, its own imperious necessities, with the general spiritual life of the community."

I know this is necessary for us to do. I don't know how we do it.

✦

Culture is an emergent property of our biology. We are social creatures—the worst punishment we can inflict, short of the death penalty, is solitary confinement—and we are successful creatures, compared to many less fortunate species, because culture has made us speed-learners. The problem lies in the speed at which these two mechanisms—culture and biology—work. Culture is fast, biology slow.

Plastics offer a good example here. They are hydrocarbons, and we've made a lot of them. Plastic particles float in the ocean as vast islands of waste. No organism can metabolize this form of hydrocarbon; yet scientists suggest that, given enough time, microbes will evolve that can break the plastics back down into their chemical building blocks, and they will enter again into the molecular flow. This will be a long time coming, too long for the human species to sit back and wait for. But in Earth's time, a biological solution will come for at least some of our cultural excess.

With our increasing awareness of the crisis of global climate change, the science thrust to the forefront of attention is, as J. Baird Callicott pegs it, "biogeochemistry, which reveals a Gaian Earth that is certainly systemic, holistic, internally related, and indeed self-organizing and self-regulating." This shift in awareness is forcing us to pose old questions about our own nature with increasing urgency: What kind of creature are we? What kind of creature might we become? What is given and what is learned? Must we operate on the principle of survival of the fittest or can we shift to survival of the most cooperative? What stories can biology give us that help us revise the story of who we can be?

✦

Nothing on this trip to San Diego was as I had expected. Why is it that my fantasies are so often stuck in the past? When I made the hotel reservations on the California coast, I pictured the place as it might have been a century ago. That small black dot on the edge of the map showed ocean blue on one side and forest green on the other, not the grid of freeways so entangled that places overlap and nothing has definition or limit. I pictured the classic stucco-and-mission-tile retreat, a place where the only shows in town are the sunstruck surf and forever blond sand, plus the bird of paradise flowers blooming with orange and blue plumage in December.

What I found was no small black dot, but a panic attack of intersecting velocities. Each town sold shirts wearing its name, and the shirts wore pictures of the classic stucco-and-mission-tile hotel. I found a flier advertising the Blessing of the Pets scheduled at St. Anne Catholic Church, "all species welcome," with cut-and-paste computer art showing turtle, parrot, cat, iguana, and dog lining up for sanctification. I found sidewalks busy with pedigreed dogs boasting perfect hairdos as they walked with their owners in the glamour of California sunlight—canine celebrities like the beauty queen Irish setter with her gleaming mahogany coat feathering off belly and legs like the chiffons of a veil dancer, and the attentive little corgi sitting upright in the driver's seat of a parked Range Rover as if he were ready to pull out into the flow.

I had come to California to observe the bonobos (*Pan paniscus*) at the San Diego Zoo. These seductive little apes, along with their cousins the chimpanzees (*Pan troglodytes*), are our closest primate relatives. We three species are descended from an alleged common ancestor, a woodland ape whose fossil remains have yet to be found, an animal dubbed *Pan prior* that lived about six million years ago. Traits carried by *Pan prior* come into the modern world—shape-shifted by time—in the bodies and minds of human beings, chimps, and bonobos. To see (more likely than not on television) a chimp displaying and slapping his way into the social group, or a bonobo gossiping, hugging, and humping her way in, is like finding an old family photo album, the faces and behavior of strangers closely resembling living relatives.

Physical violence is common among chimpanzees. Primatologist Frans de Waal writes in *Our Inner Ape* that the chimpanzee "resolves sexual issues with power." Bonobos, however, almost never show violence. The bonobo "resolves power issues with sex." Want a taste of your neighbor's food? If you're a bonobo, you don't steal it—you offer your rump, or hump your neighbor's thigh, or simply throw a reassuring arm around his shoulder. When groups meet in the forest they exchange constant chatter as if catching up on gossip. In captivity bonobos spend so much time grooming one another they may become temporarily bald. They laugh when they're tickled, they squeal in sexual pleasure, they have sex face-to-face—and in every other position imaginable—and they enjoy the solo delight of masturbation. Few bonobos are kept in captivity because they are rare and endangered. One can imagine the challenging staff meetings as zookeepers and handlers discuss the appropriate language for interpretive materials. What will we tell the children? That sex is fun and helps these creatures maintain a peaceful and egalitarian society? Perhaps this approach would play in Belgium, but with the abstinence-only regime ruling sex education in the United States, one imagines a somewhat stiffer word choice.

Although the fate of bonobos in the wild is grim, what might the story of their traits lend to our thinking about ourselves? True, we seem to have followed the pathway of the chimp with chest thumping, ground drumming, bullying, assault, and mutilation as very old habits in the primate line. That doesn't mean this is the only path we can follow through the genetic undergrowth. Our species is apparently the only one in evolutionary history to develop refined skills for language, self-awareness, and awe. Symbolic systems that embody these capacities may have developed on other worlds—worlds on which creatures have made it through the bottleneck of learning technological prowess without destroying themselves—but we are unlikely ever to know them. We're stuck with the wonder and challenge of ourselves.

De Waal, studying social intelligence, has spent thousands of hours watching bonobos and other primates. He has been dissolving the distinctions between instinct and intelligence in our distant relations, finding that they, like us, are adept at taking cues from the social prompts surrounding them. Primatologists increasingly speak of "cultural" variability among primates, and this does not apply only to learned tool use and eating habits, "such as chimpanzees cracking nuts with stones or Japanese monkeys washing potatoes in the ocean."

De Waal's most intriguing account is the experiment in which he put juveniles of two different macaque species together for five months; "the typically quarrelsome rhesus monkeys were housed with the far more tolerant and easygoing stumptail monkeys." The monkeys he expected to be aggressive clung fearfully to the ceiling of their cage, making a few threatening grunts. The stumptails weren't impressed, ignoring the challenge. De Waal writes, "For the rhesus monkeys, this must have been their first experience with dominant companions who felt no need to assert their position."

The rhesus learned the lesson "a thousand times over and also engaged in frequent reconciliations with their gentle oppressors." After five months the two species played, groomed, and slept together "in large mixed huddles." Most impressive was the fact that when the species were separated, the rhesus showed "three times more friendly reunions and grooming after fights than was typical of their kind." Peacemaking was shown to be a social skill rather than an instinct in these primates. Is there something in us, then, older than our conflicts that can bring us peace?

How it stands today, according to the World Wildlife Fund and the World Population Clock:

Bonobos: 10,000 (no reliable estimates; may be as few as 5,000 or as many as 60,000; declining rapidly)

Chimpanzees: 200,000 (estimated 172,000–299,700; once inhabited twenty-five African countries, now extinct in three or four; nearing extinction in many others)

Human Beings: 7,100,000,000 (and the clock is ticking)

Pan prior: 0

✦

The female beewolf, a European species of wasp, hunts honeybees. After paralyzing them with her stinger, she carries them to a chamber she has built in sandy soil. She paints the walls with white goo she has cultured in her antennae glands, a substance produced by *Streptomyces* bacteria that live in these glands, finding there a warm and moist habitat wherein they thrive. The beewolf lays her eggs in the nursery, where the goo prevents fungus from growing. When the young hatch, they eat the honeybees. They apply the antifungal goo to the threads of their larval cocoons, protecting themselves from the parasitic fungus that might find the warm and humid nest a welcome home. Solitary and commensal, attacking and harboring, learned and brainless, the beewolf is a study in contrasts. The beewolf *is* its relationships. It does not require thought, but it does require millions of attempts and failures at community among insects, fungi, and bacteria.

Is there sentience involved in this process? We cannot possibly know what the labor of the beewolf feels like. I can imagine the physical intensity of the hunt, the weighty work of flying the prey back to the nest, the fevered robotic housekeeping before the eggs are deposited. But I cannot imagine my way inside the beewolf's experience. Every creature, even a plant, has some degree of sentience, the capacity to read its surroundings and identify signs—"honeybee," "sandy soil," "strep goo"—that trigger what it has to do to survive. Even an amoeba can switch genes on and off in response to changes in its environment: slime your way over here for food; slime away from toxins. This is an elaborate enzyme activity based in chemistry and biomechanics. No consciousness. No decision making. No reflection. But I can't stop thinking how weird and marvelous it is that mere matter can conjure up such processes.

The simplest life form seems symphonic when I contemplate the unlikelihood of the complexity each creature embodies. If the amoeba is a symphony, then the human being ought to be a cacophony with its ten trillion cells, one hundred trillion synapses, each neuron averaging one thousand inputs. To really hear the noise of a single person, add to these human cells the one hundred trillion live-in bacterial cells (ten trillion individual bacteria of one thousand different species in the gut alone!), mostly friendly, collaborating in our bellies, hair follicles, tear ducts, and skin, each of them ecstatic in the fecundity of our bodies, each of them welcomed by our bodies, though our minds may find them disgusting, for the contribution they make to our well-being. Hookworms in the human gut, for example, appear to reduce the incidence of allergies. When I think about the complexity of my body, the biological community of my body, my idea of myself begins to wobble. I am essentially two creatures in one: the thinking, feeling, sensing creature I know as me, and the bundle of involuntary processes—electrical, chemical, cellular, rhythmic, and interorganismic—that go smoothly along beneath my recognition.

This mess of collaboration feels to me like a musical masterwork, though I do not believe any master is involved in its creation. I believe that life is a self-generating, self-complicating, self-correcting, and often self-deceiving process. What are the boundaries between my animality and the microbes that collaborate with my existence, between my voluntary and involuntary actions? There *are* no boundaries—only conflicts and resolutions, an endless process of mutual capitulation that keeps a person coasting along as if she were one discrete organism. Why call it musical? I think of the jazz chords I've been learning for the past couple of years, the sevenths and ninths and thirteenths that add a crunchy dissonance to melody by rendering it more bittersweet and beautiful because they complicate the song, creating the tension that longs for resolution, complexity that longs to know the simplicity of a major chord with nothing funky to challenge the ear. I find oddly comforting the fact that all my desires and sorrows and aspirations are nothing more than ten trillion cells interacting with each other and with what they—in the guise of an "I"—encounter. My animal heart keeps the beat without anyone counting.

Biologist Ursula Goodenough writes:

> Life can be explained by its underlying chemistry, just as chemistry can be explained by its underlying physics. But the life that emerges from the underlying chemistry of biomolecules is something more than the collection of molecules. . . . Once these molecules came to reside inside cells, they began to interact with one another to generate new processes, like motility and metabolism and perception, processes that are unique to living creatures, processes that have no counterpart at simpler levels. These new, life-specific functions are referred to as emergent functions.

Emergent functions, Goodenough says, are "something more from nothing but." Emergence is nature's mode of creativity. Atoms made in stars possess emergent properties. Planets and seas are emergent in star ash. Emergent properties abound in nonlife and life. When water turns to ice, it expresses the emergent property of buoyancy. Emergent outcomes in biology, such as motility or awareness, are called "traits." They mean that the organism has a purpose. Fly in tandem with the handful of starlings closest to your side, and the emergent property of flocking is expressed. Paralyze a honeybee and plant it with your young, and the emergent property of nurture is expressed. Write a book, symphony, sermon, prescription, or equation, and the emergent property of culture is expressed. Life insists upon purpose through a continual process of emergence.

Brain-based awareness in human beings emerges to become language. Language-based brains lead to an "I." The self does not feel like matter, but that is all it is. "I" is an emergent property of language-based brains, "something more from nothing but." Maybe it's just an accident that we have self-consciousness. Maybe the feeling we have that some people call "soul" or "spirit" is simply an intuition for the emergent, "the search for the adjacent possible," in Goodenough's words. Where are we heading in this big symphony of emergent chords? With any luck, and given enough time to develop enough collaborative relationships, we are trying to get from "I" to "we" on a global scale: from self to culture, nation to planet, history to biology.

Stuart Kauffman's 2008 book *Reinventing the Sacred: A New View of Science, Reason, and Religion* explores the significance of the idea of emergence. Kauffman offers a comprehensive theory of emergence and self-organization that he says "breaks no law of physics" and yet cannot be explained by them. "God," he writes, "is our chosen name for the ceaseless creativity of the natural universe, biosphere, and human cultures."

✦

On a 2008 visit to the Cape Cod National Seashore I heard a young naturalist speak about the condition of the piping plover, a species that nests on the beaches in May and June.

I'd become interested after walking there and finding areas roped off for "bird use," where plovers had scratched out tiny basins in the sand in which to lay eggs perfectly camouflaged by the sand grains. The parent plovers worked the tidal wash for prey; a pair of turkey vultures scanned the shore for a shot at cleaning up. On Cape Cod this nesting behavior stirs up controversy akin to the trouble roused in the Pacific Northwest by the northern spotted owl. Select bumper stickers boast "Piping Plover: You Can't Eat Just One" and "Piping Plover Tastes Like Chicken."

Cape Cod fishermen pay dearly for off-road permits to drive their Cherokees and Rams along the beach and surf-cast for bluefish and striped bass. Their beach roads coincide with the nesting ground. So the fight is on—birds versus men—though in truth the fight is between one group of citizens and another. I don't see why moderation cannot be a guide here. That appears to have been the course taken by the U.S. National Park Service with its gracefully worded sign, "Bird Use Area," which prods the visitor to consider the motto "Land of Many Uses" as incorporating the interests of species other than our own in our policies.

The lecturer, a young AmeriCorps volunteer doing noble service on behalf of ecological integrity, had been trained to foster audience participation. What I wanted were the facts, the latest research, details about what was at stake for the plovers and how they were doing against the human competition for beach space. But I bowed to the process, with one random half of the audience assigned to the "pro" plover position and the other half to the "con." I was among the pros. No contest in my mind, though I could not get anyone in my group to acknowledge that "all life forms are sacred" was an argument worth holding up to the policy fray. The cons argued "Why interfere with the natural process of evolution?" holding forth that since we are the dominant predators and since we have paid good money for our off-road-vehicle permits, it is our right to unseat the nesters.

Our lecturer floated between the two groups. One of our pro colleagues, wanting to find something tangible to hold up against a fishing license, asked her, "Do they have a purpose? I mean, it would be so much easier, if the plovers had a purpose."

Like what, I wondered? Pharmaceutical production, or mosquito control, or the higher purpose that the religious see in life? I know some people see in the science story a life without direction or ethical dimension. Why are their actions what they are? What should their actions be? The facts of life do not answer and the silence looms. I am not among such people. For me, as for my mother, the facts of life are enough of a miracle to induce religious feeling and a sense of purpose.

"No," our guide confided apologetically to the plover pros. "That's the hard part. They really don't."

I wanted to take her by the shoulders and shake her loose from this capitulation to the forces of doom, but I understood that my role here was not to be the hard hat but to understand how very far my sympathies lay from the general drift of public sentiment.

"Of course they have a purpose," I shouted into my inner megaphone. "Their purpose is to be piping plovers and to make more piping plovers! That's a sacred calling. Life is its own purpose." I remained silent, considering how terribly well my own species had followed the dictates of this imperative to make more of itself. And I sat in the sadness that the argument was not at all a simple one for this random gathering of tourists assembled at the National Seashore on a May afternoon in the first decade of the twenty-first century. If everything is sacred, then how do we know which interests to protect? Our moral philosophy is not yet sufficient to give us clear guidelines.

✦

I cannot get out of my head the little Lucy-like hominids whose bones turned up early in the new millennium on the Indonesian island of Flores. Standing a meter tall, with a chimp-sized brain, the remains were similar to *Australopithecus afarensis*, the erect walking hominid that lived in Africa 3.5 million years ago. The creature's size won it the nickname "the Hobbit." The team that had discovered the Lucy skeleton in Ethiopia celebrated their find while sitting around a campfire listening to "Lucy in the Sky with Diamonds" on a portable tape player. That's how this relic of our deep ancestry got her nickname. But the new find suggested that a similar creature lived on an Indonesian island as recently as eighteen thousand years ago. An artist's rendering of *Homo floresiensis* depicted him walking home for dinner with a golden retriever-sized rat slung over his shoulder.

How many millennia had passed since his ancestors migrated away from Africa and Asia? Three or four or five species of Old World hominids were living at the same time. *Homo erectus* was the first colonizer, making it to Java around 1.8 million years ago, according to evolutionary biologist Francisco Ayala. Modern humans are not descendants of those early migrants. The diaspora of *Homo sapiens* from Africa to Asia came much later, starting about one hundred thousand years ago. The earlier migrants appear to have had a long and relatively peaceful tenure on Flores, and they represent a different branch on the tree of life than do our ancestors. They make us contemplate the possibility that rather than a tree of hominid life, there was a thicket—many starts, many entanglements, many failures—and only we survived. Unless, of course, you believe in Bigfoot. Somehow this time-deep story grows more fascinating as the fear increases that our story may be growing short and that our species's résumé may show us to have been terrible animals, heedless devourers of the beautiful Mother that gave all Earth's beings their lives.

But thinking backward in such a time frame also calls up the question of a symmetrically long future. What if we make it? What if learning how broadly destructive the human presence has been on the planet provides us with catalyzing self-awareness? What if this sensitivity to brokenness is tweaking our intelligence to make the next leap forward in our evolutionary story, a leap that turns the runaway force of human culture toward restraint and mutual aid, toward the acquisition of knowledge rather than junk, toward a ten-thousand-year project to restore Earth to a state as close to Eden as we could come, and to grow an outlying garden on Mars? Is that not an artful technological dream that we could love? I want this to be as possible as our doom. Ten thousand years from now, I want someone to say of us, "What amazing courage they had, and what spirit. How smart they were, how inventive—and how profoundly they must have loved Earth."

Epilogue: The Gannet

I left the island one rainy Saturday, the sea a sloppy gray churn, the island shrouded in fog. A storm had come and passed, a hurricane sweeping two winter storms into its galactic arms. New York City had taken a major hit. On Grand Manan the fishermen had lashed down every boat in the harbor; the surf had raked rock against rock in front of my Castalia home. But the island had been spared. The storm spun inland and dissolved.

The laboring ferry slid northward, past the islands called the Wolves toward Blacks Harbour. The island receded in the ship's wake, its basaltic cliffs melting down to nothing in the fog. The steel hull churned on, its bulk becoming lighter and lighter, its presence smaller and smaller, against the enormity of open water. I climbed to the top deck of the *Grand Manan V*, a protected spot behind the port smokestack, to watch shearwaters and fulmars skim the water's surface, these pelagic birds so utterly at home in a place without borders or shores. When they cleared out, there was nothing to see but the bay's ever-shifting peaks and swales of motion.

The gannet was gliding low near the bow, its white, sharp, extended wings holding it in flapless glide, the black wing tips giving it elegance. Alabaster. Starlight coalesced into feathers. Surely wingtip shoes were named for this elegance. The northern gannet is one of the largest of seabirds. Its wings can stretch seven feet wide. It spends nearly its whole life in or on or above the water. The map of its breeding ground marks a rough semicircle hemming the North

Atlantic: Quebec, Newfoundland, Iceland, Ireland, Great Britain. For brief periods, large colonies gather on rocky cliffs to hatch and rear their young. For the most part, their gatherings occur at sea. Hundreds of birds swarm together in large fishing parties. They dive from more than a hundred feet in the air. They hit the water, bill first, with tremendous impact, their eyes wide open. I've seen them in something like an aerial yoga pose—bodies bunched up, feet tucked, wings arced round embracing the air for balance, heads bowed with gaze downward—as they prepare to make the plunge. When they hit the water, the lenses of their eyes shift from oval to spherical to adjust for underwater seeing. They dive seventy or more feet underwater, using feet and wings to propel them, flying through the water, grabbing and swallowing sardines or shrimp or squid as they go. There isn't much research done on pelagic species that spend most of their life at sea. They live relatively private lives.

✦

When I lived for six months in Hawaii, I became captivated by the traditional Hawaiian concept of the 'aumākua, a special guardian figure that might be assigned to a family. It could take the form of a plant or an animal. Because of its sacred descent, writes Martha Beckwith in *Hawaiian Mythology*, the 'aumākua could grant protections and supernatural powers to family members. A corpse might be offered to become a shark, "actual markings on the body of a shark singled out for worship, corresponding to the clothing in which the body of the beloved had been wrapped. Such a shark 'aumākua became the family pet. It was fed daily and was believed to drive food into fishing nets, save the fisherman from death if his canoe capsized, and in other ways ward off danger."

These guardians also had "evil uses." They could become a "fetcher to kill an enemy." An 'aumākua could bring crude justice. A bird hunter recklessly slaughtered plovers even when he didn't need them to eat. His neighbor, who worshipped the plover, got sick from contact with the smoke from his neighbor's plover-stuffed oven. The neighbor warned the plover pillager, but he did not change his ways. A flock of plovers invaded his house, pecking and scratching him to death.

✦

This singleton gannet flew due north along our port side, passing only a foot or so above the stormy chop, just riding along beside our hull as if to flaunt its comfort and ease in the vastness. Did the ship provide a windbreak? Or a draft that eased the bird's flight, so that it just kept going and going without a single flap? The bird was a perfect fit with its surroundings, moving with grace and balance, within a scale of incomprehensible enormity and constant motion. It was nothing but itself, a single life in the whole of bio-continuity. As Earth is to the universe, so one gannet is to all the wild seas.

There is no whiteness like the whiteness of the gannet gliding through storm. Ivory tusk, gardenia, cocoon, surgical gauze, Dominican's robe. If I were to live like a gannet, I'd suspend my need to know and open my arms to the future. But, no. I'm content to let the gannet be the gannet.

Notes

Page 3
Introduction

Michael J. Curley, Physiologus, Austin, University of Texas Press, 1979, p. xv.

The discovery of the mammoth tusk carvings is reported in *Science News*, December 20 & 27, 2003, and in *Nature*, December 18/25, 2003. The bird figure is designated there as "a water bird," and it looks a little like a cormorant and a little like a duck with neck outstretched. For my purposes, I made it a cormorant in honor of that bird's elegant beauty.

Page 12
"Murray Springs Mammoth"

Paul Martin's *Twilight of the Mammoths: Ice Age Extinctions and the Rewilding of America* lays out the story and theory of his research.

Page 19
"Spotted Hyena"

An account of the vexing genitalia of the female hyena can be found at the Web site of the International Union for Conservation of Nature: Hyena Specialist Group. http://www.hyaenidae.org/the-hyaenidae/spotted-hyena-crocuta-crocuta/crocuta-reproduction.html

For explication of mating, given these nonstandard genitals, see illuminating field notes at http://scientistatwork.blogs.nytimes.com/2011/07/19/how-spotted-hyenas-mate/.

Page 23
"The Sacred Pig"

The quote is from astrophysicist Robert Brownlee, who spent his career working at the Los Alamos National Laboratory. He and Robert Campbell, test director for Operation Plumbbob, gathered memories and anecdotal accounts of the experiences of men with whom they worked at the nuclear test sites. See "Caging the Dragon" at http://www.scribd.com/doc/6602337/Caging-the-Dragon-The-Containment-of-Underground-Nuclear-Explosions, a report prepared "as an account of work sponsored by an agency of the U.S. Government"—in this case the Department of Energy, Defense Nuclear Agency, Nevada Operations Office. This is a fine personal documentary and often weirdly poetic reading.

Brownlee said in a talk given at a 1981 Monterrey Containment Symposium: "It has been said that there is no such thing as history, only biography. Assuming this to be true, a description of the evolution of containment would contain the story of the people involved— their experiments, beliefs, motivations, successes, failures, foibles and idiosyncrasies. We might then be able to understand our current faith and practice, their origins in a far better way."

Page 37
"*Patativa* (Sporophila leucoptera)"

I'm grateful to the International Writing Program at the University of Iowa, which took me to Brazil on a reading tour in May 2012. In Fortaleza our group was hosted by the cultural center devoted to the work of *cordelista* and *repentista* poets. There—and everywhere—I learned about the poet known as Patativa. I'm also grateful to the work of Laiz Chen, Brazilian scholar-activist, for her work on Brazilian poetry and protest songs ("a canon of exclusion") presented at the 2010 Interdisciplinary Conference at Nottingham Trent University.

For an evocative account of a visit with Patativa at his home, see *Waiting for Rain: The Politics and Poetry of Drought in Northeast Brazil* by Nicholas Gabriel Arons.

Page 47
"Ant Art"

Dubuffet's collection is described in all its bizarre and wondrous detail in Lucienne Peiry's *Art Brut: The Origins of Outsider Art*.

Page 51
"Field Notes on Hands"

Ellen Dissanayake's work cited in For Further Reading argues for art making as an adaptive strategy, a normal, necessary, and universal behavior of human beings from the earliest times that fosters social cohesion and heightens experience, making it more memorable and significant.

For the history of the Shaker culture, one of the great American experiments in communal living, see *The People Called Shakers* by Edward D. Andrews or *The Shaker Experience in America* by Stephen J. Stein.

A fine site for information about and images of the mammoth bones structures at the Mezhirich site: http://donsmaps.com/mammothcamp.html

The Field Museum in Chicago has an excellent mammoth and mastodon exhibition that includes a scale model of a mammoth bone hut. I believe there was an exhibition in the 1980s at the American Museum of Natural History in which mammoth bone huts and villages were reconstructed and on luminous display. I can't find the reference for it, except in my memory, where the images of tallow oil light shining through bone and pelt walls have never left me.

Page 66
"Elephant Watching"

Gay Bradshaw's work is summarized in the October 10, 2008, *New York Times Magazine*. http://www.nytimes.com/2006/10/08/magazine/08elephant

Among efforts to shelter traumatized elephants is the elephant rehabilitation project in Nairobi, Kenya. http://www.sheldrickwildlifetrust.org/

Closer to home is the Riddle's Elephant and Wildlife Sanctuary in the Ozark Mountain foothills of Arkansas. http://www.elephantsanctuary.org/default2.asp

See Paul Crutzen in "Dawn of the Anthropocene," *Science Daily*, March 26, 2012.

The Language of Conservation project was sponsored by Poets House in New York City, the Wildlife Conservation Society, and the Institute for Museum and Library Services. Zoos and aquariums are among the most popular cultural institutions in the United States with over 150 million visitors each year, so this is a huge constituency for the animals. Exit interviews conducted after the first installation in Central Park Zoo found a statistically significant increase in conservation values among zoo visitors after they had viewed and read the poetry installations. The project expanded to five additional cities: Milwaukee,

Jacksonville, Little Rock, New Orleans, and Chicago. A report of the project is published by Poets House:

PDF of *The Language of Conservation: Poetry in Library and Zoo Collaborations*, edited by Poets House managing director Jane Preston

Page 90
"The Feasting"

The quote comes from the great Ralph Waldo Emerson essay "Experience," a work catalyzed by the death of the author's young son. A longer version of the fragment is this:

> "We dress our garden, eat our dinner, discuss the household with our wives, and these things make no impression, and are forgotten next week; but in the solitude to which every man is always returning, he has a sanity and revelations, which in his passage into new worlds he will carry with him. Never mind the ridicule, never mind the defeat: up again, old heart!—it seems to say,—there is victory yet for all justice; and the true romance which the world exists to realize, will be the transformation of genius into practical power."

My mother recounted this experience in her book *Darling This . . . Darling That*, which she wrote in her nineties and published in 2010 when she was 101 years old. The chapter referred to here is "Emily Birch, Persona Unique."

Page 101
"A Dog with His Pets"

This chapter began as a formal imitation of and homage to John Berger's "An Old Woman with a Pram" in *Photocopies*.

See the journal *Neuroanthropology*, August 23, 2010, for more on the dog-human connection in evolution. http://neuroanthropology.net/2010/08/23/the-dog-human-connection-in-evolution/

Also the *Online Dog Encyclopedia*, dogsindepth.com

The Clayton Eshleman references come from "Abbreviated Introduction for Juniper Fuse" on his website.

Page 106
"City of Storks"

Augustine's *City of God*, Book XIV, Chapter 28, Book XV, Chapter 4,

Book XV, Chapter 4, Book XIX, Chapter 17. Fordham University's "Medieval Sourcebook" online.

On both www.iberia/spainstorms.html and Fundacion Global Nature, I find 33,217 and 32,923 breeding pairs cited, respectively. These are 2004 numbers and I don't find anything reliable more recently. However, since stork populations in Spain are not going down (many happily feeding on dumps and not bothering to migrate), I think this is a good estimate.

Carl G. Jung, "Experiences Concerning the Psychic Life of the Child." Lecture 3, Clark University, 1909. See Classics in the History of Psychology: http://psychclassics.yorku.ca/Jung/Association/lecture3.htm

Egyptologist Louis Zabkar's study of "The Concept of the 'Ba.'" University of Chicago. http://oi.uchicago.edu/pdf/saoc34.pdf

Aesop, *The Complete Fables*, with introduction by Robert Temple (Penguin Classics), translated by Olivia and Robert Temple.

Neil Russack, *Animal Guides* (p. 48)

Page 124
"Dragon"

On the life of Saint George, see William Caxton, *The Golden Legend: On the Lives of the Saints, Volume 3* (edition of 1900, London: J. M. Dent & Sons.)

William Caxton's reference to "corn" may sound anachronistic in a text written in 1438. Corn was unknown in Europe until after explorers brought it back from the Americas, where corn is native and was first cultivated by indigenous people. The word "corn" showed up in Europe before the vegetable. It was commonly used in this pre-corn time to denote "grain" such as wheat, oats, or barley, whichever grain was most prevalent in the region.

David E. Jones, *An Instinct for Dragons*, is interesting if not convincing.

Joyce Hargreaves, *A Little History of Dragons*
Carl G. Jung, *Psychology and Alchemy*

Page 132
"Black Vulture"

Previously published as part of the essay "In the Territory of Birds" in my book *The Edges of the Civilized World* (Picador USA 1998). I traveled to Punta Chueca with ethnobotanist and writer Gary Paul Nabhan, whose work with the Seri spans several decades.

Page 139
"Liberating the Lobster"

Some material is recycled from an interview with Todd Davis: "The World, the Word, and the Inevitable Beauty of Change: An Interview with Alison Hawthorne Deming," *Interdisciplinary Literary Studies*, Vol.14, no. 1, 2012. Pennsylvania State University, University Park, PA, and from an editorial in terrain.org titled "Ruin and Renewal."

L. K. Ingersoll, "Grand Manan at the Turn of the Century" and "Lobsters Galore," Grand Manan Historical Society

The *New York Times* reports that forests are dying in Canada, Russia, Australia, the Amazon basin, and the American Southwest. The pines of Greece and the cedars of North Africa are dying. For more information, see: http://www.nytimes.com/2011/10/01/science/earth/01forest.html?pagewanted=all&_r=0

The ending echoes the end of Dante's *Purgatorio*, which W. S. Merwin translates, with Virgil speaking:

> Now you can tell how great
> must be the love for you that burns in me
> when it escapes my mind that we are empty
>
> and treat a shade as a solid thing.

Page 149
"Trumpeter Swan"

See the Cornell Ornithological Laboratory and Minnesota Department of Natural Resources websites and Neil Russack and Joseph L. Henderson, *Animal Guides* (p. 31).

Plato reports on Socrates's reflections about death and swans in his *Phaedo*.

Page 170
"Feral Children"

Giorgio Agamben, *The Open: Man and Animal*

Douglas Candland, *Feral Children and Clever Animals: Reflections on Human Nature*

Henry David Thoreau, "Walking"

Rita Carter, Susan Aldridge, Martyn Page, Steve Parker, *The Human Brain Book*, London. Dorling Kindersley Limited, 2009

Page 178
"Vervet"

Donald R. Griffin, *Animal Minds* (p. 154-5, 201, 233)

Page 184
"Chimera"

J.B.S. Haldane, *Daedelus, or Science and the Future*
Giovanni Aloi, *Art and Animals*

Page 190
"Letter from Mars"

For the arresting images sent by *Curiosity*, start here:
http://www.nasa.gov/mission_pages/mars/main/index.html
    Check out *Curiosity*'s Twitter feed here:
https://twitter.com/MarsCuriosity
    The letter was inspired by the December 20, 2012, Twitter
feeds, as well as cursory research into the concepts of "the singularity" and "friendly artificial intelligence." See the Singularity
Institute for Artificial Intelligence or *The Transhumanist Reader*
for a deeper dive.

Page 195
"Owl Watching in the Experimental Forest"

The H. J. Andrews Experimental Forest is one of twenty-six
Long Term Ecological Research sites ranging from Alaska to
the Caribbean to Antarctica funded by the National Science
Foundation. Under the leadership of philosopher Kathleen Dean
Moore and geoscientist Fred Swanson, the site has expanded its
focus to include Long Term Ecological Reflections, a two-hun-
dred-year project bringing arts and philosophers into the research
site. I'm indebted to their leadership and friendship. Our many
rich conversations about science and art, while we were walking
among the old giants there, have been deeply nourishing.
    For information about the NSF's Long Term Ecological
Research sites see: http://www.lternet.edu/.
    For information about the loose network of sites doing Long
Term Ecological Reflections see: http://www.ecologicalreflec-
tions.com/.
    Paul Crutzen, *ibid*
    Adam Gopnik, *Winter*

The translation of the words of Brazilian poet Antonio Carlos Secchin was written on a hotel notepad by Maria Jose Barbosa during our trip to São Paulo, Brazil, in May 2012, surely while we were enjoying caipirinhas and conversation.

Page 215
"The Rabbit on Mars"
For the rather unimpressive image of the actual "rabbit" on Mars, see: http://marsrovers.nasa.gov/spotlight/opportunity/b19_20040304.html

Page 218
"Field Notes on Culture, Biology, and Emergence"
The essay was written for the *Georgia Review*, Spring 2009, in a special feature responding to Scott Russell Sanders's essay "Simplicity and Sanity."

The Salman Rushdie quote is from *Joseph Anton: A Memoir*.

Edward Sapir's essay "Culture, Genuine and Spurious" is available in *The Collected Works of Edward Sapir*.

Ursula Goodenough, *The Sacred Depths of Nature*

Page 240
Epilogue: The Gannet
A team of researchers in New Zealand did some fancy underwater videography of the gannet that is native to their region. The lens of the birds' eyes, within eighty milliseconds of hitting the water, shifted from oval to spherical to adjust for underwater seeing.

See Martha Beckwith, *Hawaiian Mythology*, p. 128

"There is no whiteness like the whiteness of the gannet" echoes William Carlos Williams, who writes in "The Descent":

> No defeat is made up entirely of defeat—since
> the world it opens is always a place
>   formerly
>   unsuspected. A
>   world lost,
>   a world unsuspected,
>   beckons to new places
>   and no whiteness (lost) is so white as the memory
>   of whiteness   .

For Further Reading

Aesop, *The Compete Fables*
Giorgio Agamben, *The Open: Man and Animal*
Giovanni Aloi, *Art and Animals*
Roland Barthes, *Mythologies*
John Berger, *Photocopies*
John Berger, *Why Look at Animals*
Jorge Luis Borges, *The Book of Imaginary Beings*
Douglas Candland, *Feral Children and Clever Animals:*
    Reflections on Human Nature
Frans de Waal, *Our Inner Ape*
Peter Demetz, *Prague in Black and Gold*
Jacques Derrida, *The Animal That Therefore I Am*
Ellen Dissanayake, *Art and Intimacy*
Ellen Dissanayake, *Homo Aestheticus*
Dennis Dutton, *The Art Instinct*
Marija Gimbutas, *The Goddesses and Gods of Old Europe*
Allen Ginsberg, *Kaddish*
Ursula Goodenough, *The Sacred Depths of Nature*
Donald R. Griffin, *Animal Intelligence*
Donald R. Griffin, *Animal Minds*
J. B. S. Haldane, *Daedelus; or, Science and the Future*
Carl Gustav Jung, *The Essential Jung: Selected Writings* and
    Psychology and Alchemy
Stuart Kauffman, *Reinventing the Sacred: A New View of*
    Science, Reason and Religion
Stephen Kellert, *Birthright*
Marianne Moore (tr.), *The Fables of La Fontaine*

Max More and Natasha Vita-More, *The Transhumanist Reader*

Rainer Maria Rilke, *Duino Elegies*

Neil Russack and Joseph Henderson, *Animal Guides in Life, Myth and Dreams* (Studies in Jungian Psychology by Jungian Analysts)

Rafe Sagarin, *Learning from the Octopus*

Visnu Sarma (tr. Chandra Rajan), *The Pancatantra* (Penguin Classics)

Elaine Scarry, *On Beauty and Being Just*

Paul Shepard, *Coming Home to the Pleistocene*

Paul Shepard, *The Others: How Animals Made Us Human*

Thomas Singer and Samuel Kimbles (eds.), *The Cultural Complex: Contemporary Jungian Perspectives of Psyche and Society*

C. P. Snow, *The Two Worlds* and *A Second Look*

Jakob von Uexküll, *A Foray into the Worlds of Animals and Humans*

Leon Wieseltier, *Kaddish*

Acknowledgments

The book began with a series of short pieces written at the invitation of Peter Blaze Corcoran for the inaugural Rachel Carson Distinguished Lecture Series on Sanibel Island, Florida, in 2004. The event, sponsored by Florida Gulf Coast University's Center for Environmental and Sustainability Education, had as its theme "The Ethics of Sustainability." I was to share the stage with Mary Evelyn Tucker, whose inspiring work in ecology and religion carries on that of the late Thomas Berry. I knew I could not imagine sustainability without imagining a place for animals in both the material and the spiritual world, and so the work began. I must begin by giving thanks to Peter and Mary Evelyn for their vision and dedication, for years of impassioned conversation and leadership in bringing aesthetic and spiritual values front and center in considering the human and earthly future.

So many friends and colleagues have supported me, egged me on, and challenged me in this work that I cannot begin to let everyone know how grateful I am for your thoughts and art and science and companionship in one place or another that has been essential to this work. Barbara Hurd, Kathleen Dean Moore, Charles Goodrich, Fred Swanson, Steve Akers, Robin Kimmerer, Bill Fox, Kim Stanley Robinson, Richard Katrovas, Gary Paul Nabhan, Alan Weisman, David Orr, Mitchell Thomashow, Scott Russell Sanders, Chris Impey, Diana Liverman, David Rothenberg, Lauret Savoy, Gail Browne, Chris Cokinos, Ander Monson, Aurelie Sheehan, Adela Licona, Maria Jose Barbosa, Cornelius Eady, Alan Heathcock, Chris

Merrill, Stephen Corey, Elizabeth Bernays, Stuart Kestenbaum, Luci Tapahonso—you know where you are on or behind these pages. What a beautiful mélange you make!

Sandra Alcosser, Lee Bricetti, and Kelliann Whitney: what a great privilege and pleasure and spur to this writing it was to work with you curating the poetry installation at the Jacksonville Zoo and Gardens.

H. Emerson Blake and the community surrounding *Orion* magazine have provided nourishment and inspiration for the past twenty years. And the best part of it is the friendship and purposefulness that has always been at the heart of *Orion*'s mission.

To Patrick Burns, I owe thanks for research on cheetahs.

The University of Arizona has continued to be a welcome home for me, a place of dynamic collaboration across disciplinary lines, and I'm grateful for the 2011 sabbatical that provided the time and focus for a major revision of the book.

To my agent, Laura Blake Peterson, I owe thanks for attending with care to how this book would come into the world. And to Patrick Thomas, my editor at Milkweed, I owe a tremendous debt of gratitude for his enthusiasm for the project and his perspicacious editorial eye. The book is far better than it would have been thanks to his attentive reading and commentary. Real editors have become a rarity in publishing. I count myself most fortunate.

The ghosts of my brother, Rodney Macnab Deming, and my mother, Travilla Macnab Deming, both of whom died during the writing of this project, have been gentle companions throughout. I'm grateful that they invited me into their final days. Their struggles with that passage guided me toward framing grief in both intimate and planetary perspectives, and taught me to cherish every vexing day of life.

To my daughter, Lucinda Bliss, and her family—William, Lincoln, and Raymond—you're the future that makes all of this matter for me.

Publications

I'm grateful to the publications in which chapters of this book first appeared, sometimes in earlier versions.

Journals:

Ecotone, "The Pony, the Pig, the Horse"

Eleven Eleven, "The Sacred Pig"

The Georgia Review published "Cormorant" (included in the Introduction here), "Wolf Spider," "Dogtags," "Ant Art," "My Cat Jeffrey," and "The Storks of Alcalá" (now expanded as "City of Storks") as a segmented essay titled "With Animals in Mind" in Fall 2005.

"On Nature, Culture, and Emergence" appeared in their Spring 2009 issue and was awarded the Best Essay Gold by the Southeast Magazine Association's GAMMA Awards.

"Bobcat," "Chimera," and "Patativa" were published as "Fool for Life"

Hawk and Handsaw, "The Finback"

The Haystack School of Crafts Monograph Series, "Field Notes on Hands"

Isotope, "The Rabbit on Mars"

OnEarth published "The Owl, Spotted" (now included in "Owl Watching in the Experimental Forest") and "Brief Encounter on the Savannah" (now the first section of "Elephant Watching")

Orion, "Spotted Hyena"
Terrain.org, "The Cheetah Run"
Threepenny Review, "A Dog with His Pets"
Water~Stone Review, "T. Rex"
Western Humanities Review, "Hood River Oyster"

Anthologies:
Best American Science and Nature Writing, "The Rabbit on Mars"
The Haystack Reader: Essays on Craft, "Field Notes on Hands"
Moral Ground: Ethical Action for a Planet in Peril, "The
     Feasting"
The Way of Natural History, "Field Notes from the Experimental
     Forest"

ALISON HAWTHORNE DEMING was born and raised in Connecticut. She is the author of the poetry books *Rope, Genius Loci, The Monarchs: A Poem Sequence, Science and Other Poems,* and the nonfiction books *Writing the Sacred into the Real, The Edges of the Civilized World,* and *Temporary Homelands.* Her honors include the Walt Whitman award, Wallace Stegner Fellowship, Bayer Award in Science Writing, Fine Arts Work Center Fellowship and the National Endowment for the Arts Fellowships. She is Professor in Creative Writing at the University of Arizona and Senior Fellow at the Spring Creek Project at Oregon State University. She lives in Tucson, Arizona and on Grand Manan Island, New Brunswick.

Interior design & typesetting by Mary Austin Speaker
Typeset in ITC New Baskerville

New Baskerville is a revival of the eighteenth-century typeface Baskerville. Revived in 1923 by Stanley Morison of Monotype, New Baskerville was released by the Mergenthaler Linotype Company in the late 1970s and adapted for digital typography in 1982 by ITC. Baskerville is a transitional typeface designed in 1757 by John Baskerville, who sought to improve upon the typefaces of William Caslon. The design of Baskerville influenced the design of later typefaces Didot and Bodoni.